The LIBRARY

The LIBRARY

An Illustrated History

Stuart A. P. Murray

Introduction by Donald G. Davis, Jr.

Foreword by Nicholas A. Basbanes

SKYHORSE PUBLISHING

ALAEditions

AMERICAN LIBRARY ASSOCIATION
CHICAGO, 2009

To Els

Visit our website at www.skyhorsepublishing.com.

10 9 8 7 6 5 4 3 2

Paperback ISBN: 978-1-61608-453-0

Library of Congress Cataloging-in-Publication Data

Murray, Stuart A. P.
The library : an illustrated history / Stuart A.P. Murray ; introduction by Donald G. Davis, Jr. ; foreword by Nicholas A. Basbanes.
  p. cm.
Includes bibliographical references.
ISBN 978-1-60239-706-4 (alk. paper)
1. Libraries—History. 2. Libraries—Pictorial works. I. Title.
Z721.M885 2009
027.009--dc22
2009012126

ALA edition ISBN: 978-0-8389-0991-1

Printed in China

Frontispiece: "The Bookworm," by Carl Spitzweg (1808–85)

CONTENTS

FOREWORD

During the darkest days of the Great Depression, a noted bibliophile named Paul Jourdan-Smith wrote a heartfelt tribute to the eternal power of reading in which he offered a passing commentary on the continuing misery he saw everywhere around him.

"This is no time for the collector to quit his books," he observed. "He may have to quit his house, abandon his trip to Europe, and give away his car; but his books are patiently waiting to yield their comfort and provoke him to mirth. They will tell him that banks and civilizations have smashed before; governments have been on the rocks, and men have been fools in all ages. But it is all very funny. The gods laugh to see such sport, and why should we not join them?"

Published in 1933 in a work aptly titled *For the Love of Books*, Jourdan-Smith's observation came at a time when people throughout the United States were using their local libraries in record numbers for precisely the reasons he had perceived, turning to them as sanctuaries of first resort during times of particular need. And the widespread reliance on these remarkable institutions of cultural preservation—five thousand years in the making, as we learn in Stuart Murray's most useful survey—continued through the long trauma of World War II.

A week after the Japanese attack on Pearl Harbor in 1941, the charismatic mayor of New York City, Fiorello H. La Guardia, took to the airwaves on radio station WNYC for a series of Sunday night broadcasts in which he would speak directly to his constituents, keeping them apprised of world events, giving them all an encouraging pep talk in the process. At the end of each program, it was the custom of the man affectionately known as the "Little Flower" to conclude his remarks with the words "patience and fortitude," calm advice that he felt would see everyone safely through the long ordeal that lay ahead.

So inspirational was La Guardia's message of comfort and hope that "Patience and Fortitude" were adopted as the unofficial names of the majestic lions carved from pink Tennessee marble that guard the entryway to the New York Public Library on Fifth Avenue in Manhattan. With concern in some myopic quarters arguing that technology has rendered twenty-first-century libraries quaint and archaic, these names have taken on renewed significance, especially as a financial crisis of monumental proportions took its toll during the early months of 2009. As conditions worsened, news reports began to crop up that libraries were busier than ever, a circumstance made especially curious by the fact that so many of them were among the first to suffer severe cutbacks in funding.

In New York, attendance for 2008 was up 13 percent over the previous year, with circulation reaching 21.1 million items, an increase of close to four million. Similar patterns were evident from coast to coast, with the American Library Association reporting more active borrowing cards in use nationally than at any other time in history. Americans visited their libraries some 1.3 billion times in 2008, and checked out more than 2 billion items—an increase in both figures of more than 10 percent. "It's a national phenomenon," ALA president Jim Rettig told NBC News. "Library use is up everywhere." Too bad, he might have added, that it takes hard times for some people to appreciate the indispensability of this remarkable institution. What follows is an eloquent account of this noble history, as it has unfolded from its earliest times to the present. "A great library cannot be constructed," the nineteenth-century Scottish historian John Hill Burton reminded us in *The Book-Hunter,* "It is the growth of ages."

Nicholas A. Basbanes

INTRODUCTION

L ibraries, or collections of recorded knowledge, are the collective memory of the human race. The story of libraries is the saga of what our predecessors thought was important enough to write down and preserve in order to inform or enlighten future readers. Thus, all libraries are acts of faith—faith that coming generations will make use of the contents of those libraries.

The record of human cultural achievement is found primarily in the writings and graphics preserved from previous generations. Archival and library collections enable us to understand our monuments and artifacts and to interpret their meaning and the context in which they came to be. The history of libraries is a cultural world history, seen through library-colored lenses. The present volume is a brief historical survey that serves as a modest introduction to human history as it relates to the transmitted record of civilization.

Beginning with the origins of writing, and the resulting early records and books, this volume summarizes vast periods of time and a multitude of regional and national traditions, ending with the globalization of information resources. Current strides in accessible electronic information are an extension of the library's classic role of bringing patrons and materials together, not only for pleasure, but as an engine for the production of still more knowledge.

After a chapter on ancient libraries, this survey continues with a balanced treatment of worldwide library development to the middle of the second millennium. Thereafter, following the arrangement of many library historians, the narrative combines a chronological treatment with relevant continental and national concerns. The emphasis is on libraries in the United States, but the rest of the world is hardly slighted. Well-supported libraries of all types predominate in Europe and America, and of special interest is the rise of public libraries that provide popular materials and media for all levels of society. A section with brief sketches of notable and representative libraries (more than fifty, in all) concludes the book.

The difficult choices to be made in preparation of a short work that reaches for such breadth and scope should not be underestimated. Telling the intriguing story of the production, transmission, preservation, organization, and utilization of cumulated human knowledge—and telling it in a style that appeals to the widest spectrum of readers—is both a challenging and a most worthy task. No one—from library historians and cultural scholars to the general public and young readers—will agree on what should be included in or omitted from the text and illustrations. Least of all will librarians themselves be of one mind—of that we can be sure! But the effort to tell this story, however sketchy and even idiosyncratic, is well worth it.

Several audiences will find this volume helpful. There will be patrons of libraries who will be curious about how collections came to be and how they developed through history. Others will find this book a stimulus to read and study further about libraries. And, finally, there may well be readers and lovers of libraries who will be stimulated by text and illustrations to visit some of the libraries mentioned in this overview.

With whatever perspective a reader comes to this work, and to whatever purpose it is put, those who are drawn to its pages can agree on one thing: Libraries remind us of our humanity, preserve our legacy as a species, and provide the intellectual building blocks for the future.

Fqpcnf "I0"Fcxku."Lt0
Professor Emeritus of Library History
School of Information & Department of History
University of Texas at Austin

"For the Dedication of the New City Library, Boston"

Behind the ever open gate
    No pikes shall fence a crumbling throne,
No lackeys cringe, no courtiers wait, —
    This palace is the people's own!

Oliver Wendell Holmes
1888

▲ This seventh-century carved alabaster panel from Nineveh shows
Assyrian king, Assurbanipal, closing on his quarry during a lion hunt.

THE ANCIENT LIBRARIES

On a December night in 1853, gangs of diggers labored with pick and shovel by the light of oil lamps to fill baskets and handcarts with sandy rubble. An ancient palace was thought to be under their feet, part of the ruins of Nineveh, capital of mighty Assyria from the ninth to seventh centuries BCE. Nineveh had been destroyed by the Babylonians in 612 BCE, razed, and left to the desert wind and sand.

The men worked after dark, in secret, because this ground was reserved for a competing French archaeologist—one who had neglected it too long but who could expel them if he found them here. Directing the laborers, who were from nearby Mosul, was Hormuzd Rassam (1826–1910), an Assyrian Christian and a native of that city. Rassam, who had studied at Oxford, was funded by the British Museum, which financed several ongoing excavations and took delivery of the best finds. If Rassam's diggers found something important, the established archaeologists' code would permit them to keep excavating, and the museum could claim first choice of any discoveries.

In a memoir, Rassam wrote about his worries that night as he watched the men work and as morning approached. If he were evicted before finding a structure, he would be accused of poaching, would be ridiculed, and the museum trustees surely would fire him. Then, there came the shout, "*Sooar!*"

meaning "images." "[T]o the great delight of all we hit upon a marble wall," Rassam wrote.

The work continued, excitement mounting. A "beautiful bas-relief in a perfect state of preservation" appeared, showing a king carved in alabaster, armed with bow and spear, standing in a chariot as he hunted lions. The digging soon revealed a long, narrow room, a "saloon," as Rassam termed it.

Suddenly, an embankment attached to the sculpture fell away and fully "exposed to view that enchanting spectacle." Rassam felt the excitement surge "through the whole party like electricity":

> They all rushed to see the new discovery, and having gazed on the bas-relief with wonder, they collected together, and began to dance and sing my praises, in the tune of their war-song, with all their might. Indeed, for a moment I did not know which was the most pleasant feeling that possessed me, the joy of my faithful men or the finding of the new palace.

That momentous find would lead to more sculptures and larger halls, to entire city walls with entrances paved with marble, decorated by carved rosettes and the lotus. So began the unearthing, shovel by shovel, of the palace of Assurbanipal (625–587 BCE), last ruler of Assyria. In the king's "lion-hunt room" Rassam would find all the walls covered with carved alabaster scenes, and also something less dramatic:

> [I]n the center of the same saloon I discovered the library of Assur-bani-pal, consisting of inscribed terra-cotta tablets of all shapes and sizes; the largest of these, which happened to be in better order, were mostly stamped with seals, and some inscribed with hieroglyphic and Phoenician characters.

In the presence of such exquisite bas-relief scenes, it was no wonder Rassam mentioned only briefly the terra-cotta tablets. These, however, were part of

A weary digger, pick at his feet, rests from his labors excavating an ancient Nineveh palace. ▶

4

the royal library, which would eventually number 30,000 tablets and fragments. This would prove to be the earliest-known "cataloged" library, organized into sections: government records, historical chronicles, poetry, science, mythological and medical texts, royal decrees and grants, divinations, omens, and hymns to the gods.

Scholars would learn vastly more about the ancient past from those unobtrusive stacks of tablets with their wedge-shaped writing than from all the glorious sculptures and palace rooms discovered in the long-buried ruins of Nineveh.

▲ This detail from a second-millennium BCE Babylonian stele, inscribed in cuneiform, proclaims Babylonian government regulations.

The first libraries appeared five thousand years ago in Southwest Asia's "Fertile Crescent," the agricultural region reaching from Mesopotamia's Tigris and Euphrates rivers to the valley of the Nile in Africa. Known as the "cradle of civilization," the Fertile Crescent was the birthplace of writing, sometime before 3000 BCE.

The earliest writing was done on various materials: bones, skins, bamboo, clay, and papyrus. It consisted of images (pictographs) representing a subject or idea. From the start, written documents needed storage and organization—libraries.

In ancient Mesopotamia, written documents were clay tablets inscribed by using a stylus when the clay was damp. *Cuneiform,* the name for this technique of ancient writing, comes from *cunea,* Latin for "wedge," because the characters were made by cutting small wedges into the clay. Groups of wedges indicated words or terms. At least fifteen ancient Mesopotamian languages have been discovered on tablets inscribed with cuneiform.

The earliest clay tablets recorded business transactions and government matters, such as taxes paid and owed, armies raised and supplied. In time, literature developed—epics and myths, as well as scientific, historical, and philosophical tracts. Clay tablets contain the ancients' knowledge of astronomy, geography, and medicine, and reveal the earliest myths, such as the *Epic of Gilgamesh,* the creation story of Babylon, Mesopotamia's great city. Clay tablets were the first books.

About an inch thick, tablets came in various shapes and sizes. Mud-like clay was placed in wooden frames, and the surface was smoothed for writing and allowed to dry until damp. After being inscribed, the clay dried in the sun, or for a harder finish was baked in a kiln, much like pottery. For storage, tablets could be stacked on edge, side by side, the contents described by a title written on the edge that faced out and was readily seen. Some ancient libraries used baskets to hold tablets, while a library at Babylon stored them in earthenware jars.

When it came to the archives and libraries of ancient cities, conquest by invaders usually resulted in the victors carrying off the tablets or burning down the buildings that housed the libraries. Since clay tablets do not burn, they endured when left undisturbed in the arid climate of Southwest Asia. Over time, the encroachment of the desert buried many an abandoned tablet-library under drifting sand, to be hidden for thousands of years.

▲ The excavated ruins of the third-millennium BCE West Asian city of Ebla have yielded 20,000 inscribed clay tablets from the oldest known library.

Archaeological expeditions have excavated scores of ancient libraries, notably at Ebla, Nineveh, Nimrud, and Pergamum. The daily life of legendary civilizations has been revealed by the discovery of the clay tablets. The oldest known library was found in the lost ruins of Ebla, in northern Syria. A major commercial center by 2500 BCE, Ebla was destroyed twice. After the second time, around 1650 BCE, it never recovered and wind covered the ruins—and their libraries—with the desert's sand. Ebla was no more than a legend until the 1970s, when it was unearthed by archaeologists who eventually recovered 20,000 clay tablets with cuneiform writing.

Typical of ancient libraries, Ebla's tablets had been arranged on shelves built into the walls. When Ebla's library shelves were burned by the invading army, or decayed over time, they collapsed under the tablets' weight. According to one researcher, the tablets "settled on top of one another, in horizontal heaps, like cards in a file." They were discovered in exactly that way.

Many Ebla tablets were inscribed with a previously unknown dialect termed Northwest Semitic, or "Old Canaanite" (also named "Eblaite"). Other tablets were in Sumerian, a language much studied and well understood by archaeologists. Among the tablets were vocabularies that intermixed words from the two languages, which allowed for the translation of Eblaite.

Ebla's tablets documented the economic and cultural life of the city's 250,000 inhabitants, who had commercial relations with the peoples of eighty other lands. One library storeroom contained lists of food and drink, apparently keeping the accounts of official messengers and state functionaries. Other tablets dealt with the textile trade, Ebla's prime business, while many were concerned with taxes. Some tablets contained legends, hymns, magical incantations, and scientific records and observations—including writings on zoology and mineralogy. Ebla's tablets also held the first known references to the city of Jerusalem.

In the seventh century BCE, Assyrian king Assurbanipal established one of the greatest ancient libraries at Nineveh, on the Tigris River. Assurbanipal's royal library of more than 30,000 clay tablets, written in several languages, often were organized according to shape: four-sided tablets were for financial transactions, while round tablets recorded agricultural information. (In this era, some written documents were also on wood and others on wax tablets.)

Tablets were separated according to their contents and placed in different rooms: government, history, law, astronomy, geography, and so on. The contents were identified by colored marks or brief written descriptions, and sometimes by the "incipit," or the first few words that began the text.

The Nineveh library was Assurbanipal's passion, and he sent out scribes to the distant corners of his kingdom to visit other libraries and record their contents. These were among the first library catalogs. The king also organized the copying of original literary works, for he sought to study the "artistic script of the Sumerians" and the "obscure script of the Akkadians." In so doing, Assurbanipal hoped to obtain "the hidden treasures of the scribe's knowledge." Assurbanipal's library also held the *Gilgamesh Epic*. In the coming ages, libraries would be increasingly revered as sources of knowledge and wisdom—spiritual, magical, and earthly—and whoever controlled books and libraries possessed a unique power.

Assurbanipal died in 627 BCE, and the Assyrian empire weakened. Nineveh was attacked and destroyed in 612 BCE, its people massacred or driven away, the city razed to the ground, and a great fire ravaged the library.

By 3000 BCE Egyptians had developed hieroglyphics, which combines pictographs with symbols (glyphs) that represent syllables when spoken aloud. *Hieroglyphics* means "sacred engraving," the term given to this form of writing by Greeks, who discovered examples of it in Egyptian temples and funeral sites. There are some six thousand known hieroglyphs from Egypt, where they were in use until the fourth century.

▲ "Sacred engravings," carved Egyptian hieroglyphics is a form of writing that combines glyphs that symbolize spoken sounds with pictographs.

▲ This fourteenth-century ʙᴄᴇ scene from *The Book of the Dead* shows a scribe, followed by his mother and wife, meeting Osiris, the Egyptian god of the dead.

In Egypt, papyrus rolls were used for writing on rather than clay tablets. Papyrus—from which the term "paper" derives—is a tall, reedy plant that grows in abundance in the delta of the Nile River. To produce a writing surface, papyrus stalks were opened, exposing the interior pith, which was then pounded flat into a sheet. The sheet held together because of the reed's stringy consistency, and when two sheets were overlaid, crisscrossing, the resulting page could be made durable and smooth. Papyrus sheets were glued in sequence, making a scroll which received writing only on one side.

Library papyrus rolls were stored in wooden boxes and chests, piled on shelves, and also kept in wooden cases made in the form of statues. In some civilizations, they were kept in large clay jars. Scrolls were organized and grouped according to subject or author, and identified by labels that specified their contents. These labels, often made of clay, like thin pieces of pottery, were attached by a string to the end of the scroll. Labels made it possible to identify the contents without having to take down and unroll the scroll.

Papyrus was resilient enough to be reused when the writing was wiped off. Unlike clay tablets, it was lightweight, and since papyrus grew abundantly in the region, it was also inexpensive. Papyrus grew almost exclusively in Egypt; this meant that Egyptians controlled its distribution, which influenced the development of books and writing in the civilized world.

The English term "library" derives from *liber*, Latin for "book." The Greek term for a papyrus roll is *biblion*, and a container for storing rolls is called a *bibliotheke*. In some languages, the word for library is a variant of *bibliotheke*, a place where books are kept.

Unfortunately, papyrus was susceptible to deterioration, so few ancient scrolls survive. Conversely, archaeologists have discovered more than 400,000 clay tablets, buried in Fertile Crescent cities abandoned long ago and surrendered to the sands.

Clay tablets and papyrus scrolls kept in temples were maintained and organized by priests and their scribes (professional writers and copyists). The scribe worked in his "scriptorium," or writing chamber. One task was to prepare funerary scrolls for the wealthy by copying the texts of original books, the most revered of which was *The Book of the Dead,* a sacred guide to the afterlife. A copy of this text was an essential component of the deceased's burial wares and treasures. The funerary papyrus scroll was buried in a tomb, often in a mummy's sarcophagus, and expected to endure longer than a carved stone, or *stele*, which stood aboveground, exposed to the wind and weather.

The scroll was engraved with symbols, and often with writing. Scribes who wrote biographical literature were considered to have a kind of mystical ability

▲ This drawing, taken from a lost second-century Roman bas relief, shows papyrus or vellum scrolls stacked in a library.

In this drawing copied from a wall painting decorating an Egyptian tomb, scribes are portrayed working in a Memphis writing chamber. ▶

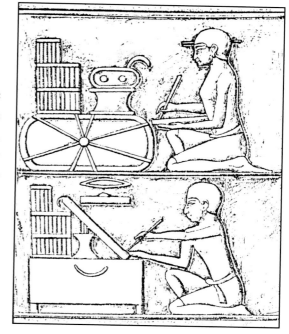

to transcend time and death because their writing would last beyond the lifetime of the subject—king, noble, or priest. The scribe's name was usually included on the scroll, occasionally accompanied by his family heritage, which could be quite lengthy if the scribe were important enough in his own right.

The best scribes were valued by nobles and governments, and it was a status symbol to have their signatures on one's family documents. The scribe was highly regarded for superior, almost magical, reading and writing skills. His written words were a link to the ancestors, to the future, even to the gods themselves. As an ancient Egyptian poem put it, "The wise scribes of the time[,] their names endure forever," even though they built no pyramids or "stelae of stone."

> They chose not to leave children
> to be their heirs and perpetuate their names:
> they appointed as their heirs
> the books they wrote and the precepts therein. . . .
>
> Man vanishes, his body is buried in the ground,
> all his contemporaries depart this earth,
> but the written word puts the memory of him
> in the mouth of any person who passes it on to the mouth of
>   another.
>
> A book is better than a house
> or the tombs in the West.
> It is more beautiful than a castle
> or a stele in a temple.

The profession of scribe was a difficult one, its demands all-consuming, as exemplified by what an Egyptian instructor told his student: "I shall make thee love writing more than thine own mother."

Legend has it that when the preeminence of Egypt's Alexandria library was challenged by a new library at Pergamum in Asia Minor, the Egyptians refused to export papyrus to their competitors. As a result, Pergamum developed a writing material of its own, made from the skin of calves, sheep, and goats, called *parchment* (it is *pergamenum* in Latin and *pergament* in Germanic languages, harking back to its origins in Pergamum).

Parchment's smooth surface took ink and paint better than papyrus, facilitating beautiful designs and calligraphy on the book page, and it was also more durable. The finest quality parchment is *vellum,* generally made from calfskin. By the fifth century in Europe, parchment, in its various forms, had replaced papyrus as the leading writing material.

In ancient Greece, library and archival collections flourished by 600 BCE, and within the next three centuries the culture of the written word rose to a pinnacle there. By the closing centuries BCE, writing and books were not only essential to human progress, but cultures also won prestige according to the size and worth of their libraries. Private book collections in homes and temples, and handsome structures to contain them, were being built by the leading citizens of Greece.

The Greeks were the first to establish libraries for the public, not just for the ruling elite. By 500 BCE, Athens and Sámos were developing public libraries; however, the majority of people could not read, so even these early public libraries served just a small part of the population.

In addition to government-sponsored Greek libraries, private libraries came to be assembled by wealthy book lovers, called *bibliophiles,* who appreciated beautiful scrolls and well-appointed library rooms. Private libraries were also built by professionals, such as doctors and scholars, who needed information close at hand. Greek city-states founded specialized libraries for medicine, philosophy, and the sciences.

The scholars Plato, Euripides, Thucydides, and Herodotus owned large personal libraries, pioneering a custom that blossomed in Roman days, when beautiful private libraries were essential centerpieces in the homes of the wealthy and the noble class.

One of the most celebrated libraries belonged to the philosopher Aristotle, who permitted his students and fellow scholars to use it. The fate of Aristotle's library is the stuff of legend, for it is said to have been brought generations later to either Alexandria or Rome, or perhaps even later to Constantinople. Becoming the spoils of war was the precarious destiny of many a library in classical times, when books and the knowledge they held were coveted by both the educated and the avaricious.

In his short lifetime, Macedonian king Alexander the Great (356–323 BCE) conquered Greece and most of the known world. Alexander laid claim to the mantle of Greek, or Hellenic, culture and to its educational tradition, rich in reading and writing and libraries.

Alexander's conquests facilitated the vast spread of Hellenic culture, which took root in the cities he captured or founded from the Mediterranean to the Himalayas. His victories, on the other hand, often resulted in the destruction of major libraries. A third-century Persian text describes how Alexander brought to the land "severe cruelty and war and devastation," sacking the capital city of Persepolis with its large library of ancient books. The account states that his forces seized an archive of holy works "written upon cow-skins and with gold ink," and "burned them up."

Although dozens of cities were named after Alexander, his enduring imperial jewel was founded in Egypt, at the mouth of the Nile: Alexandria. The most renowned cultural treasure of Alexandria was its Great Library, or Royal Library, established by Ptolemy I Soter, a Macedonian general who assumed kingship of Egypt upon Alexander's death.

Ptolemy's Alexandrian library was founded by 300 BCE and became a world center for scholarship, literature, and books. The Great Library acquired—often by laborious copying of originals—the largest holdings of the age, although historians debate the precise number of scrolls. The highest estimates claim 400,000 scrolls at the Great Library, while the most conservative estimates are as low as 40,000, which is still an enormous collection that required vast storage space.

▲ Scholars and library staff work with papyrus and vellum scrolls in the Alexandria library.

Over the centuries, the Great Library and several other major Alexandrian libraries suffered from fires and conquest, but for seven centuries the city was famous as the world's leading repository of learning and wisdom. Alexandria retained this status even during Rome's ascendancy. From the second century BCE to the first centuries of the Common Era, Romans looked to Alexandria for learning and for books.

Alexandria remained the intellectual capital of the Western world during the rise of Christianity in the second and third centuries. With the fall of the city to Arab invaders in the fourth century, the heart of learning shifted back to cities in Mesopotamia—Damascus and Baghdad—where scholars still studied the ancient texts, and libraries were essential to intellectual exploration and scientific advancement.

The Alexandrian Great Library was essentially a temple, dedicated to the Nine Muses, the goddesses of the arts—among them poetry, music, singing, and oratory. A building so dedicated was more than a place for records and books, but was termed a *museum,* a place of the Muses, a place of culture.

There were several major libraries in the city, of which the Great Library was the most prominent. The Ptolemaic dynasty, down through Queen Cleopatra of the first century BCE, stimulated Alexandria's libraries to flourish. The leading philosophers, teachers, and scholars of the age made their way to the city to teach and to learn. Just as Rome became the capital of the empire, Alexandria could be considered the capital of knowledge and learning.

Alexandria's library administrators collected scrolls from all over the world and organized and copied them—not always returning those they borrowed. In one notorious case, Athens loaned the library some extremely important original scrolls so they might be copied, and, as a guarantee of their return, Alexandria gave an enormous sum in gold to the people of Athens. Alexandria's desire for original books was so strong, however, that only the new copies were shipped back to the Athenians, who had to be content with keeping the gold and the copies.

For all his love of books and libraries, Roman emperor Julius Caesar (100–44 BCE) was reputedly responsible for the inadvertent destruction of thousands of scrolls during a battle for Alexandria in 48 BCE. According to his memoirs, Caesar's forces torched ships in the harbor, but the fire spread to buildings on land. Later historians claim that the fire engulfed thousands of books stored there. Historians have attempted, inconclusively, to establish whether the books actually were in the Great Library or were in warehouses at the seaport—destined to be shipped by Caesar himself, back to Rome. The only certainty is that many works were tragically lost in the fire.

In spite of enduring legends, no single fire destroyed the Alexandrian Great Library. After Caesar's blunder, several major fires, and even earthquakes, damaged Alexandria over the centuries. Periodic wars and destructive riots by anti-pagan Christian mobs cost the city's libraries further damage and loss. The Alexandrian book collections steadily diminished as a result of natural causes, war, and wholesale theft by corrupt administrators.

By the fourth century, the Alexandrian libraries—both books and buildings—had faded away, until only the legend remained.

Far to the south of Alexandria, in the lands some knew as Ethiopia, lay the kingdom of Aksum, a trading and maritime power. Fifth-century BCE Greek author, Aeschylus, wrote of this region as "a land at the world's end, where tribes of black people live."

Established by the first century as a trading hub for Europe, Asia, and Africa, Aksum rose beyond tribalism to become a militarily potent empire. In the following centuries, its far-ranging navy and merchant fleet operated from bustling ports on the Red Sea. Rich in gold, iron, and salt, the third-century Aksumite Empire was considered equal to the three other major empires: Rome, Persia, and China.

Towering stone stelae stood throughout Aksum, the tallest reaching one hundred feet in height. These obelisks were engraved to identify royal gravesites or to mark important places. With a unique written language,

▲ An illustration from a manuscript Bible depicts Moses receiving tablets inscribed with God's law. The Bible is written on parchment and in Ge'ez, the liturgical language of the Ethiopian Orthodox Christian Church.

Ge'ez, Aksum possessed its own translation of the Bible, and its libraries contained important Christian documents. Many such works were translated by Aksum's Coptic monks between the fifth and seventh centuries. The pre-Christian *Book of Enoch* exists only in Ge'ez. Aksum scholars and scribes also taught calligraphy and manuscript illumination—decoration with designs, colors, and miniature images—and they highly esteemed the composition of poetry.

Aksumite rulers, who often spoke and read in Greek, put great store in written documents and in libraries to keep them, which allowed the history of Aksum to survive. Thousands of Aksumite documents have been preserved, including theological tracts and medical treatises, as well as important writings on natural history that were studied by contemporaries in Europe.

Aksum was cosmopolitan, with a diverse population of Ethiopians, Nubians, Sudanese, Hebrews, Arabs, Indians, and Egyptians. Aksum's faiths included Christianity, Islam, Buddhism, Hinduism, Jainism, and Judaism, as well as Greek polytheism and animist beliefs. The kingdom is said to have been home to the fabled tenth-century BCE Queen of Sheba, known to Ethiopians as Makeda, and the honored guest of King Solomon of Israel.

According to local lore, the Hebrews' Ark of the Covenant is secreted in an Aksum church and guarded by priests. This sacred container, said to have been created at the direction of God, is believed to hold certain sacred articles, including the tablets of stone bearing the Ten Commandments given to Moses.

In the fourth century, Aksum became the first significant empire to accept Christianity when King Ezana (320–350) was converted by his slave-teacher, Frumentius (d. 383), a Greek Phoenician. The zeal of Frumentius for proselytizing the people of the Red Sea persuaded the Patriarch of Alexandria to ordain him Bishop of Aksum.

The kingdom declined after the seventh century, giving way to Islamic powers, agricultural failures, and the rise of new trading empires that exploited the Persian Gulf rather than the Red Sea. Aksum would be more commonly referred to by medieval writers as Ethiopia, remembered as an educated, literate society that cherished libraries.

The Roman republic, and later the empire, embraced the culture of the Greeks, including the Hellenic virtues of acquiring a broad education and of building libraries. As the empire flourished, between the first century BCE to the fourth century, Romans established libraries throughout the known world.

The finest Roman libraries contained books in both Latin and Greek. In keeping with Hellenic tradition, the classical Roman library was constructed in the form of a temple and usually had separate rooms for Greek and Latin works. These rooms were joined by a covered esplanade where visitors and scholars could sit in the shade and read or hold discussions. Roman libraries were even placed in public baths, a token of the luxurious lifestyle of the empire's wealthiest citizens who grew up with a love of books and literature.

Emperors Augustus, Tiberius, Vespasian, and Trajan all created great libraries, emulating Julius Caesar, the first emperor who aspired to establish a library for the public. Caesar's assassination in 44 BCE cut short his ambitions, but his successors built public and private libraries with books gathered from around the empire. Although scribes copied thousands of books, and Roman scholars and thinkers came to write their own important works as

▼ The second-century facade of a library and tomb still stands in Ephesus, Turkey, testimony to Tiberius Julius Celsus Polemaeanus, governor of Asia, whose 12,000 scrolls were once kept here.

The Roman poet Cicero writes in his library, where shelves hold both scrolls and bound codex books. ▶

successors to the Greeks, many libraries were founded, or enlarged, by bibliophile generals who carried off books as war booty.

Roman libraries and their scribes and scriptoria suffered along with the decline of the empire and the ravages of invaders. Of course, some conquerors of Rome, such as the Ostrogoths, were themselves educated, and they built new libraries or preserved existing ones. By the fourth century, Rome had been diminished, and the focus of the empire moved eastward to the city of Constantinople, the next great center of learning and libraries.

With the rise of Christians to political power, many Roman book collections were wantonly destroyed as unholy, pagan teachings that revered more than one god. Yet, the tradition of writing books and maintaining libraries persevered, for the book proved an effective means of propagating and spreading the newly dominant faith. New libraries were established at churches and monasteries, often containing ancient pagan books that had survived persecution and destruction—although these were not for public view.

The fall of Rome brought a cultural and intellectual darkness over much of the Western world by the sixth century, as the church was acquiring worldly power and influence. As the outside world suffered intellectual oppression, scribes were working as hard as ever in Christian libraries and scriptoria, copying old and new books and manuscripts for future collections.

Among the greatest achievements of these far-flung scriptoria, from Britain to the Black Sea, was the advance of the art of illumination. Book-making moved from papyrus scrolls to vellum bound pages inscribed on both sides—and new arts arose in the craft of bookbinding, calligraphy, and design.

Memoria de sco ypofozo. ant

Sancte ypofo
ir martir
ihesu ypristi
qui pro eius
nomine pe

na pertulisti opem confer in
seris atqz mundo tristi. qui
celestis glorie regna meruisti
ypofozi sancti speciem quicui
qz tueretur illo nempe die nul
lo sanguioze grauetur. confer
solamen et mentis tolle gra
uamen. Judicis examen fac
mite sic omnibus. Vz Oza
pro nobis beate martir ypo

EUROPEAN LIBRARIES
OF THE MIDDLE AGES

Roman libraries which were open to readers other than colleagues of the owner or benefactor—and termed "public"—laid the cornerstone for the future libraries of Europe and the Mediterranean countries. At the height of the old Roman Empire it was said that public libraries made authors' "talents a public possession."

By the close of the fourth century, the Roman Empire was divided into western and eastern realms, with Rome and Constantinople the respective capitals. In the fifth century, Rome fell to invaders, and Constantinople dominated what remained of the original empire: parts of southern Europe, Anatolia, and much of the Mediterranean coast.

The Middle Ages in Europe—from the fifth to the fifteenth centuries, known as the medieval era—was a time of decline in civilization. The period from 500 to 800 is often considered the "Dark Ages," when cities and towns were swept away by warfare and neglect, and barbarity overcame Rome's intellectual heritage. Although there were few open libraries anywhere between the sixth and ninth centuries, hundreds of small, private libraries were struggling to survive and even to grow. It would be long after the end of Rome's dominance before libraries would again be open to the public.

Yet, all was not darkness and loss. This era saw the rise of the Roman Catholic Church in the West, and the Byzantine, or Orthodox, Church in the East. As early as the second century, monastic communities dedicated to the

◀ This page from a late 1470s "book of hours" shows a butterfly with the plants speedwell and periwinkle. The Latin text is a devotion to Saint Christopher.

contemplative life were being established, many devoted to book learning, which prepared monks and nuns to understand and teach the faith. Monastery scribes, both monks and nuns, labored to carefully copy and preserve books so that even the Dark Ages were not completely devoid of learning or of libraries.

In the fifth century, while the Roman Empire of the West was crumbling, the libraries of Constantinople, capital city of the Byzantine Empire, were gathering classical Greek and Roman works. In Byzantine libraries they were protected from destruction by invaders or by Christians hostile to "pagans"— the term used for anyone not a Christian, Muslim, or Jew.

In Roman times, the term *librarii* meant publishers, copyists, and booksellers (the book trade), not buildings or book collections. At first, the future of the book trade looked promising under Constantinople's rule, for the flourishing of Christianity inspired believers to produce new writings; however, that promise was not to be fulfilled. For one thing, Christian writers generally published their own books, and in very limited numbers, circulating them mainly among friends and associates.

Another circumstance adverse to the book trade was the steady crumbling of the eastern empire's economy, embattled by wars on several fronts. Economic decline contributed to the ruin of publishing, which had already been struggling because of the high cost of book production. Parchment was scarce and expensive, as were the services of professional scribes and bookbinders.

Perhaps the most decisive factor in the demise of the Byzantine book trade during the medieval era was Christian opposition to pagan works that challenged its doctrines. With the persecution of non-Christian writers, and the banning and destruction of works from the classic Greco-Roman era, the book business virtually collapsed. Libraries suffered in kind. One contemporary observer remarked that once-thriving libraries had closed up and were "like tombs."

An illumination from a late tenth-century Byzantine manuscript of the Christian Gospels, Matthew, Mark, Luke, and John. ▶

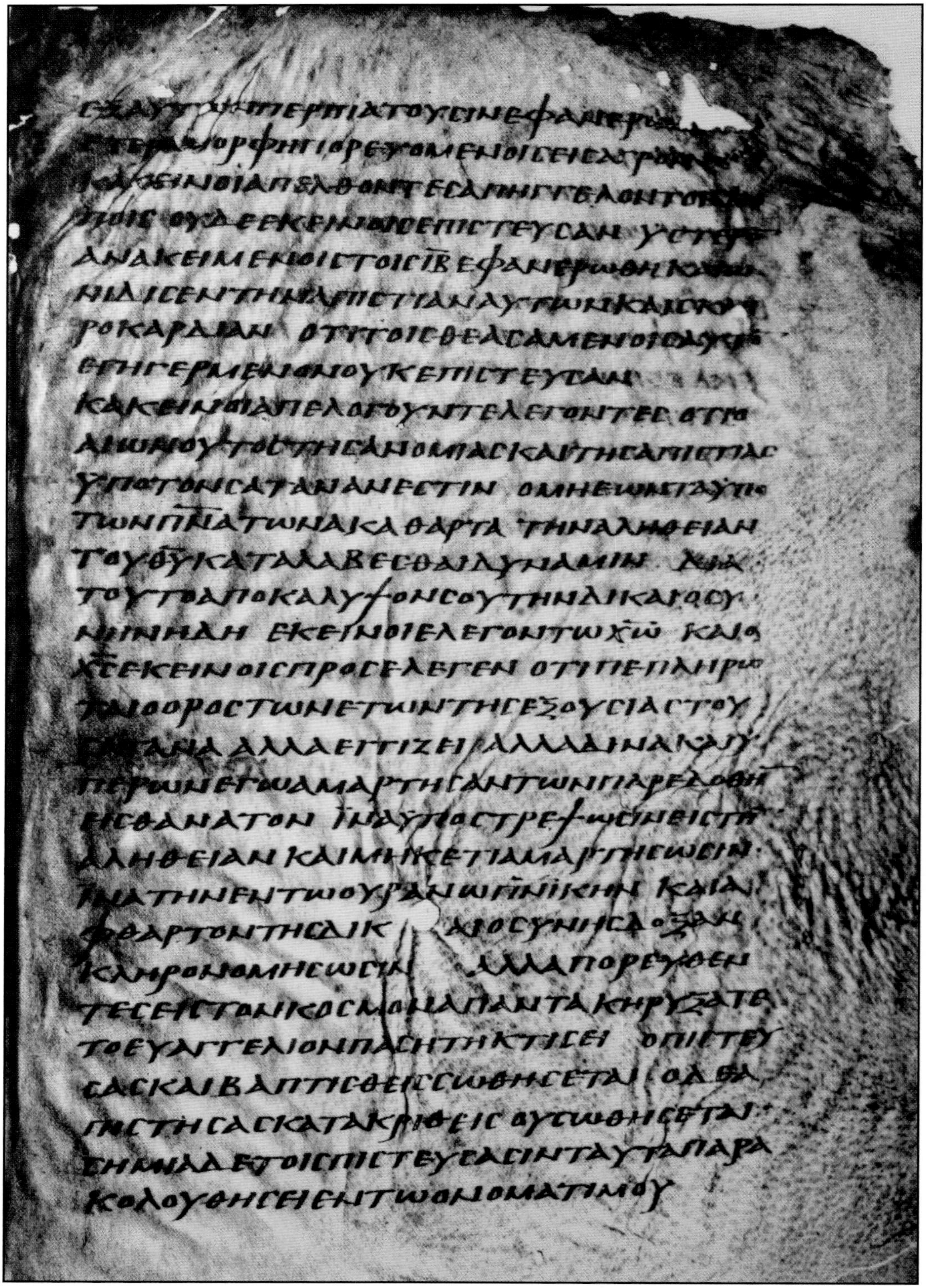

Despite Christian suppression of pagan texts, the upper classes of the Byzantine Empire possessed refined taste, admired learning, and appreciated beautiful books. In the fifth century, Constantinople's rulers maintained a great imperial library of several thousand books on diverse subjects, which were made available to scholars. These were parchment scrolls for the most part, rather than the increasingly popular new form of book, the bound *codex,* with pages. Constantinople's imperial collection was said to have a scroll of Homer's works one hundred and twenty feet long, written in gold ink.

The Romans invented the *codex* form of the book, folding the scroll into pages which made reading and handling the document much easier. Legend has it that Julius Caesar was the first to fold scrolls, concertina-fashion, for dispatches to his forces campaigning in Gaul. Scrolls were awkward to read if a reader wished to consult material at opposite ends of the document. Further, scrolls were written only on one side, while both sides of the codex page were used.

Eventually, the folds were cut into sheets, or "leaves," and bound together along one edge. The bound pages were protected by stiff covers, usually of wood enclosed with leather. *Codex* is Latin for a "block of wood"; the Latin *liber,* the root of "library," and the German *Buch,* the source of "book," both refer to wood. The codex was not only easier to handle than the scroll, but it also fit conveniently on library shelves. The spine generally held the book's title, facing out, affording easier organization of the collection.

The term *codex* technically refers only to manuscript books—those that, at one time, were handwritten. More specifically, a codex is the term used primarily for a bound manuscript from Roman times up through the Middle Ages.

From the fourth century on, the codex became the standard format for books, and scrolls were no longer generally used. After the contents of a parchment scroll were copied in codex format, the scroll was seldom preserved. The majority that did survive were found by archaeologists in burial pits and in the buried trash of forgotten communities.

Christians favored the codex format for their books, especially the Bible (its name derived from the Greek *biblion,* meaning "book"). One emperor commissioned a special production of fifty codex Greek Bibles. The scroll remained a

◀ Greek text from a fourth- or fifth-century Gospel of Mark.

symbol of Judaism, however, with the Laws of Moses inscribed on the Torah scroll—the most sacred document of the Jews.

Although book publishing and libraries did not prosper as in classical times, the Byzantines still possessed a stock of fine old books in both scroll and codex format, often from the classical Greek and Roman eras. Constantinople was known for exporting books, many of which went to Arab and Persian libraries where they were translated and studied by scholars who were participating in an intellectual blossoming. Thus did Constantinople preserve classical knowledge and pass it on to the Islamic libraries.

In 476 a major fire broke out in Constantinople, and the Byzantine imperial library burned, leaving monasteries and churches as the main repositories of old books.

Across Europe, Christian monastic orders were joined by thousands of men and women devoted to a contemplative way of life. ("Monasticism" derives from the Greek *monos*, meaning "alone.") Monastic dwellers spurned earthly possessions in favor of piety, poverty, and isolation. Scribes and copyists in monasteries painstakingly reproduced books and slowly increased the size of their libraries.

The sixth-century Order of Saint Benedict, adherents of Italian priest Benedict of Nursia (480–543), became the most influential with regard to the world of books and libraries. Their own guidebook, *Rule of Monks*, set out the principles and duties of the monastic community, advising members to practice moderation in all things—eating, religious devotion, and fasting—and to read every day. The *Rule of Monks* required each monastery to have at least one book for every brother.

The *Rule of Monks* also admonished Benedictines to never be idle and to set aside "specified periods for manual labor as well as for prayerful reading." Even at meals the Benedictine monks were exposed to the written word as a brother read aloud to them—often narratives from the lives of the saints.

The Benedictines established monasteries throughout Europe, from southern Italy to islands off Scotland. Many monasteries began to build

The illuminated Gospel *Codex Aureus of Lorsch,* from the Biblioteca Apostolica Vaticana, was written between 778 and 820, an era that included Charlemagne's rule of the Frankish Empire. ▶

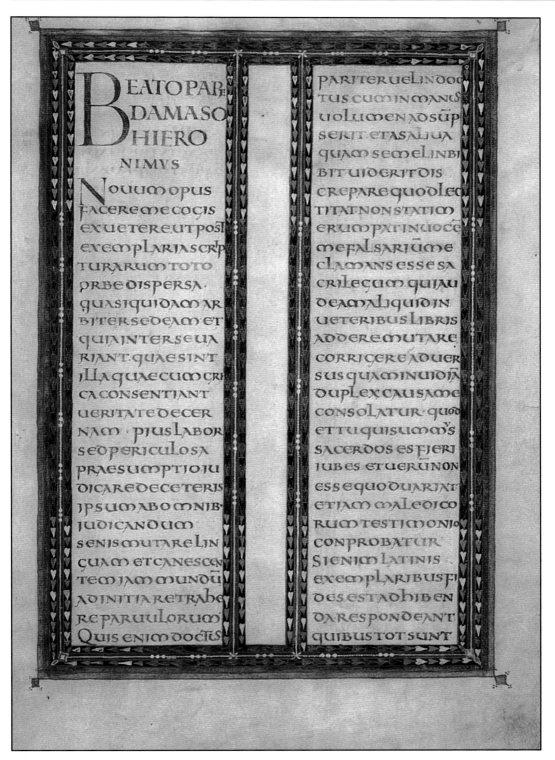

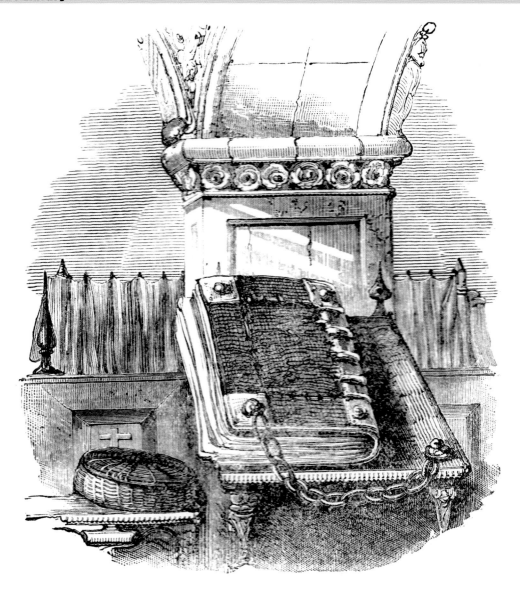

▲ A chained book in Cumnor Church, Leicestershire, England.

libraries, with the most notable at Monte Cassino and Bobbio in Italy; Fulda and Corvey in Germany; St. Gall in Switzerland; and Canterbury, Wearmouth, and Jarrow, in England. The first monastery libraries usually had fewer than a hundred books, and collections of three hundred were considered remarkably large. Many titles were duplicates, produced by and for the community.

Some Benedictines not only read every day but also wrote, employed as scribes copying texts or translating Greek works into Latin. Benedictine scriptoria became the most productive of the Middle Ages, as their far-flung monasteries industriously turned out copies of important titles—at first mostly theological. Over the centuries, monks copied thousands of manuscripts and books: the Scriptures, stories and works of the Church founders, psalters (versions of the *Book of Psalms*), missals (books of prayers or devotions), the Gospels, and writings of church leaders.

In the sixth century, the Roman Catholic Church asserted its authority over the monasteries, making their libraries the communal possession of all churches. As a result, books were more freely distributed among the monasteries, which used them for copying or exchanged them in trade for other books.

At first, most copying was done in Latin, the language common to the educated across Europe. In later centuries, texts were translated into regional languages that were maturing—Spanish, French, English, and German, in particular. Such translations made books available to a much broader audience.

In the ninth century, after conquering much of Western Europe, Charlemagne (742–814), king of the Franks, encouraged a rejuvenation of scholarship and intellectualism. A true bibliophile, Charlemagne urged clerics to pursue the "study of letters," to teach grammar and music, and to translate Christian creed and prayers into the vernacular. So much copying was accomplished as a result of this royal exhortation that virtually every ancient European manuscript that had survived until then was likely to be preserved.

At this time, increasing numbers of secular books were being produced, including chronicles and histories of various peoples, anthologies of Greek and Roman poets, and titles for studying canon and civil law, theology, medicine, rhetoric, prose composition, music, verse, agriculture, and surveying. Many private libraries were established during Charlemagne's reign, built up by aristocrats and churchmen.

Books were in demand—so much so that monastic libraries even loaned them out on occasion, as long as something of equal value was left as a deposit (often another book) to guarantee the title's timely return. Borrowers were

▲ A January day for exchanging gifts is shown in this richly decorated fifteenth-century "book of hours," commissioned by Jean, Duc de Berry, around 1410.

usually nobles or government officials, or individuals who were benefactors of the monastery. This was as close to a public library as monastic libraries ever became in this era.

Increasingly, the children of the nobility and the rising merchant class were coming to monasteries and the newly built cathedrals to be taught by the clergy, mainly in language arts, civil law, and medicine. New generations of educated officials and administrators were needed as cities and towns began to thrive and commerce expanded.

With renewed economic and cultural progress in Europe, there arose a hunger for books and education, and the ancient wisdom and contemporary knowledge they imparted.

Book production was done almost exclusively at the larger monasteries, where monks and lay brothers were the copyists and bookbinders. Outside specialists were also employed, particularly as artists to illuminate pages with elaborate capital letters, pictures, and designs. A substantial monastery might have as many as forty scribes at work in its scriptoria, the average scribe copying two books a year.

▲ Scriveners are portrayed in this Library of Congress mural by John White Alexander (1856–1915), part of his "Evolution of the Book" series.

In the early Middle Ages, monasteries lacked money and valuable possessions; even so, most were self-sufficient, growing crops, brewing beer, and raising livestock. The frugal monks and nuns put everything to good use. Scribes wrote on parchment made from the skins of the monastery's own animals, using quills from its geese. As the centuries passed and gave way to a time of reawakening and rebuilding, many monasteries became rather prosperous. This wealth came, in part, because their scriptoria were substantial sources of income, as new clients ordered books or engaged scribes to write or translate for them.

And there were ever more exquisite books, written and illustrated in gold, silver, and purple ink, with gold leaf overlaid on ornate initials, and bound in covers of ivory and metal mounted on wood. Such books were illuminated by the most skilled artists, with entire pages given over to artwork alone. These were the tomes commissioned by feudal nobility and high churchmen, books fine enough to be the gifts of vassals to liege lords, of kings to fellow kings.

A *Book of Hours* was an appropriate gift for any important personage. This was a collection of texts, prayers, and psalms to guide daily devotions, including a calendar with the holy feast days to be observed that year. The illuminations, though, were not always after religious themes. Often, there were scenes of country life, of changing seasons, and of knights and ladies in their fine castles.

Irish monks living in seacoast monasteries created especially beautiful books famed for decorations and

◀ A page from the *Book of Kells*, showing the incipit, *"In principio erat verbum."*

 Much of the *Book of Kells* may have been produced by monks of the early ninth-century Abbey of Kells in County Meath, Ireland, north of Dublin.

motifs that recalled an ancient Celtic heritage. Some wealthy monasteries had won such high repute by the ninth century that they brought about their own destruction. The first eruptions of Scandinavian Vikings knew the monasteries on remote islands and inlets were easy prey. The monks were helpless when longships appeared unexpectedly from the sea, and the Vikings stormed ashore to kill and pillage.

In the Middle Ages, every book was made by hand.

Each component required several tedious tasks, from carefully cutting sheets of parchment to writing the script, binding the pages, and protecting them with a cover. The scribe's writing duties were especially demanding, requiring meticulous care and long hours. Just copying the Bible took fifteen months of toil.

Working in daylight from a nearby window, the copyist sat down with a writing board laid across the arms of his chair (most scribes were male). He tried to sit close to the fire or beside a basin of hot coals, for heat was needed

▲ A scrivener's writing desk and chair with cushion at the historical site of Walraversijde, near Oostende, Belgium.

to dry the ink as well as keep the copyist warm. A deerskin thong, stretched across the writing board, held sheets of parchment in place.

To begin, the parchment was scraped clean, smoothed with a pumice stone, and imperfections removed with a sharp blade. Next, using ruler and awl, the scribe marked out lines and columns on the sheets. When the parchment was ready, the scribe dipped a hollow goose-quill pen into ink in an ox horn fitted into a hole in the board, and the writing began.

General rules in a scriptorium forbade the use of candles to limit the danger of fire. No unauthorized persons were allowed into the room, and idle chatter was not permitted. The toilers needed all their powers of concentration to assure accuracy. Furthermore, in a scriptorium of the Benedictines, silence was deemed an expression of piety.

The monastic scriptorium's only sounds might be the scratching of pens, occasional coughs, or the scrape of a chair against the floor. The evening bells called monks and lay brothers away to meals and prayers, and finally, to bed.

Ezra the scribe is at work in this illumination from the *Codex Amiatinus*, the earliest surviving manuscript of the complete Bible in the Latin Vulgate version. ▶

CODICIBVS SACRIS HOSTILI CLADE PERVSTIS
ESDRA DO FERVENS HOC REPARAVIT OPVS

Before dawn, they arose with the morning bells to resume their hushed labors in the scriptorium, which went on day after day except for the Sabbath.

Though the scriptorium of a monastery was silent, there was no sacred silence in a bustling, rowdy medieval town for a scribe—copyist, clerk, secretary, or scrivener, whichever he was called. Most writing chambers of the tenth and eleventh centuries were in the noisy center of fast-growing cities, near the scribe's clients, or at a newly built cathedral or growing university.

Some scriptoria belonged to lords, schoolmasters, or scholars, who commissioned the writing of poetry, prose, songs, and historical chronicles—most of which were known only by word of mouth until then. In such a scriptorium the copyist would not always be at work on fragile old manuscripts, but would also serve as the lord's secretary, writing his letters and recording his memoirs. Nor were his finished books always illuminated or beautifully bound. For the most part, common books were only columns of text, plain and legible, on pages bound between wooden boards. Sometimes several books were bound between the same boards—perhaps for the scholar who needed books but was short of money.

When working with an author, the scribe often copied drafts of text that had been written on wax tablets or chalked slates. Parchment was too rare and too costly to use for rough drafts, but wax could be wiped down or melted and slate could be cleaned and used again. Some authors dictated to the scribe, who wrote on wax and later transferred this work to parchment.

Whether in a private house near the city's center or at a secluded monastery, the scriptorium was a place of hard, patient labor. Many a medieval manuscript testifies to this with comments left by scribes, who were permitted to place a personal colophon, or inscription, in the margin at the close of the text:

> I have made an end at last,
> And my weary hand can rest.

Another, likely a professional copyist rather than a monk, scribbled:

> Now that I an end have made,
> See that what I'm owed is paid.

Whether the scribe was a professional copyist or a monk is not clear in this inscription:

> May the writer continue to copy,
> and drink good wine.

Most often, the copyist's comment was simply, "Finished, thank God."

With the appearance of cathedral schools and a dynamic mercantile class that sought both education and entertainment in reading, books were more sought after than ever before. It followed that books, both plain and fancy, were prime targets for thieves, whether criminals who broke into a library or impoverished students who could not resist pilfering and selling titles from the libraries they patronized.

A library's most-used books were not only chained to desks and lecterns to prevent theft, but they were often protected by a "book curse" to scourge whoever damaged or stole them. After finishing the copying, the scribe usually added such a curse to the final page, warning that eternal damnation or prolonged physical suffering awaited any would-be perpetrator.

Book curses are as old as writing—or at least as old as libraries. For all the reputed propriety and patience required of their calling, librarians have historically wished the worst of punishments on book thieves, as if they were no better than murderers or blasphemers. Ancient librarians called down the wrath of the gods of Mesopotamia, Egypt, Greece, and Rome upon book thieves and vandals. A comment on a Babylonian scroll threatened anyone who erased its writing in order to reuse the papyrus:

> In the name of Nabu and Marduk, do not rub out the text!

(Nabu was the Semitic god of writing, and Marduk his father.)

One ancient curse warned of the direst consequences if patrons even dared lend a borrowed book to someone else:

NABU

He who entrusts [this book] to [others'] hands, may all the gods who are found in Babylon curse him!

In medieval Europe, the most fearsome curse was the threat of expulsion from the church and eternal damnation. Librarians and scribes considered neither punishment too extreme for a miscreant. Calling down hellfire was considered a potent and essential protection for a library's books. One drastic (and still popular) curse invoked to protect an entire Spanish library warned:

> Him that stealeth, or borroweth and returneth not, this book from its owner, let it change into a serpent in his hand and rend him. Let him be struck with palsy, and all his members blasted. Let him languish in pain crying out for mercy, and let there be no surcease to his agony till he sing in dissolution. Let bookworms gnaw his entrails [and] let the flames of Hell consume him forever.

◀ American architectural sculptor Lee Oscar Lawrie (1877–1963) created this bronze of Nabu, the Semitic god of writing, for the east entrance of the Library of Congress's John Adams Building in Washington, D.C.

The scribe who completed the last book of the Bible, entitled Revelation, closed with a fiery admonition against altering what had been written:

> I warn everyone who hears the words of the prophecy of this book: if any one adds to them, God will add to him the plagues described in this book, and if any one takes away from the words of the book of this prophecy, God will take away his share in the tree of life and in the holy city, which are described in this book.

Other, more standard curses called for the perpetrator to be "frizzled in the pan," "broken on the wheel," or, somewhat more mercifully, just hanged. And many a witty book curse was in rhyme:

> Steal not this book my honest friend
> For fear the gallows should be your end,
> And when you die the Lord will say
> And where's the book you stole away?

وانيسي في دنياي واخرتي اللهم

اجعل القران لنا في الدنيا قرينا وفي

القبر مونسا وفي القيمة شافعا و

على الصراط نورا وفي الجنة

رفيقا ومن النار سترا وحجابا والى

الخيرات كلها دليلا برحمتك يا ارحم

صدق الله العلي العظيم

ASIA AND ISLAM

In South and East Asia, writing and books developed along with the spread of religion and philosophy. Chinese emperors promoted the copying of Confucian texts and of new works on the sciences and history. By the late Middle Ages, Chinese printing and papermaking—far in advance of the West—gave rise to a dynamic book culture in East Asia.

In West and Central Asia, the spread of Islam, founded in the seventh century, linked distant China with Europe. By the mid-fifteenth century, Islamic conquests had captured Constantinople and absorbed the Byzantine Empire with its books, libraries, and ancient learning. The writings of Islamic scholars and teachers spread both classical works and new scientific discoveries into Europe. Major Islamic centers of learning, not seen since Roman times, grew up from Baghdad to Cairo and Cordoba—cities with splendid libraries where Muslims, Christians, and Jews studied and taught law, science, theology, and philosophy.

China's art of papermaking was acquired by the Muslims of Persia, who eventually transferred this knowledge westward until it took hold and flourished in late Medieval Europe. For students and those without financial means, books began to become more affordable, thanks to the production of paper.

◀ Near the end of a c.1550 Persian Qur'an, this prayer in Arabic is appropriate for the completion of a reading session.

Asian religious and philosophical movements, such as Buddhism, Confucianism, Daoism, and Jainism, stimulated learning, printing, and book collecting.

Jainism, emerging in the sixth century BCE, was one of the major faiths of the Indian subcontinent—along with Islam, Buddhism, and Hinduism. With a strong tradition of religious, scientific, and cultural scholarship, Jainism's early adherents produced scriptural writing by the first century BCE, and established some of Asia's earliest libraries. These library collections, at first mainly housed in temples, were later termed "Jain Knowledge Warehouses." Jain libraries eventually developed under private ownership, and by medieval times, "knowledge warehouses" had preserved hundreds of thousands of handwritten manuscripts on Indian society, theology, philosophy, and art.

As in Europe, monks copied texts and maintained much of India's book learning and scriptural studies. The Indian subcontinent's bookmaking

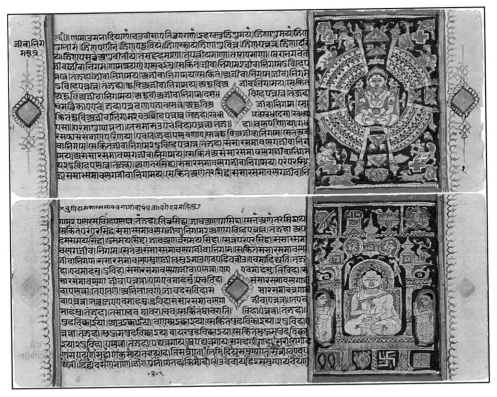

▲ With miniatures in gold, red, and lapis lazuli, this image is from the *Surya Prajnapti Sutra*, a Jain astronomical work dating to the third or fourth century BCE.

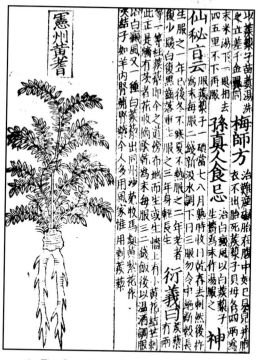

▲ The Song Dynasty *Bencao,* writings on traditional Chinese medicine, was printed with woodblock in 1249.

tradition was especially rich, featuring beautifully illustrated manuscript texts. There was, however, virtually no mechanical printing of books in India until the sixteenth century, decades after printing appeared in Europe. Printing came to India in 1556, brought by Jesuit missionaries.

In China, paper had been invented by the second century. The "classic" works of sixth-century BCE philosopher, Confucius, were inscribed in stone tablets—similar to customs in the civilizations of the Fertile Crescent. The Chinese achieved an early form of printing by pushing soft paper into the stone text and applying ink to the back of the sheet. The result, when the paper was withdrawn, was a black background with white letters. Many Confucian adherents made personal copies of the classics by this "stone-rubbing" method.

The craft of block printing was widespread in China by the eighth century. A carved woodblock—with the characters in relief—was inked, and then paper was placed on the block and rubbed with a brush to print the characters. In the tenth century a major Buddhist canon, the *Tripitaka,* was published in 5,000 volumes using more than 130,000 individual woodblocks.

Movable type—single letters or characters that can be placed alongside others in a printing form, or frame—was first developed in China in the eleventh century. Three centuries later, the Koreans established the first type foundry for casting movable type in metal, and Japan soon followed suit. Movable type did not, however, permanently catch on in East Asia. For centuries, woodblocks remained the leading printing method in China, Korea, and Japan.

In India, woodblocks and paper were not widely used until the fourteenth and fifteenth centuries. Books were mostly handwritten on sheets made of narrow palm leaves held together with a cord.

▲ Thirteenth-century Korean movable type, made of brass, iron, copper, and wood.

Every Chinese empire compiled its own official written archive. From the earliest Qin reign (third century BCE) through the Manchus (seventeenth to twentieth centuries), emperors decreed which philosophical texts, which accounts of history, which rituals of faith, and what poetry and literature would be permitted in their realms.

The first Qin emperor was especially fierce in his attempts to eradicate the teachings and texts of Confucianism, then an emergent philosophy of statecraft and self-cultivation. Accounts written in later years by Confucian scholars claim the emperor burned countless Confucian texts and buried alive nearly five hundred scholars, physicians, and mystics who had criticized Qin rule or refused to submit to its authority.

This "burning of the books and burying of the scholars" legend was part of a tradition in Chinese chronicles in which the following regime writes its own version of its predecessor's history. In the Han era that followed the Qin, Confucianism was celebrated as state orthodoxy. The bias of Confucian historians of the Han era must be accounted for when considering the burning and burying legend, but heavy-handed intellectual orthodoxy was the rule in Chinese imperial history.

When orthodox Confucianism came into collided with fast-spreading Buddhism during the Han reign, the emperors opposed the publication of Buddhist texts without imperial permission. As in the West, important religious tracts were copied in monasteries—in this case, Buddhist—and kept secret during times of persecution by the rulers.

Confucian and Buddhist writings were brought from China to Korea and Japan as early as the sixth century. This cultural interchange in books led to the further development of East Asian book publishing and the building of libraries.

Some Confucian Chinese emperors were open to other religious influences, such as Buddhism and Daoism. As a result, so-called orthodox, or official, Confucian doctrine could change from emperor to emperor. Studying and mastering current Confucian teachings was essential for anyone wishing to become an imperial official.

A formal examination was the government's way of finding young men whose superior knowledge of Confucian classics qualified them to be civil servants. Naturally, this exam fluctuated in content, according to the changes in Confucian doctrine.

The Tang dynasty of the sixth to tenth centuries, known as the golden age of imperial Chinese history, saw the growth of private collections of books and texts. Some collectors opened their libraries to help young men who were studying for the civil service examination. These collectors included successful candidates who had passed the examination and were awaiting an official post. Others were retired government officials, and some were professional tutors. The collections themselves became known as "academy" libraries, where scholars came to study for the civil service exam.

Academy libraries were important aspects of the Chinese "meritocracy," or merit system, which used competitive examinations and objective evaluations to certify its civil servants. The merit system was not commonly used until the nine-

◀ The *Tripitaka Koreana,* a thirteenth-century Korean collection of Buddhist scriptures, is carved into 81,340 wooden printing blocks. The world's oldest intact version of Buddhist canon in Chinese script, it is stored in a South Korean Buddhist temple.

teenth century in the West, where hereditary, privileged classes controlled all levels of government.

The spread of wood-block printing during the Tang era made more affordable texts available, promoting growth in the size and number of academy libraries. By printing editions of classical and new texts, an academy could build its prestige, attracting the patronage of local gentry and their student sons.

Likewise, privately collecting books demonstrated one's cultural refinement and was a way to acquire social esteem. For those with the financial means to collect books but who were from lower classes—such as merchants and military men—book collecting could help pave the way to higher social status.

One of the most remarkable Asian libraries was hidden away for centuries in western China in the Mogao Grottoes, which became known as the "Caves of the Thousand Buddhas."

Discovered by Western archaeologists in the early twentieth century, these caves formed a complex of almost 500 temples, with half a million square feet of religious wall murals. The complex contained more than 15,000 paper books and 1,100 paper bundles, each of which held dozens of scrolls. This library had been sealed up in the eleventh century, perhaps to protect it from invaders, or perhaps because the books had been discarded after having been copied and then republished.

It is said the name of the caves comes from a vision experienced by a fourth-century Buddhist monk, who imagined a thousand Buddhas, inspiring the creation of the shrines. For centuries the monks collected texts from the known world—a task facilitated by close proximity to the Silk Road, the 5,000-mile trade route between the Far East and Asia Minor. Along this route journeyed merchants from Constantinople, China, Rome, Egypt, Persia, the Indian subcontinent, and Mesopotamia.

Found in the caves were books from the Fertile Crescent, including a version of the Old Testament written in Hebrew. There were also Tibetan scrolls as well as Buddhist texts, written in Sanskrit, the ancient South Asian language with links to European tongues. The world's oldest-known printed book, dating from the ninth century, was found in the Caves of a Thousand Buddhas.

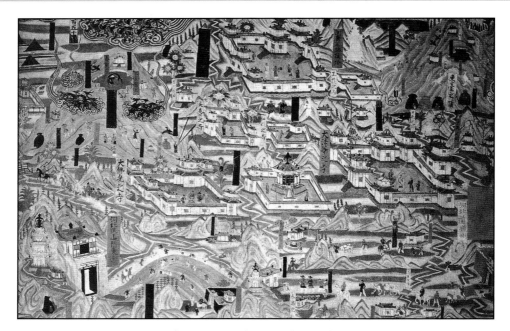

▲ This tenth-century Chinese mural from the "Caves of a Thousand Buddhas"—the Mogao Caves (or Grottoes)—depicts Tang dynasty monastic architecture.

In the fifteenth century, Chinese imperial authorities ordered many of the texts housed in the caves to be copied and published in the form of an encyclopedia that numbered 11,000 volumes. Three centuries later, another encyclopedia of 36,000 volumes was produced from this same library.

Between eastern and southern Asia and Europe stood the lands newly dominated by Islam, which had essentially enveloped Central Asia. Islam spread along the northern coast of Africa, and Constantinople—along with much of southern Europe, Sicily, and Iberia (Spain and Portugal)—fell under Muslim control.

With this conquest, Muslims had access to the books and libraries of the Byzantines, the heirs of much classical Greek and Roman culture. While in Christian Europe, pagan books were generally allowed to languish and were not copied (and therefore perished); they had been preserved by the Byzantines and later by the Muslims, who were great admirers of books and learning.

Public libraries appeared in major cities of the Muslim world, where most books were made of paper and published in codex form. The world of Islam acquired the art of papermaking in the eighth century, taught by Chinese prisoners who had been taken during eastward expeditions. Eventually, the Muslims brought papermaking to the Indian subcontinent and to Europe.

A widespread love of books, especially of beautiful books, stimulated the development of private libraries in Islamic lands. Since the faith frowned upon making graven images, Islamic titles lacked the colorful illumination of European books. Instead, the art of calligraphy flourished and became one of the most elegant aspects of Islamic books.

Most Islamic libraries were incorporated with mosques and were important to devotional study, especially of the Qur'an, the Muslim holy book. As in European monasteries, a prime function of the mosque library was the copying of books by scribes, in this case from Greek, Persian, Sanskrit, and Latin into Arabic. In turn, Arab science was translated into Latin by visiting scholars from Christian Europe. This science was partly obtained from books

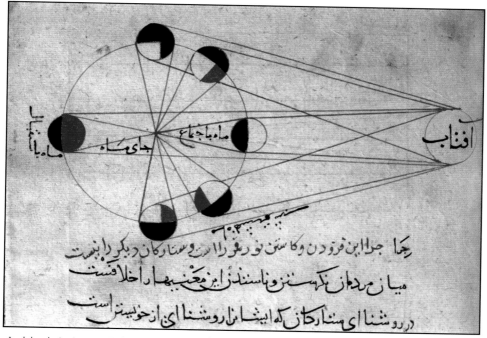

▲ Islamic texts on astrology, cosmology, medicine, and mathematics were illustrated by Persian polymath and scholar Abu Rayhan Biruni (973–1048); shown are phases of the moon.

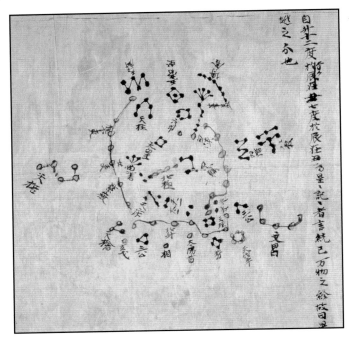

◄ This eighth-century star map from the Tang Dynasty is part of a set that contained 1,300 stars; the maps are from the Caves of a Thousand Buddhas.

surviving from classical times, but the ancient knowledge was greatly improved upon by Muslim intellectuals and inventors.

For several centuries Islamic learning flowered. Commerce between civilizations helped promote European education and science, both much less advanced than that of the Muslim world. Christian monasteries in close proximity to Islamic libraries sent scribes there to copy and translate books. These copies, in turn, were disseminated widely throughout Europe.

Muslim Spain had at least seventy libraries, with the greatest at Cordoba, a city second in size only to Constantinople. Cordoba attracted so many Christian scholars that it helped stimulate the establishment of universities in Europe.

Among the Islamic works of special interest to European readers were texts on astrology, astronomy, and cosmology—studies that were highly developed with Muslim scholars. Islamic books on medicine and mathematics also were well regarded in Europe, as were Muslim inventions such as advanced navigational instruments. In libraries from southern Russia to Sicily and Spain, cooperation flourished among scholars of the three faiths: Christianity, Islam, and Judaism. Known collectively as "People of the Book," each religion was guided by the written word: Christianity and Judaism by the Bible, and Islam by both the Bible and the Qur'an.

The era of these religions studying in peace came to an end with the Crusades (eleventh through thirteenth centuries), as Christian armies invaded and occupied the Holy Land. The books and libraries previously shared in open cooperation suffered the depredations of relentless war and religious persecution.

Many Islamic libraries were ruined during the two centuries of war that saw the fall of Jerusalem and the massacre of its people by Crusaders. Even the Christian city of Constantinople was captured and sacked by a wanton Crusader rampage in 1204, its monasteries and libraries looted. Constantinople's Eastern (Greek) Orthodox books were considered heretical by Crusaders, and many thousands were stripped of their rich covers and bindings and burned.

On the positive side, decades of Crusader occupation in West Asia had led to considerable cultural interaction and exchange between Islam and Roman

▲ King Abu 'abd-Allah Muhammad XII (c.1460–1533) surrenders in 1492 to the Catholic forces of Ferdinand and Isabella, who had besieged the city during the *Reconquista* of Iberia.

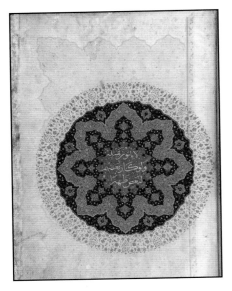

Illuminated folio, color and gold on paper, from a sixteenth-century Persian Qur'an.

Catholicism—including books. The Crusaders were defeated by the mid-thirteenth century, but the almost-constant warfare had exhausted the Muslim peoples. As a result of the prolonged hostilities, Mesopotamia and the Levant were left weakened and vulnerable when a Mongol invasion struck. In 1258, Mongol hordes destroyed Baghdad and its thirty-six public libraries, the pillagers tearing books apart so the leather covers could be used for sandals.

A further demise of Islamic libraries was brought about by the fifteenth-century expulsion of Muslims from the Iberian Peninsula. Muslim books were burned wholesale by Catholic Spain. Of Western Europe's Islamic written heritage, little more than the Latin translations of Arabic books, housed at the religious and intellectual centers of Cordoba and Toledo, remained. Yet it was Arabic translations of classical Greek texts that preserved ancient works of philosophy and science which otherwise might have been lost to the West. Arabic

Interior of the Great Mosque at Cordoba.

renditions of Plato, Aristotle, and Galen were cornerstones of European educational advancement, which subsequently led to the Renaissance of the fourteenth and fifteenth centuries.

It is said that when the angel Gabriel first appeared to Muhammad late in the sixth century, his instruction to the prophet was, "Read."

Gabriel, the messenger of the Lord, is believed to have dictated the Qur'an to Muhammad, and ever since, Muslims have practiced their faith by closely reading all 120,000 words of their holy book. Thus, every Muslim believes he or she is able to interact directly with the divinity and to follow a personal path in Islam.

Throughout the Middle Ages, the Qur'an (like the Bible) was widely copied and distributed. The art of writing—calligraphy—rose to an apex in the Islamic world by the ninth century, inspired by the need to copy the Qur'an. Various writing styles achieved an elegance that was comparable to the fully illuminated texts of Christian Europe. Expert calligraphy and elaborate bindings imparted visual appeal and beauty to the finest Muslim books. Bindings were of board or heavy paper—not of leather or animal skins, which was prohibited by the faith.

Eventually, some of the more-sweeping calligraphic styles became so stylized that they were considered too showy for use in a holy scripture.

By the tenth century, many Islamic cities had major libraries, and one of the largest, with an estimated 400,000 to 600,000 books, was at Cordoba, capital of Al-Andalus, the Muslim-ruled lands of the Iberian Peninsula. The oldest mosque library, and among the most important, was the Sufiya in Aleppo, northern Syria, where a local prince had personally bequeathed 10,000 titles.

Some mosque libraries were open to the public and named "Halls of Science." At Baghdad was a library known as the "House of Wisdom," which held thousands of Greek and Roman manuscripts. The House of Wisdom,

▲ This scene by an Iberian Muslim artist was taken from the thirteenth-century "Tale of Bayad and Riyad," a love story about a young man from Damascus and an aristocratic lady in Al-Andalus—Muslim Spain.

sponsored by the caliph (one who is both a spiritual and worldly ruler), was also a university with many scholars and copyists translating works into Arabic. There were astronomical observatories, important for Islamic culture, which was advanced in the sciences.

Islamic libraries were rich in diversity, allowing scholars from other lands to share the facilities. These libraries were known for their attractiveness and comfort, many adorned with the classic Islamic dome, some surrounded by walkways and landscaped with ponds. Among the most legendary libraries was that of the Persian city of Shiraz, where there were more than three hundred chambers furnished with plush carpets. The library had thorough catalogs to help in locating texts, which were kept in the storage chambers and organized according to "every branch of learning."

The Shiraz library was described by a contemporary Muslim as being unequaled in East or West: "No educated person entered it but was enchanted, nor any learned person but his imagination was filled with the delights and perfumes of paradise."

By the late Middle Ages, the realm of books and libraries was undergoing a major change, as papermaking was brought from China via the Muslim world.

Paper was at first called *bagdatikos*, meaning "from Baghdad," because of its introduction through this city on its way to the West. The craft of papermaking reached Spain in the twelfth century, and at subsequent hundred-year intervals arrived in Italy, Germany, and England. Yet, for centuries after paper became widely available in Europe, vellum and parchment were preferred for documents that had to be long-lasting.

Much cheaper and easier to produce than parchment or vellum, paper revolutionized book manufacture and stimulated production. For example, up to 40 percent of the cost of a book made in Constantinople had been in the parchment alone. The increased use of paper drastically reduced publishing costs. A skilled papermaker could turn out thousands of sheets in the time that a few skins could be made into vellum or parchment.

The basic ingredients of paper were linen and cotton, soaked in water and beaten into a smooth pulp, or slurry. As the pulp was drained through a wire screen, the slurry's interlocking fibers matted together, ready for the next step. First, a press squeezed out water from the sheet, preparatory to drying; then, the application of a gelatin coating readied the sheet's surface for ink.

In this same era, European scribes changed over from large script (majuscule), to small script (minuscule), allowing for many more words on the page. The use of paper and smaller script made more books available, and the advent of the printing press in the fifteenth century began a publishing revolution. Libraries benefited from the greatly increased production of less-costly books and acquired more copies, which were needed to meet the demands of the growing number of scholars attending the many new colleges and universities.

EUROPE'S HIGH MIDDLE AGES

Europe saw the rise of cities, monarchies, and a princely merchant class during the "High Middle Ages," which encompassed the eleventh through thirteenth centuries. In this time, schools run by cathedrals grew and prospered, developing into universities with prized libraries.

Universities fostered an educated and literate class, many instilled with a hunger for learning, for reading, and for exploring the fascinating works of ancient Greece and Rome. Scholars and intellectuals across Europe sought to understand the nature of the human being, and from this quest arose the inquiring philosophy of "humanism." By the late thirteenth century, human-ist-inspired education in the liberal arts—languages, sciences, philosophy, and history—brought about a *renaissance*, or rebirth, of learning and refined culture.

During the era in Europe termed the "Renaissance"—the fourteenth to sixteenth centuries—many wealthy individuals established private libraries, some housed in outstanding buildings. There was, however, a significant difference between the libraries of Roman times and those of the Renaissance:

◀ *The Very Rich Hours of the Duke of Berry,* a lavishly decorated book of hours, contains daily prayers to be said by the lay faithful. The book is considered the most important surviving illuminated manuscript of the fifteenth century.

While the Romans often considered book collections as tokens of power and authority, Renaissance collectors (especially the "humanists") had a true love for books and the exploration of knowledge they contained.

As humanists built book collections and university libraries developed, the book trade grew to meet this unprecedented demand for reading matter. Around 1450, impelled by the need for books, Johann Gutenberg (c. 1400–1468) developed the printing press in Germany. Within fifty years, millions of printed books were in circulation across Europe.

▼ Alcuin (center) joins Frankish Benedictine monk, teacher, and author Raban Maur (780–856), who presents his work to the archbishop of the city of Mainz.

Books and libraries would never be the same, nor would the realm of ideas, now influenced by a torrent of printed books and pamphlets.

Monastery schools were closing their doors to the public during the High Middle Ages, as fewer young people chose the monastic life. Instead, cathedral schools became the main centers of learning. Cathedrals were headquarters for church leaders, and their schools were seminaries for religious training, but the teachers also began to educate the sons of nobles and merchants who wished to study civil law and medicine. Cathedral school libraries grew, stocking books required by the increasing number of scholars.

One of the finest cathedral schools was at York in northern England. Founded in the seventh century, York was known for teaching theology as well as the seven liberal arts: grammar, rhetoric, logic, geometry, arithmetic, music, and astronomy. York won fame because of its administrator, Flaccus Alcuinus (c. 735–804). Known as Alcuin, this teacher, scholar, and poet was instrumental in preparing the way for the development of university education in Europe.

Alcuin, called Albinius in France, became confidant and advisor to Charlemagne, Frankish ruler of the Holy Roman Empire. Alcuin transplanted his York educational methods—and his esteem for libraries—to Charlemagne's royal court in Aachen. Tutoring Charlemagne and the emperor's sons, along with other young noblemen and clerics, Alcuin taught the liberal arts and theology, with courses in his special field: astrology. He became the most prominent figure in what is known as the Carolingian Renaissance, an intellectual and cultural revival that presaged the Italian Renaissance of five centuries later.

"Faith is a free act of the will, not a forced act," Alcuin told Charlemagne when discussing the subject of compulsory baptism. "You can force people to be baptized, but you cannot force them to believe."

Alcuin once described, in rhyme, the contents of the York cathedral school library, paying homage to classical times:

Iazze haglagolo connic · lufeh Zu&ih
Zlodeiu · luzemiego deuuih · luzeh ɫ moki·
delom · Iuzem iego Damirafttc napomoki
lepocam · Tofe uue brti· kibogu moih gre
ruiu ubog uze mo chou · Dabim cifto iz
goki · lu iega Zin; pouued Ztuoril · lod
lu Zuueti duh·Dara puztic otboga priel·
tri imena · edin bog Bogu uhe mogo kemu·
gozpod Zuueti· iZpouuede uhe moie
ife Zuori nebo·lh greche· lfce marie·
emlo · Tofe izco ie yzeh nepraudnih del·
ga milofhti· lfce inepraudnega pomifleza·
mariae· lfce mic ɫfe iehem uuede Ztuo
habela· lfce pe ril· ili neuuede·nudmi
tra· lufeh bofih Zl. ili lubmi Zpe ili bde.
lufeh bofih mofe Yhprtnih rotah· Vlifnih
nic· lufeh ɫ Za refih· vtatbinah· Yhmaf

Carolingian minuscule script was used to write the tenth-century Freising Manuscripts, the first Latin-script document in a Slavic language: Slovene.

There shalt thou find the volumes that contain
All of the ancient fathers that remain:
There all the Latin writers make their home
With those that glorious Greece transferred to Rome—
The Hebrews draw from their celestial stream.
And Africa is bright with learning's beam.

Alcuin recites the names of authors, from Jerome back to Comminian, adding that there are "many more . . ."

. . . masters of old lore,
Whose many volumes singly to rehearse
Were far too tedious for our present verse.

When students and instructors at a cathedral school formally organized themselves, their association was named a "university," which derives from a legal term for a united body. "University" eventually came to mean an institution of higher learning that is empowered to confer degrees and has a community of teachers and scholars under common administration.

By the thirteenth century, universities had been established at most cathedrals. In contrast to the isolated rural environment of medieval monasteries, cathedrals were located in bustling cities—in France, for example, at Chartres, Orleans, and Rheims. The cathedral school at Paris, known for theology, became one of the first universities in Europe, as did the cathedral school in Bologna, Italy, known for the study of law, and at Salerno for medicine (a point of contact with Islamic lands).

This view of a convention of doctors at the University of Paris decorated a medieval manuscript of *chants royaux,* a medieval French verse form. ▶

64

Some educational institutions were termed "colleges," groups of individuals living under prescribed rules. The College of the Sorbonne was founded in Paris around 1257 by French clergyman Robert de Sorbon (1201–74), who persuaded many wealthy patrons to contribute books for a library. Eventually to become a college in the larger University of Paris, the Sorbonne built one of Europe's finest library collections and established a large fund to purchase books for students. It became common practice in universities to loan sets of books to students for the academic year.

By the end of the fourteenth century, more than seventy-five European universities had been established, each with a library. Major university libraries generally had a reading room—termed a "great library," and often handsomely appointed—where instructors and scholars could study. There was also a "small library," which lent out books to members of the university, but was more of a storeroom than a reading room.

Since books had to be protected from theft, the titles in the great library were held by chains. Chaining library books was a common practice throughout Europe, although it often led to crowding and awkwardness when several readers had to stand side by side, at times reading from the same book.

Universities prepared secular students as officials to govern the fast-growing towns, and also to serve in royal administrations. University libraries were built to suit the various areas of study: theology, canon and civil law, and medicine. Each required specific book collections. Whenever the curriculum broadened in scope—for instance, to include natural sciences such as geography and astronomy—so did the selection of library books.

In many cases, books were available to students through what were termed "stationers' shops," which copied, bound, and published titles as well as loaned them for a fee. Stationers loaned books out in sections so they could be studied or copied, then returned in exchange for the next section. Some

◀ Humanists and bibliophiles, scholars and clergy, are depicted in this imaginary scene set in a Renaissance-era Christian library.

65

stationers were so successful that the university library was not much used by scholars whose studies went beyond the most commonly used course books, which were available at the stationers.

It was helpful that the technical skills for producing eyeglasses had been developed by the thirteenth century, enabling both readers and writers to make the most of the written word.

Books of history, science, medicine, theology, literature, and poetry had an ever-widening audience by the thirteenth century. The Old English oral legend, *Beowulf*, was written down by a monk and copied and recopied for readers who were thrilled to read the adventures of an ancient warrior doing battle with mythical monsters.

By the fourteenth century, English readers also could enjoy the *Anglo-Saxon Chronicles* in their own language, and Geoffrey Chaucer's entertaining *Canterbury Tales*, as well as stirring poetry about legendary King Arthur and his knights. Among the most popular theological titles were commentaries by Italian philosopher and priest Thomas Aquinas, and English philosopher-scientist Roger Bacon.

Widespread interest in the Scriptures made the Bible an ever-present book in Europe's libraries. During this time, mounting challenges to the Church's strict dogma brought calls for the Bible to be translated from Latin into common tongues so that readers might arrive at their own understanding of the scripture. Since the seventh century, parts of the Bible had been translated into Old English, but it was not until the close of the fourteenth century that a full Middle English translation appeared. English theologian and lay preacher, John Wycliffe (c. 1325–1384), led the efforts of this first translation of the Bible into vernacular English in 1382.

"The Knight's Tale" page from the fifteenth-century Ellesmere Manuscript of *Canterbury Tales* by Geoffrey Chaucer, belongs to The Huntington Library of San Marino, California.

▲ The writings of Greek philosophers such as Aristotle, as contained in this 1570 book printed in Lyon, were widely influential with the intellectuals of Renaissance Europe.

The fourteenth century saw growing enthusiasm for book learning, especially for the works of classical Rome and Greece. Ancient texts were sought after in private libraries and dilapidated monasteries, usually to be translated into evolving languages such as French, German, Spanish, English, and Dutch.

This intellectual interest led to the study of humanity and human values, including philosophy and religion. Classical texts acquired the name "humanities," and the belief that human beings possessed free will was at the heart of humanism. Also, humanists believed that the individual was an integration of body, mind, and soul, and not only (or primarily) a soul, which had been generally accepted. Open-minded criticism of ideas and religion and the study of languages were cornerstones of humanism, whose adherents made fresh assessments of Aristotle and the Bible.

Humanism, and the humanists who embraced this new way of thinking, accelerated the gathering of old manuscripts from the known world, and also were instrumental in the building of libraries. Humanism was especially strong in Italy, where the scholar Francesco Petrarch (1304–74) was

Petrarch, Italian scholar, poet, and humanist, is pictured in his library. The drawing is after a fifteenth-century manuscript illumination. ▶

one of the movement's founders. An important book collector, Petrarch searched for manuscripts of classical writings and personally copied them for his own library, which he referred to as "my daughter." He bequeathed his collection to Venice, where it became the foundation of a future public library.

All aspects of religion were influenced by humanism. Rigid dogmas and rules were challenged and often rejected. In concert with humanism, there emerged an intense interest in rediscovering classical culture, a "rebirth" of ancient Greek and Roman ideals. This impulse became so pervasive and enduring that the fourteenth and fifteenth centuries earned the name "the Renaissance," or revival.

The Renaissance, with its deepest roots in Italy, was a transition period between the Middle Ages and modern times. Art, architecture, philosophy, science, music, and libraries; All were transformed, enriched by a widespread yearning for education and for books.

Bibliophiles, such as Petrarch's acquaintance, English bishop Richard de Bury (1281–1345), gathered books (manuscripts) wherever and however they could. De Bury was a tutor of royalty as well as a diplomat and clergyman. As a high official of King Edward III, de Bury was showered with gifts and bribes from those who desired his favor and influence with the royal court. The best bribe, however, was a book. He wrote:

> Indeed, if we had loved gold and silver goblets, high-bred horses, or no small sums of money, we might in those days have furnished forth a rich treasury. But in truth we wanted manuscripts, not moneyscripts; we loved codices more than florins, and preferred slender pamphlets to pampered palfreys.

▲ The translation of the Latin text on the bishop's seal of Richard de Bury reads, "Of Durham: Bishop Richard: by the grace of God."

In keeping with Benedictine monastic customs, de Bury had someone read to him when he was at a meal. It was difficult to walk through de Bury's residences because they were so crowded with piles of manuscript books—more, it was said, than all the English bishops put together. He was happiest when surrounded by scholars and authors.

In the final years of his life, de Bury compiled a volume of essays—attributed to him, but perhaps written by others—about his fervor for books and his methodology for finding and acquiring them. De Bury's *Philobiblion,* meaning "the love of books," included chapter titles such as: "That the Treasure of Wisdom is Chiefly Contained in Books"; "The Degree of Affection That is Properly Due to Books"; and "Why We Have Preferred Books of Liberal Learning to Books of Law."

De Bury founded Durham College at Oxford as a "house of studies" for Benedictine monks, to whom he bequeathed his books. The monks built a new library for the acquisition.

"The same man cannot love both gold and books," wrote de Bury in his *Philobiblion,* where he affirmed an "ecstatic love [that] has carried us away so powerfully, that we have resigned all thoughts of other earthly things, and have given ourselves up to a passion for acquiring books."

As one method of finding old books, de Bury became a patron of mendicant monks, whose wide travels brought them to distant, lonely convents and monasteries. There, in run-down, forgotten libraries were neglected books of great value—at least to de Bury, whose monkish agents "found heaped up amid the utmost poverty the utmost riches of wisdom."

Upon the bishop's own visits to clergymen who sought his favor, the libraries of the most famous monasteries were thrown open, cases were unlocked and caskets were undone, and volumes that had slumbered through long ages in their tombs wake up and are astonished, and those that had lain hidden in dark places are bathed in the ray of unwonted light. These long lifeless books, once most dainty, but now become corrupt and loathsome, covered with litters of mice and pierced with the gnawings of the worms, and who were once clothed in purple and fine linen, now lying in sackcloth and ashes, given up to oblivion, seemed to have become habitations of the moth.

Philobiblion was completed shortly before de Bury's death in 1345, but not published until 1473. This "little treatise," as he described it, has been regularly reprinted in every century following, and generations of kindred book-loving spirits have acquired and cherished their own copies of *Philobiblion.*

European books, publishing, and libraries underwent a radical change after 1450, when German goldsmith Johann Gutenberg turned his metal-working talents to the manufacture of "movable type." At his workshop in the Rhineland city of Mainz, Gutenberg fashioned individual letters that could be assembled as words and locked into a framework that was placed on a printing press to turn out pages—thousands of pages, all identical.

Eventually, Gutenberg associates and former employees dispersed over Europe, teaching and developing these new methods for duplicating the written word. Printing caught on like wildfire, from the British Isles to Italy and Greece, from Spain to Constantinople. By 1500, approximately 260 printing establishments were in operation. Within a few decades after Gutenberg's achievement, the enormous output of the printing press stimulated

▲ *The Printing Press,* one of six paintings in the Library of Congress's "Evolution of the Book" series by John White Alexander (1856–1915), portrays Johann Gutenberg and his press.

▲ A seventeenth-century German printing house is seen in this contemporary engraving published in Frankfurt for an historical chronicle.

increased reading, as well as original new scholarship and writing on every sort of subject.

One estimate calculates that 40,000 book editions had been published by the start of the sixteenth century. Figuring an average print run of 500 copies of each edition, as many as 20 million books could have been printed. Although half the titles were Bibles or Christian texts, many were literary works by the likes of Italian poet, Dante Alighieri, and England's Chaucer. Other titles offered valuable scientific and historical information, until then impossible to find without hunting endlessly through libraries and archives.

It was significant that every copy of a printed edition was exactly the same, unlike handwritten manuscripts, which were susceptible to copying mistakes or differences in translation. Printed books made it possible to discuss and compare texts, the readers knowing their fellows were using exactly the same material.

Relatively large numbers of book buyers, both wealthy and lowly, were found all over Europe during the Renaissance era. Humanists of means were inspired to acquire all the Latin and Greek literature they could find, and scholars sought the latest volumes on scientific, philosophical, and social thinking. Thousands of students and teachers converged on the great university centers, such as those at Rome, Padua, Bologna, Milan, and Naples, and they all needed books.

Print shops, which were also booksellers, became vibrant gathering places where scholars, teachers, translators, authors, and editors met. They congregated with the printer-publishers, who themselves often had a scholarly interest in the works they printed. One of the great humanist editors and authors was Holland's Desiderius Erasmus (c. 1466–1536), who advised major printers, such as the prolific Italian, Aldus Manutius (1449–1515), on which manuscripts to publish.

The rapidly expanding business of publishing was a dominant topic of discussion at printing establishments. One profitable book-trade occupation was the search for significant handwritten manuscripts that could be sold to printers. These works were then set in type and published as books that were proudly touted as the latest gems resurrected from classical times.

Libraries, more than ever, became repositories of collected human knowledge, and not only for Church-approved religious texts and law books.

Gutenberg's pioneering work with movable type and the printing press was eagerly taken up by inventors, craftsmen, and designers, who steadily improved the process.

One of the most important innovators was Italian academic, Aldus Manutius, born around the time Gutenberg's movable type appeared in

Movable metal type: Some characters are loaded into a composing stick, and other metal type is stored in a type case, ready for use.

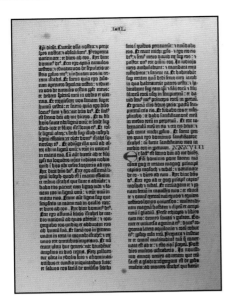

"Gutenberg Bibles"—those printed by Gutenberg's early movable type methods—became treasures of later rare book collectors.

the mid-fifteenth century. Known as Aldus, he was passionate about translating original Greek works into Latin and printing them as books and pamphlets. He often produced small-format editions that were cheap and sold readily. These inexpensive books—the first paperbacks—were, as ever, a boon to scholars.

Aldus's agents searched Europe for manuscripts, and through times of war and upheaval, his Aldine Press in Venice faithfully published the works of the classical authors. Aldus sought out manuscripts by both the famous and the lesser known, from Aristotle, Plato, and Plutarch to Pindar and Athenaeus. He also printed first editions of Hippocrates, Strabo, and Galen.

In the course of running his publishing operation, Aldus devoted himself to designing type, creating the distinctive and elegant typeface that bears his name. Said to have been styled on Petrarch's handwriting, Aldus remains an extremely popular typeface.

—❖—

During the fourteenth and fifteenth centuries, immense wealth came to many powerful families of the aristocracy and the merchant class. Among them were book lovers who spent fortunes establishing collections that would become the cornerstones of great national libraries.

Humanists led the quest for new values founded on classical open-mindedness and intellectual honesty. Some humanist libraries were modeled on the ancient bilingual libraries, with separate Latin and Greek chambers. In keeping with the Renaissance spirit of free inquiry and scholarship, these collections were often made available to the public.

By the mid-sixteenth century, books produced by printing presses dominated European libraries, yet no respectable collection was complete without a number of beautifully handwritten manuscripts. As popular as printed titles were, for several more decades, book collectors favored handwritten texts over printed works.

The love of illuminated books still flourished, a passion exemplified by the fabulously wealthy Medici family of Florence. The Medicis bought valuable books printed on parchment and then had them illuminated by the finest Florentine miniaturists.

Federico da Montefeltro (1422–82), Duke of Urbino, was another major Italian collector, one who desired only books "written by the pen." Urbino employed dozens of copyists who wrote on costly vellum. Their work then was illuminated by miniaturists and bound in crimson covers with silver decoration. Although the duke's seventeenth-century descendants willed his collection to the city of Urbino for a public library, the Church interceded and brought the books to the Vatican library.

Urbino's rival in collecting was Cosimo de Medici (1389–1464), and together they were the most notable library builders of the age. Cosimo, a patron of the arts, erected libraries at his Florentine estate and at the nearby monastery of San Marco. He believed libraries should be open to all scholars, and his San Marco collection was the first public library in Italy.

▲ Portrait in marble of Cosimo de' Medici by Italian sculptor and goldsmith Andrea del Verrocchio (1435–88).

San Marco's library was designed with graceful elegance, featuring Ionic columns, central arches, white walls, and tall windows for ample daylight. To build the collection, Cosimo purchased the library of the late bookseller and collector, Niccolò Niccoli, formerly his personal librarian and one who had spent a lifetime in search of antiquities and Greek manuscripts.

The more than eight hundred Niccoli manuscripts acquired by Cosimo would become the cornerstone of a later Florentine library—the Laurentian—founded by Cosimo's grandson, a merchant prince aptly known as "The Magnificent."

RENAISSANCE TO REFORMATION

Aunique characteristic of some Renaissance libraries was that they were open to the public. As in classical times, these libraries were places where ideas were exchanged and where scholarship and reading were considered both pleasurable and beneficial to the mind and soul.

Freethinking was a hallmark of the age, and many libraries contained a wide range of writers, ancient and contemporary. Classical texts could be found alongside humanist writings, and religious tomes accompanied new books on philosophy and science and recent literature such as poetry and novels. Kindred spirits formed "academies"—associations—of scholars, especially in the major cities of northern Italy, where nobles such as Cosimo de Medici served as sponsors and patrons. The Renaissance academy hearkened back to Plato's fourth-century BCE Athenian school of philosophy, established at Akademia, a sanctuary dedicated to Athena, goddess of wisdom. Renaissance academies were likewise dedicated to higher learning and philosophy.

These informal associations of intellectuals—with their insatiable appetite for ancient texts, theoretical discussions, and libraries—profoundly influenced Renaissance culture. Yet, the unregulated and uncontrolled nature of academies disturbed and unsettled dogmatic Church leaders. Although several important figures in the Church were themselves benefactors of academies, the religious establishment leaders felt threatened. They became

◀ The ceiling of the Piccolomini Library, attached to the Cathedral of Siena in Italy, is decorated with sixteenth-century painted panels showing mythological figures.

▲ A view of the Biblioteca Laurenziana and its draped reading benches is presented in this eighteenth-century engraving.

angry when academy members appeared to favor classical culture and pre-Christian, pagan ideas and books over the approved doctrine of the Catholic Church.

One unbridled Roman academy of the late 1400s counted a papal librarian among its "neo-pagan" adherents. Pope Paul II (1417–71), an opponent of humanist learning, arrested members of this academy, accusing them of conspiracy against him and of irreligion and immorality. They were pardoned upon repentance and allowed to go free.

Famous Renaissance book collectors who endorsed the humanist ethos included Paris-born Giovanni Boccaccio (1313–75), author of a popular collection of novellas, *The Decameron*. Boccaccio persuaded librarians at southern Italy's Abbey of Monte Cassino—famed for its Greco-Arabic medical works—to open their collection to nonclerical scholars. Boccaccio also copied classical Roman works owned by the monastery and sent them to his bibliophile friend, Petrarch.

Another humanist was French diplomat Jean Grolier de Servin (1479–1565), who collected more than three thousand books and was a patron of printer Aldus Manutius and of expert bookbinders. Grolier had an obsession for fine bindings with beautifully worked designs in their leather or fabric covers. Grolier's books, dispersed after his death, became enduring treasures to collectors, libraries, and museums around the world.

Hungary's fifteenth-century king, Matthias Corvinus (1443–90), built a great library of three thousand titles in his capital city of Buda, on the Danube. His royal court had a number of Italian humanists who—along with his queen Beatrice of Naples (1457–1508), a humanist and book lover—guided the establishment of the Corvinian Library. As was the fate of many a great collection, the Corvinian was destroyed and dispersed by conquest, in this case by the Turks in 1526.

The spirit of inquiry continued to challenge the dogmas, doctrines, and authority of the Church, inspiring a powerful "reformation" of religion that was well under way by the mid-sixteenth century. The hostility arising from conflicting religious ideas brought about political upheaval. Religious wars would ravage Europe for generations, invariably destroying books and libraries in order to stamp out the ideas they contained.

Although the spirit of inquiry and free-ranging scholarship was abroad in Europe during the Renaissance, there were those who despised intellectual or religious freedom. To them, such wantonness of thought went hand in hand with licentiousness, ungodliness, and blasphemy.

Among the most aggressive zealots, whose fierce righteousness likened him to a Crusader, was the Italian priest and Franciscan missionary, Bernardino of Siena (1380–1444). Destined for sainthood, Bernardino was an inspired

▲ The marble *Oratorio di San Bernardino*, sculpted in the mid-fifteenth century for a Perugia, Italy church, portrays Bernardino of Siena preaching at a "bonfire of vanities."

◀ Girolamo Savonarola works at his writing table in this fifteenth-century woodcut from a publication about "simple Christian lives."

orator who railed against such ungodly, immoral vanities as mirrors, cosmetics, fine clothing, musical instruments, unapproved books, and classical manuscripts. Born to a noble Tuscan family, this priest journeyed around Italy, ministering to the sick and participating in a dynamic religious revival, with audiences numbering in the thousands. Several miracles were attributed to his power of faith.

Often, as Bernardino preached, the sites of his sermons would be alight with bonfires consuming mirrors, sculptures of unrobed figures, gaming tables, chess pieces, fine hats, Greek poetry, and many, many books. These blazes earned the label "bonfires of the vanities." With flames of purification roaring in accompaniment, Bernardino enthralled listeners with his oratory against sin and sinners. He rose in stature and authority among the Franciscans but never rested from ministerial labors or bonfires, dying in Naples while on the road to another revival.

Bernardino's mission was taken up by others, and "bonfires of the vanities" continued to delight those disposed to the eradication of sin. The Dominican priest Girolamo Savonarola (1452–98) of Florence, another nobleman, was an especially enthusiastic book burner, famed for his hatred of Renaissance art. Paintings of Botticelli and Michelangelo were said to have been reduced to ashes in Savonarola's pyres. Then, after describing the Church as a whore, he was excommunicated for heresy and sedition at the command of Pope Alexander VI.

Savonarola was hanged and his body burned in the same Florentine square that had been the site of his bonfires.

Readers and book collectors of the sixteenth and seventeenth centuries were driven by both a love of learning and a love of books as treasured possessions—even if the ideas contained inside were not in keeping with their own beliefs. The Dutch philosopher and scholar, Erasmus—consultant to

A contraption known as a "book wheel" sits next to a window in this sixteenth-century French illustration. Developed by an Italian military engineer, this revolving book stand enabled readers to study several heavy volumes at one location.

publisher Aldus—expressed the sentiments of many who were passionate about books: "When I get a little money I buy books; and if any is left, I buy food and clothes."

That books served various intellectual functions is suggested by the English jurist, statesman, scientist, author, and philosopher, Sir Francis Bacon (1561–1626): "Some books are to be tasted; others swallowed; and some few to be chewed and digested."

Danish physician A. Bartholini (1597–1643), who was devoted to literature, wrote: "Without books, God is silent, justice dormant, natural science at a stand, philosophy lame, letters dumb, and all things involved in darkness."

—❈—

While Renaissance-era scholars, philosophers, physicians, and jurists needed books and haunted libraries, few could afford a private collection of much consequence. Some of the richest bibliophiles, however, built libraries as temples to books and knowledge. A number of libraries appeared as manifestations of immense wealth joined with a love of books. In some cases, cultivated library builders were also committed to offering others the opportunity to use their collections.

Prominent aristocrats and princes of the Church created great libraries for the use of their entourages, or courts. Termed "court libraries," these

◀ Even the most elegant and genteel of libraries, such as the Laurentian, kept their most-used books securely chained, to be read from benches.

were housed in lavishly designed monumental buildings decorated with ornate woodwork, the walls adorned with frescoes. Appropriately, since Italy was at the heart of the Renaissance, court libraries were built at Naples, Modena, and Cesna, with one of the most spectacular being the Piccolomini Library at the Cathedral of Siena. Another was Florence's sixteenth-century Laurentian Library, designed by Michelangelo (1475–1564) for Cosimo de Medici's grandson, Lorenzo de Medici (1449–92), styled by contemporaries as "Lorenzo the Magnificent."

Court libraries became ever more splendid, decorated with paintings, statues, and frescoes of subjects that inspired Renaissance ideas: classical mythology, Christian saints, Church fathers, historical events, and scenes from early Church struggles. These motifs mingled with everyday views of the city and countryside. Frescoes were created by a new generation of artists who found ample employment with popes and kings, bishops, merchants, and book publishers.

Several royal and ecclesiastical libraries would become the foundations of new national and university libraries. France's Charles V (1338–80), known as "the Wise" and a humanist, possessed a manuscript collection considered one of the largest in Europe. His royal library eventually became a cornerstone of the Bibliothèque nationale de France, in Paris, a fitting location, that city was also a center of humanism during the Renaissance. One of Europe's finest church libraries, that of the Monastero di San Nicholas di Casole in Italy, would not survive. It was destroyed during a 1480 massacre by the Ottoman Turks.

A c.1477 fresco commemorates the appointment by Pope Sixtus IV (1414–84) of Bartolomeo Platina (1421–81) as prefect of the Vatican Library. ▶

TEMPLA DOMVM EXPOSITIS:VICOS:FORA MOENIA PONTES:
VIRGINEAM TRIVII QVOD REPARARIS AQVAM.
PRISCA LICET NAVTIS STATVAS DARE COMMODA PORTVS:
ET VATICANVM CINGERE SIXTE IVGVM:
PLVS TAMEN VRBS DEBET:NAM QVAE SQVALORE LATEBAT:
CERNITVR IN CELEBRI BIBLIOTHECA LOCO.

Perhaps the greatest court library was that of the Vatican in Rome, after it was renewed by Pope Nicholas V (1398–1455). The papal library had languished for a century until Nicholas (Tomaso Parentucelli) came to the throne and contributed hundreds of his own manuscripts to the collection. Nicholas himself had once been a professional librarian, and had played an important role in establishing Cosimo de Medici's library.

The pope also set about renewing the city of Rome, cleaning and paving streets and reconstructing its once-famous aqueducts, destroyed by invaders in the sixth century. Nicholas's municipal efforts included rebuilding St. Peter's Basilica. This renaissance for Rome coincided with Nicholas's humanist efforts to shape a liberal Renaissance library. He employed hundreds of scholars and copyists to translate Greek works, whether Christian or pagan, into Latin. His efforts at compiling an incomparable reservoir of knowledge resulted in a papal library of nine thousand volumes.

One unfortunately illiberal component of Nicholas's worldview was his official declaration that "Saracens [Muslims], pagans, and any other unbelievers" could be rightfully bound by Christians to hereditary slavery. This genteel bibliophile and library founder was also instrumental in legitimizing the enslavement of sub-Saharan Africans.

As his Vatican librarian, Nicholas appointed scholar Giovanni Andrea Bussi (1417–75), editor of many classical texts. Bussi acquired titles by using the particularly effective method of ordering monasteries to give up any works he or Nicholas wanted for the collection. Vatican agents traveled around Europe, searching monasteries and private libraries for rare or otherwise important manuscripts, buying and selling as they went. Titles were often found in some dusty corner of a neglected monastic library. They might be purchased outright or borrowed for copying.

It often happened that the pope's agent—usually a respected man of the cloth—simply hid a desired book under his robes and left with it. One particular papal secretary, who scoured northern Europe for manuscripts, justified outright theft by asserting the work had been rescued from "neglect" and "captivity" in the libraries of "Teutonic barbarians."

Pope Nicholas succeeded in acquiring many Greek texts which otherwise would have been lost to posterity. It was excruciatingly painful to him when the Muslim Ottomans captured Constantinople in 1453, cutting off a vital stream of classical manuscripts. The fall of this center of Greek literature and culture to Saracens, a friend wrote to Nicholas, "is a second death to Homer and Plato."

Political events made Nicholas's papacy turbulent and difficult in his last years. He ruefully reminisced about his previous life as Thomas, the librarian, when, "I had more happiness in a day than now in a whole year." He did not live long enough to know that many Greek scholars from devastated Constantinople would make their way to Rome and his Vatican library, carrying precious manuscripts for translation.

A century later, at a secluded monastery northwest of Madrid, Philip II of Spain (1527–98) founded a library that would compete with the Vatican's in content, quality, and grandeur: El Real Monasterio de San Lorenzo del Escorial.

The cornerstone of the king's monastery and palace, known as the Escorial, was laid in 1563. When finally completed in 1654, the Escorial would have more than 80 staircases, 9 towers, a church, cloisters, cells, and a library of 40,000 volumes, including several thousand manuscripts. The royal library was conceptualized by Philip, a devout Catholic and scholarly humanist. He was not only passionate about the rare and handsome books he personally collected from far and wide, but he also researched and recorded information about previous owners.

The grand hall of the library at the Royal Monastery of El Escorial. ▶

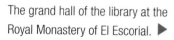

▲ The entrance to El Real Monasterio de San Lorenzo del Escorial, near Madrid.

The library's great hall, fifty-four meters long and ten high, was decorated with frescoes and friezes, with carved bookcases, marble floors, and vaulted ceilings. Frescoes on the hall's ceilings illustrate the seven liberal arts: grammar, rhetoric, logic, geometry, arithmetic, music, and astronomy.

A room on an upper floor contained banned books confiscated by the Inquisition, which Philip himself authorized, to root out heretics and Muslims and their beliefs. The forbidden titles he collected were thus protected from destruction at the hands of his armies and Inquisition agents, who burned at least 70,000 volumes. This remnant, preserved for posterity, included more than 1,800 Arabic titles, most of them acquired by the persecution and expulsion of Muslims from Islamic Iberia.

The Escorial library introduced an unusual method of arranging book-cases, or "book presses," as they were termed in monastic libraries. Until then, most presses stood perpendicular to the exterior walls and were often combined with "carrels"—desks with bookshelves and seats. Known as the "stall system," this arrangement allowed light from windows to illuminate the shelves. Philip's library initiated a "wall system," with bookcases standing parallel to walls or against them.

Contemporary users of Philip's royal library found it difficult to locate or browse the titles, but not because of the quality of illumination. For one thing, his chief librarian customarily glued large, descriptive labels to spines, overlapping and blocking the view of adjacent books. Furthermore, Philip

◀ The Bibliothèque Mazarine in Paris is seen in this turn-of-the-twentieth-century photograph of the library interior.

himself had the habit of reshelving books with spines facing inward, to protect them from sunlight.

In 1671, a disastrous fire broke out in the Escorial library, and the monks threw books out of the windows to save them. Inadvertently, a flaming banner that had been captured in the 1571 Spanish victory over the Muslim Ottomans at Lepanto was also thrown outside. It landed on the books and set many ablaze.

An essential tool of Renaissance librarianship was the catalog that listed, described, and classified a library's books. Libraries were organized according to the whims or knowledge of the individuals in charge. Sometimes books were arranged by language, or by whether they were printed books or handwritten manuscripts. The more scholarly librarians arranged books into generally recognized categories such as Scriptures, the writings of the Church Fathers, the saints, canon law, Greek and Roman philosophers, rhetoric, mythology, mathematics, and astrology.

The Sorbonne library in Paris was among the first to list titles alphabetically under each subject area. This cataloging organization was an improvement, but became cumbersome as the library grew. New acquisitions had to be entered in the margins of the catalog list until a new catalog was laboriously compiled. Further, it was common for several books to be bound in one volume, whose cover bore only the title of the first work. If the librarians were unfamiliar with the volume's contents, most of its works would likely be forgotten—unless the library possessed an in-depth catalog.

Major French and Austrian libraries began to grow in this era, notably Cardinal Mazarin's collection in Paris, Bibliothèque Mazarine, and the Habsburg court library in Vienna, Hofbibliothek. Each employed brilliant directors, scholarly and methodical, who labored at classifying and organizing the collections. Despite the heroic and obsessive efforts of library staff, the immense task of cataloging holdings invariably lagged far behind the acquisition of titles.

A shared characteristic of sixteenth-century pioneers in librarianship was a combination of compulsiveness for organization and broad knowledge of scholarly subjects. One of the first was the accomplished Swiss bibliographer, Conrad Gesner (1516–65). A physician and naturalist who compiled a Greek-Latin dictionary at the age of twenty-one, Gesner produced the *Bibliotheca universalis* in 1545. This *Universal Bibliography* listed 10,000 titles by 1,800 authors (including all known Latin, Greek, and Hebrew writers). A companion to the *Bibliotheca universalis* was published in 1548, with 30,000 entries, cross-referenced and grouped under appropriate subheadings. Known as the "father of bibliography," Gesner's work remained invaluable to librarians for centuries.

Typical of the best early bibliographers, Gesner was accomplished in several disciplines and languages, eventually writing or editing more than seventy books. He was an expert in physics and theology and was an outdoorsman who resolved to climb one mountain a year—for his health as well as for his love of nature, and to study plants and animals. His friends knew him as a botanist, even though his works in this field were not widely published until the eighteenth century. He did publish, in his lifetime, a vast work on zoology— the illustrated four-volume *Historia animalium*—which won him recognition as a founder of that science.

Gesner died of a plague that swept Europe in 1565.

Originally a reading room, the eighteenth-century baroque *Prunksaal*, or "splendor hall," of Vienna's former court library (now Austria's national library) has become a museum. ▶

As libraries grew in size, catalogs became increasingly important. One of the essential tasks of the librarian was to revise the catalog regularly. Lists of holdings, including bibliographical descriptions and summaries, were copied and exchanged for the catalogs of other libraries.

Good catalogs facilitated locating works in other collections, including those with titles for sale. Catalogs were especially important to publishers who needed writings to set in type and mass-produce via the printing press. The simultaneous growth in literacy and printing brought about a surge in published treatises on narrow subjects—monographs and pamphlets— which were bought up by the reading public.

Monographs could have been extremely influential with the scholars and religious reformers of the day. By the early sixteenth century, spiritual and philosophical controversy stimulated increasing opposition to the Church. The rise of Protestantism was influenced by the printing press and the revolutionary ideas it disseminated—ideas often in keeping with the Renaissance values of open-mindedness and free inquiry.

At the same time, the Church used the duplication power of the press to print thousands of so-called letters of indulgence, purchased by the devout in hopes of spending less time in purgatory after their earthly lives. Opposition to indulgences and to the absolute authority of the pope spurred on the Protestant Reformation, led by German monk and theologian, Martin Luther (1483–1546).

Luther published a pamphlet in 1524 that called upon all German cities to establish schools to teach children—schools that needed libraries free of the Church's rigid dogma. "Discard all such dung," he said, urging citizens to acquire books for studying the Scriptures and for learning Hebrew, Greek, and Latin, as well as the local vernacular. Luther called for libraries with books on religious commentary, law, and medicine, and for histories that "help in observing the marvelous works of God."

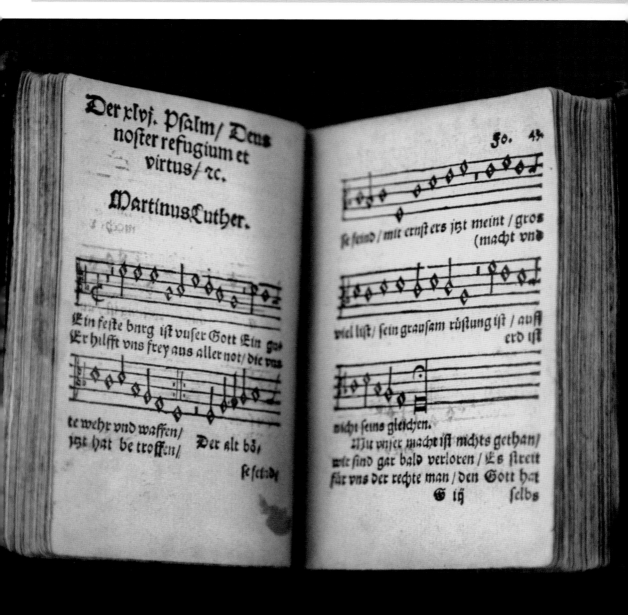

▲ A very rare early edition of Martin Luther's famous hymn, "A Mighty Fortress is our God" from the second printing.

Seven years earlier, Luther had sparked the Protestant Reformation by nailing his "Ninety-five Theses" to the door of a church in Saxony. The theses, first written in Latin, were translated into German, printed, and distributed throughout Northern Europe. They initiated furious controversy and also gained Luther support, shaping popular opinion in favor of religious reformation.

The stage was set for more than a century of wars in which armies of Protestants and Catholics rampaged through much of Northern Europe. Towns and villages were razed, cities besieged, pillaged, and taken. Churches, universities, monasteries, and colleges were mercilessly devastated, and libraries large and small were left amid the ashes, or—more often—carried off to glorify the victorious commander's own collection. Books and libraries were eagerly sought out as valuable spoils of war, and every European university or religious institution within reach of armies in the field was under threat of destruction. Many a famous library in safer regions profited from books thus looted during the religious wars of the sixteenth and seventeenth centuries.

▲ Ruins are all that remain of Fountains Abbey, a twelfth-century Cistercian monastery in Yorkshire, England, which operated until 1539. At that time, Henry VIII ordered the "Dissolution of the Monasteries" and the buildings and land were sold by the Crown.

The Reformation began as a movement to change the Roman Catholic Church, but the foundations of its bitter conflicts lay in centuries of warfare that long before had set peoples against peoples and princes against princes. Wars may be brought on by religious hostility, pitting Calvinists and Lutherans against Catholics, but the battles often were between old foes, whether Russians against Swedes, Germans against French, or Dutch against Spanish.

Confiscation of monastic property, in particular their libraries and scriptoria, took place in many Protestant lands, such as Sweden, Switzerland, and Denmark. The Jesuits, whose libraries were among the best, suffered especially severe losses. Religious conflict also swept through England, where reformers had the upper hand.

The "Suppression of the Monasteries" between 1536 and 1541 was part of a methodical campaign to eradicate Catholic monasticism in England, Wales, and Ireland. King Henry VIII considered the links of many monasteries and abbeys to the French monarchy (whose throne he claimed) as a threat to his reign. If monasteries could afford to pay royal fines, however, they were allowed to carry on. In the 1530s more than 300 monasteries were threatened with dissolution, but approximately 70 were able to pay the fines and avoid being shut down.

The destruction of England's monasteries and other Catholic institutions was incomplete, but the 5,000 friar positions extant in England during the fourteenth century had dwindled to 1,000 by the sixteenth century. Abbots who resisted royal demands to dissolve their monasteries were executed for treason. And much was confiscated—especially the libraries, whose books were sold, appropriated, or else transferred to non-Catholic foundations, such as those associated with the universities at Oxford and Cambridge.

In the case of the cathedral at Worcester, only six books survived out of six hundred in the library. The monastery library at Durham College, founded by Richard de Bury and stocked with his life's collection of manuscripts, was among those dispersed. Many de Bury titles are believed to have gone to the university library at Oxford.

Doomed monasteries were legally dismantled, their stone walls, lead roofs, stained-glass windows, and furnishings sold off along with their libraries. The king benefited financially from the confiscation and sale of monastery property. Further, the legal destruction of certain monasteries inspired mobs to attack and tear apart other monasteries, hauling off whatever could be carried. Books were destroyed for their valuable bindings—including manuscripts of church music that had not yet been printed by the Gutenberg method, and now never would be.

Hatred of Catholicism was so intense that many books suffered ignominious and foul fates. One memoirist of the day wrote about pages used as toilet paper—"to serve their jakes"—others "to scour candelstyckes, and some to rubbe their boots," while many were sold to grocers and soap sellers. This loss of library and scriptorium heritage is considered one of the worst cultural disasters of the English Reformation.

In general, English parish churches were permitted to remain open during this episode, but the elimination of abbeys and monasteries was a disaster to hundreds of communities. Abbeys and monasteries had been centers of education, their libraries essential to scholar and priest alike. In several parts of Britain, the people rose up in rebellion against this destruction and calls went out for a Catholic monarch to take Henry's throne.

The leaders of uprisings were soon executed, but a spirit of resistance had developed—a spirit that convinced Philip II, Spain's humanist-Catholic monarch, to send an armada to conquer Protestant England, then ruled by Henry's daughter, Queen Elizabeth I. Philip hoped to raise a Catholic army from this undercurrent of resentment, but no such rebellion ever developed. The Spanish Armada was defeated in 1588, but wars of the Reformation era continued, spilling over to the newly planted European colonies around the world.

Wars of empire in South and Central America already had cost other libraries dearly, as invading Europeans destroyed native records. In the fifteenth century, Spanish conquistadores in Peru tried to destroy all evidence of the Inca system of knots (*quipu*), used to keep records. To the Spanish, quipu represented Inca religion and therefore was forbidden as idolatry.

In 1562, Spanish conquistadors and priests pressed on with their sanctifying work in the Yucatan, burning 27 Mayan codices along with more than 5,000 idols. In the face of this destruction, controversial Spanish Dominican priest, Bartolomé de las Casas (1484–1566), protested government policy, earning the enmity of colonial authorities. He became, however, a regional folk hero as a Spanish missionary who fought against repression and opposed the importation of African slaves.

Las Casas not only wrote extensively on the peoples of Central America and the Caribbean, but he is also said to have saved several native codices from the fires.

PEOPLE OF THE BOOK

Wherever Islamic armies and holy men went, they brought with them books and libraries. From the Arabian Peninsula and Mediterranean regions, Muslims swept north toward Russia, south into sub-Saharan Africa, and eastward to Central Asia, reaching the Himalayas by the eleventh century. Impelled by conquest and by conversion, Islam spread rapidly toward South Asia, and reached East and Southeast Asia by the thirteenth century.

Yet Muslims were not one people under only one leader, and the faith itself split into two major camps: Sunni and Shi'a. Powerful Islamic dynasties arose in Cairo, Baghdad, Damascus, and Isfahan (Persia), and wars for domination pitted Muslims against Muslims. The great Kurdish leader and bibliophile, Saladin (c. 1138–93), presaged his defeat of Crusader kingdoms in the Holy Lands by first wresting control of Egypt from the Islamic Fatimid dynasty at Cairo. He promptly incorporated the most valuable Fatimid books into his own private collection, and allowed his viziers (ministers or advisors) to take what they wished from the rest. Saladin continued this custom whenever he captured a city. One vizier amassed 30,000 books—not all plunder, however, for many were purchased or commissioned from copyists.

In the thirteenth century the mighty force of fast-riding Mongols burst out of Central Asia to devastate Persia, West Asia, and Eastern Europe. Other Mongol hordes headed eastward to China and South Asia. Most

◀ The Sri Guru Granth Sahib is the holiest literature in the Sikh religion. This illuminated folio with gold and colors on paper is from the late seventeenth to early eighteenth centuries.

Mongols were adherents of shamanism or were animists—attributing souls not only to humans but to animals, plants, geographical features, and natural phenomena. Those first Mongol armies also included many Christian and Buddhist recruits.

In time, a major Mongol leader, or *khan,* named Berke (d. 1266) converted to Islam, yet he could do nothing to stop a rival (Christian-led) Mongol horde from sacking Baghdad, Islam's greatest city. The invaders slaughtered hundreds of thousands and ravaged the metropolis, throwing so many books into the Tigris that for a year the river ran black with ink.

The destruction of a revered city and its sacred Islamic books, including many a Qur'an, so infuriated Berke that he struck an alliance with the Muslim Mamluks defending the Levant, Palestine, and Egypt. Berke's aid helped defeat the Mongol horde, saving Jerusalem and Cairo and Islam's holy cities on the Arabian Peninsula, all of them with irreplaceable libraries.

As a "People of the Book," Muslims founded centers of scholarship and libraries wherever their faith took root. After the Spanish expulsion of Islam from the last remnant of Al-Andalus at the close of the fifteenth century, the migration of many highly literate Muslims led to the establishment of libraries in other Islamic lands. Libraries developed in Muslim towns and trading centers, including deep in West Africa, far from Islam's spiritual heartland of Arabia and the Levant.

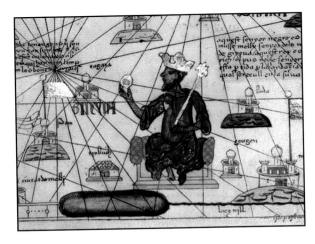

In the fourteenth century, the devout and scholarly sultan of Mali, Mansa Musa (r. 1312–37), built a royal residence at Timbuktu and used it as a tower for the city's Great Mosque. This *mansa* (emperor) was

◀ Mali's King Mansa Musa (r. 1312–37) holds a gold nugget in this illustration from a 1375 map of Africa and Europe.

Mosque
architecture in the
city of Timbuktu. ▶

famed for his 1324–25 *hajj*, or pilgrimage to Mecca, accompanied by a vast
caravan of 60,000 men preceded by 500 slaves clad in Persian silk and bearing
staffs of solid gold. The people of Cairo long remembered the mansa from
Mali, whose free spending flooded the city with so much gold that it was
devalued for years to come. Mansa Musa was also a generous benefactor of
Islamic studies wherever he went on his hajj.

By the sixteenth century, Timbuktu and other West African cities were
held in high repute for their many scholars and their impressive book collections. Founded as a trading post by Tuareg peoples in the eleventh century,

Timbuktu was a sprawling, thriving city of mud-brick buildings with thatched roofs, many rising in elegant shapes and arches. The grandiose Great Mosque, of cut stone and mortar, stood at the center of the city and had its own extensive library. When the Vatican's correspondent, Leo Africanus, arrived in the 1520s, he knew the city was a center of Islamic learning and of the book trade, for he had been there before, as a Muslim.

Africanus began life as Hasan ibn Muhammad al-Wazzan al-Fasi (c. 1488–1554), a Moor of wealthy family living in the Iberian Peninsula Kingdom of Granada. Al-Fasi was a young man when he and his family were expelled by the Spanish conquest of 1492. He resumed his education at the Islamic university city of Fez in Morocco, where the library contained one of the largest and most important Muslim book collections of the day. In company with his diplomat uncle, he traveled widely in Africa, stopping at Timbuktu. Later captured by pirates, he was sold to the Vatican as a learned slave. Before long, he was freed and baptized as Johannes Leo de Medici by Pope Leo X—Giovanni de Medici (1475–1521).

Pope Leo commissioned Johannes Leo to journey through Africa and write, in Italian, about his experiences. He wrote as Leo Africanus, describing Timbuktu, its university and *madrassas*—mosque schools—and the library with its scriptorium and Greek texts. The city's prosperity showed in bountiful markets and well-fed people, who loved to stroll until late in the evenings and play musical instruments. That prosperity was also manifested in the paper used by some scriptorium copyists—paper manufactured in Europe.

Africanus wrote about the ruler's golden plates and scepters, and about Timbuktu's "great store" of learned men, including skilled doctors and clerics, many of them authors in their own right, who had studied in Mecca:

> There are in Timbuktu numerous judges, teachers and priests, all properly appointed by the king. He greatly honors learning. Many hand-written books imported from Barbary are also sold. There is more profit made from this commerce than from all other merchandise.

Books were, indeed, a valuable commodity in Timbuktu, even in this land of gold. This was a land where salt, too, was precious, for it was carried from the seacoast 500 miles across the Sahara. Actually, Timbuktu's profit from trade in books was subordinate to trade in gold and salt, but books were cherished just as highly. The city's leading families possessed more than 100,000 manuscripts, then considered one of Timbuktu's greatest treasures. Written mostly in Arabic, and many of them pre-Islamic, these works were the source of a young scholar's education, particularly in religion, commerce, astronomy, botany, and music.

An old West African Islamic proverb expresses the importance of Timbuktu's libraries to the region's Muslims, and the sanctity of the written word to the faith: "Salt comes from the north, gold from the south, but the word of God and the treasures of wisdom come from Timbuktu."

By the sixteenth century, a new West African commodity was rising in value, as seafarers and traders from Europe reached around the coasts of the continent and entered her great rivers. That commodity was slaves. Africanus wrote about the reigning monarch, whose palace was in Timbuktu:

> This king makes war only upon neighboring enemies and upon those who do not want to pay him tribute. When he has gained a victory, he has all of them—even the children—sold in the market at Timbuktu.

Increasingly, the slave trade became the source of prosperity for African kings and chiefs. In the seventeenth century, 100,000 Africans were shipped annually to the Spanish New World, while 1,500 slaves were taken each year to British colonies. Between 1550 and 1800, more than 2.5 million Africans were shipped as slaves to Portuguese Brazil. By 1700, slaves were the most lucrative African commodity.

A century before, Timbuktu—conquered and reconquered—had passed its peak, commercially and culturally. The sultan of Morocco captured the city in 1591 and persecuted Timbuktu's scholarly class, which he correctly believed was disaffected with his rule. Many were killed, and Timbuktu's stature as a flourishing intellectual center rapidly declined thereafter. Famine, further conflict, and epidemics took their toll, until the former population of 40,000 numbered fewer 10,000 by the end of the eighteenth century.

Yet, Timbuktu's library tradition never came to an end, as families preserved their old books, storing them in cases and boxes, sometimes hiding them in caves. People of other West African cities, including Gao and Kano, had a similar book-loving culture. Along with Timbuktu's people, they preserved private collections from generation to generation—precious heirlooms that amounted to hundreds of thousands of books. Future generations would discover them, a cultural treasure that endured despite centuries of slave trade that sapped so much of West Africa's wealth and substance.

Those ancient family libraries bear witness to distant ancestors, who still speak from the books they wrote, as does Leo Africanus, who converted back to Islam.

In South Asia, Southeast Asia, and East Asia, Islam, at first, competed with the major established faiths of Hinduism, Buddhism, Shintoism, Daoism, and Confucianism. In Central Asia, Islam overwhelmed the Zoroastrians, whose adherents mainly fled to India. It was usually the sword that decided whose teachings would be supreme in any given land.

Invariably, libraries of one faith or the other suffered from warfare, but a defeated adversary's books often were retained, even read. In times of peace, scholars of differing religions shared knowledge and books, borrowing and copying,

▲ A Khangah (or Sufi) library is found inside Pakistan's Lahore Fort, citadel of the city of Lahore. The citadel was built in the sixteenth-century, during the reign of Mughal emperor, Akbar.

This miniature shows a shah swearing fealty to emperor Babur in the sixteenth century. ▶

so that cultures and ideas mingled. The Sufi order, dynamic missionaries of Islam, sought to discern and discuss where various religious ideas and worship converged or held similar principles.

In India, the powerful Islamic dynasty known as the Delhi Sultanate, which reigned between the thirteenth and sixteenth centuries, developed several types of libraries. These included the Khangah (or Sufi) library; large court libraries; and academic, mosque, and private libraries. These rulers, ethnically Turkish for the most part, encouraged the establishment of libraries in the realm, which encompassed Hindus, Buddhists, and Jains, as well as the dominant Muslims. Mosque libraries were generally open for public use.

The sultanate instilled Turko-Persian-Islamic culture in South Asia. A similar cultural impulse had appeared once before, with the arrival of Persian and West Asian peoples fleeing the depredations of the Mongols. The sack of Baghdad in 1258 sent surviving Islamic scholars, doctors, writers, architects, teachers, and musicians to Delhi, which became the great center of Islamic culture.

Turko-Mongolian invaders took control of northern India early in the sixteenth century and deposed the Delhi Sultanate. Yet, book and library traditions continued in India, perhaps more vigorously than ever, for this generation of Mongols chose to build libraries rather than pillage them. The new imperial dynasty was known as the Mughals, and their first ruler was Babur (1483–1531). Although a great military leader, Babur was far-removed

◀ Mughal father and son, Akbar (right) and Jahanghir, would successively rule South Asia as emperors who loved libraries and education—soldier-scholars also bred for war.

from the brutal war-road mentality of his ancestor, Genghis Khan (c. 1162–1227), founder of the Mongol empire.

Babur brought to India the fused culture of Central Asia's Turko-Mongolian military class and Persia's sophisticated civil society. That society had nurtured him, instilling a love of art and books, and he became an accomplished writer, whose memoirs (the *Baburnama*) are considered Islamic literature's first autobiography. Babur established the Imperial Library at his Delhi palace, a library that would be patronized and supported by subsequent Mughal emperors. As would his successors, Babur built many mosques, and with them came libraries and madrassas.

Libraries and fine books were prized royal possessions for the Mughal dynasty. Jahangir (1569–1627), educated in language, mathematics, and science by renowned soldier-scholars, collected art for the Imperial Library. Aurangzeb (1618–1707), although a harsh ruler, expanded the Imperial Library's holdings in jurisprudence, Islamic law, and theology. The reign of Akbar (1542–1605), one of the greatest Mughal emperors, was distinguished by good relations between often hostile Hindus and Muslims, and also by library expansion and organization.

Akbar formed a department exclusively for cataloging and arranging the Imperial Library's 24,000 volumes. He did much of the work himself, classifying the books under three main groupings: first, poetry, medicine, astrology, and music; second, philology, philosophy, Sufism, astronomy, and geometry; and third, commentaries on the Qur'an, general theology, and law. This system was comparable to the classification of most Muslim libraries of the era.

Akbar's rule promoted books and libraries in several other significant ways. For one, the generous patronage of his court, with its many bibliophiles, encouraged bookbinding to become a high art, producing beautifully decorated covers. Akbar also established a library exclusively for women, and he decreed that schools for the education of both Muslims and Hindus should be established throughout the realm. Yet, for all his love of libraries and his passion for education, Akbar could neither read nor write.

A warrior and virile sportsman, Akbar was also an able ruler and an erudite master of jurisprudence. After the long day's demands of governance and court, his evenings were spent listening to experts on scientific studies and architecture. Leisure time also was devoted to literary matters—readings of Persian translations, poetry and religious writings, including the New Testament.

▲ The text of this fifteenth-century manuscript, written in Persian, is verse attributed to Persian poet Rumi, admirer of the Sufi Whirling Dervishes.

Persian poets were favored by Mughal emperors, who especially appreciated the verse of Sufi mystics. These works were prized possessions of the imperial household, often given as gifts by family members. Among the most loved was Rumi (1207–73), the Persian poet and theologian, patron of Sufism's "Whirling" Dervishes. A young refugee from the Mongol destruction of Baghdad, Rumi became a teacher and a mystic poet who composed in couplets. His most famous works include the six-volume *Masnavi I Ma'navi*, in which he warns of "being puffed up with vain conceit of cleverness," a fitting admonition for any emperor such as Akbar, who so appreciated him.

Rumi soon follows with the advice to seek "inspired" knowledge before relying on information contained in books, or "borrowed knowledge." One particular ancient who failed to do so was washed away in the Great Flood of Noah's age:

> Would he had been less full of borrowed knowledge!
> Then he would have accepted inspired knowledge from his father.
> When, with inspiration at hand, you seek book-learning,
> Your heart, as if inspired, loads you with reproach.
> Traditional knowledge, when inspiration is available,
> Is like making ablutions with sand when water is near.

Make yourself ignorant, be submissive, and then
You will obtain release from your ignorance.

Eventually, Akbar parted ways with Islam, if not with Rumi, and studied
other faiths, including Zoroastrianism and Christianity. He invited representatives of diverse religions to debate in his presence. One of his most
notable audiences was given in the 1580s to Portuguese Jesuit missionaries
in order that he might be instructed "in their faith and its perfection." The
Jesuits failed in their attempt to convert the emperor, whose "obstinacy
and . . . restless intellect," they asserted, "could never be quieted by one answer
but must constantly make further inquiry."

It might be said that Akbar's "restless intellect" was emblematic of the age,
as the seventeenth century opened. From India to Europe, the printing press
was disseminating published accounts of travels to unknown lands, monographs on new scientific developments, controversial religious dissertations,
and perhaps the fastest-growing genre, popular literature—verse and fiction.

▲ The Golden Temple or Temple of God, in the city of Amritsar, India, is the
most sacred place of worship for Sikhs and one of the oldest *gurdwaras*—or
"doorways to the *guru* (teacher or guide)."

In general, South Asia's Hindu culture had fewer books and libraries than did Islam during the sixteenth and seventeenth centuries, but the elites owned many private libraries. Court libraries were maintained in palaces from Kashmir southward, throughout the Indian subcontinent.

There was little in the way of secular writing in South Asia, for most Hindu, Jain, and Buddhist libraries were associated with monasteries and temples, and therefore religious in content. In many cases, priests regularly sold off or burned books of other faiths.

To strengthen Hindu scholarship, students often were required to deposit their notes with the school or in library archives so they would be of use to others. This practice fostered the growth of Hindu libraries, although the caste system frowned upon educating the lowest levels of society. Thus, Indian libraries were not open to all.

The Sikh faith (*Sikh* is Sanskrit for "disciple," or "pupil") developed in South Asia in the late seventeenth century, its members most numerous in northwest India's Punjab Region. In Sikh places of worship, called *gurdwaras*, the faithful hear devotional hymns and recitals from Sikh scripture. Gurdwaras offer a free community kitchen to all comers, regardless of race or creed, and invariably have a library of Sikh literature available to all. Key tenets of the Sikh faith are belief in one immortal being and in a succession of ten *gurus*—teachers who have great knowledge and wisdom.

The ebb and flow of South Asia's sixteenth-century religious cultures—Muslim, Hindu, Buddhist, Sikh, and Jain—determined the flourishing and fading of libraries throughout the early modern age. It was much the same in East Asia and the East Indies—except in those parts of the world, the libraries were, for the most part, in service only for the elite.

As the Mughals built their Turko-Mongol-Persian empire in South Asia, to the west, in Central Asia, the Safavid dynasty—of Azerbaijani and Kurdish heritage—sought to resurrect high Persian culture. Established as rulers in the sixteenth century, with their capital at Isfahan, the Safavids built mosques, libraries, and schools, and re-created once-beloved Persian gardens. They, too, cherished books. One emperor's private library numbered three thousand beautifully bound and illuminated volumes.

The Safavids cultivated a "Persianate society"—one grounded in the Persian language, customs, literature, and arts. Persian culture, spread by poets, artists, architects, scholars, holy men, and jurists, had strongly influenced West, South, and Central Asia for centuries, and reached as far as Central Europe and southern Russia. Persian culture permeated the Islamic world, as attested to by the importance of Persian books in Islamic libraries.

The Delhi sultans and Mughal emperors of India, with their roots in Persia, modeled mosques, palaces, and tombs on Persian designs and stocked libraries with Persian works on science, language, literature, and discourses on Islamic values. The leading Muslim poets—including those living in the sprawling domains of the Ottoman Empire—wrote in Persian.

The Ottoman Turks first rose to importance in the fourteenth century and built upon the foundations of the former Byzantine Empire. The Safavids challenged the power of the Ottomans, engaging in conflict after conflict. The Safavids were Shi'a and the Ottomans Sunni. It's no wonder the two nations clashed; the Byzantines, too, had been in constant conflict with the Persians.

The Ottomans reached a height of power in the late sixteenth and early seventeenth centuries, ruling from their capital at Constantinople, the great crossroads of armies and cultures. Ottoman sultans controlled the eastern Mediterranean, most of North Africa, Southeast Europe, Mesopotamia, and

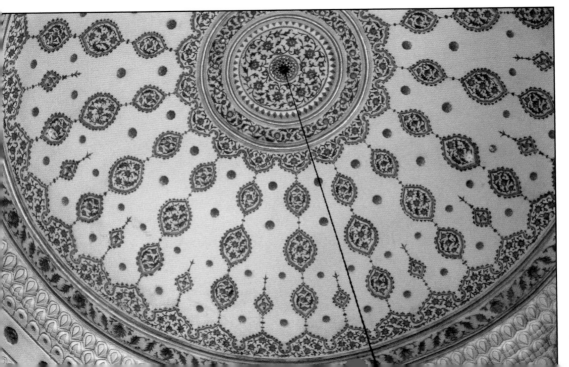

lands beyond the Black Sea. Their domains included the cities of Baghdad; Cairo; and Damascus, the Muslim spiritual centers of Mecca and Medina; as well as the Christian holy city, Jerusalem, which was also sacred to Islam.

By the seventeenth century, a mingling of cultures and ideas imbued Ottoman lands with a dynamic intellectual impulse. Muslim scholars were attracted to the new mosques, and colleges and libraries were established there, mostly open to the public in accord with the Islamic policy that believers should read (at least approved works). Book collections grew, many privately owned, with salaried library staff that included assistants to the librarian and bookbinders. Library growth was spurred on by the Islamic tradition of *waqf*—wealthy individuals offering endowments for the public good. Typical beneficiaries of this type of wealth were hospitals, schools, public fountains, and also libraries.

Among the significant Ottoman library developments was the 1678 establishment of a major library in a dedicated building in Constantinople. Also, the magnificent Topkapi Palace was simultaneously building up the largest collection of illuminated Arabic manuscripts in the world.

Mechanical printing presses would not be employed by most Muslims for two more centuries because Islam favored elegant handwritten works over machine duplication. The transcendent value of such books to Ottoman bibliophiles was attested to by "mausoleum libraries," book collections built beside the deceased owner's place of eternal rest.

In an age characterized by warfare that was becoming ever more scientific as gunpowder and firearms dominated battlefields and waterways, the Ottomans wielded great military power over a vast empire. Around the close of the seventeenth century, they resolved to assert their identity as Turks, choosing to give up Persian as the official court and administrative language. Instead, they spoke Turkish, the language of the Seljuks who had founded their dynasty.

This extreme step shocked Persianized Muslims, especially the Mughals of Delhi, which was still considered the center of Islamic culture. Yet, the Ottomans' decision was not so much a rejection of Persian culture as it was

◄ The dome at Istanbul's Topkapi Palace, which houses the Enderun Library, built in the eighteenth century for officials of the royal household.

an assertion of Turkish power. Turkish language and literature began to come into its own, finding a more prominent place in Turkish libraries.

※

In East Asia, Mongols were a threat for generations, rampaging around the Great Wall built to keep them out of China. When Mongols conquered much of China in the thirteenth century, they largely adopted Chinese customs and culture, and their rulers became the Yuan dynasty. Mongol rule brought years of peace to the "Silk Road," a network of routes linking China and the West.

Over that road journeyed the Venetian merchant, Marco Polo (1254–1324), who lived and traveled in the domain of Yuan emperor, Kublai Khan (1215–94). Polo recounted those seventeen years in foreign countries in his book, *Description of the World*, also known as *The Travels of Marco Polo*. First published in 1298, Polo's memoir was soon printed by the thousands and translated into many languages. It was one of the most popular and influential books of the age, essential to every European library, and stirred a hunger within its readers for voyages to and adventures in distant lands.

The Yuan continued their aggression late in the thirteenth century, with Kublai Khan attempting seaborne invasions of Japan, which were repulsed. The Yuan's eastward push had been stopped, but they turned south to Indochina and the island kingdoms of the Malay Archipelago and South China Sea. Kublai Khan sent an invasion fleet of a thousand ships against the Hindu kingdom of Majapahit on Java, but again was repulsed. Indochina, too, fought against Yuan control, eventually throwing off Kublai Khan's successors in the fourteenth century.

◀ A page from *The Travels of Marco Polo* (*Il milione*), originally published in the late thirteenth century and frequently translated and reprinted.

In this 1287 painting, the garb
of Archbishop John of Cilician Armenia displays
a Chinese dragon, suggesting the region's
commercial and cultural ties with
the Mongol empire. ▶

Islam was gradually brought to the Malay Archipelago and the surrounding region by peaceful means—Muslim trading vessels and Sufi missionaries. The faith joined Buddhism and Hinduism in Malay and Javanese culture, which already had temple libraries throughout the islands. By 1500, Arabic strongly influenced the Malay language and was used for trade and diplomacy by peoples from Southeast Asia to Sumatra, Java, and the southern Philippines. Arabic script was also used to write books here.

A distinctive form of manuscript illumination developed among the Malays, an art influenced by Chinese Islamic manuscript illumination and Arabic script. The Malays also followed traditional Muslim methods of book design and layout—symmetrically decorated double pages and beautifully illuminated colophons (brief, informative texts about the book or author).

The texts usually were in Malay or Arabic, but sometimes used other regional languages such as Acehnese or Javanese. The Majapahit Kingdom's fourteenth-century *Nagarakertagama* is one of the principal manuscripts of this culture. A poem in several parts, it describes a unique Hindu-Buddhist civilization, with integrated temples, palaces, and ceremonies, and a unique Shiva-Buddha deity that incorporates the Hindu and Buddhist divine beings.

In this era, Islam's Qur'an was reproduced by Malay scholars and artists, who invariably put forth great effort for their holy book. Considerable cost was expended to produce as elegant an edition as possible. Some locally made Qur'ans were written in Malay and others in Chinese. After the failed Yuan invasion, many Muslim Chinese migrated to the islands, which soon would become known to European seafarers as the East Indies.

This fifteenth-century scroll depicts Beijing's Forbidden City, residence of the emperor. Since yellow is the emperor's color, most roofs are yellow. But this library's roof is black—a color associated with water—and thus with fire-prevention.

In China, the Yuan were, in turn, succeeded in the fourteenth century by the Ming, who came to power after decades of rebellion. The Imperial Library in Beijing was maintained and, in fact, grew during both dynasties, and many private libraries prospered, as did the academy libraries, which educated scholars who would become civil servants.

The era spanning the tenth to seventeenth centuries is known as China's "period of encyclopedists." The government employed many hundreds of scholars to compile massive encyclopedias of collected knowledge, the largest of which—completed in 1408—totaled almost 23,000 folio volumes in manuscript form.

Late in the seventeenth century, emperor K'ang Hsi (1662–1722) initiated a campaign to develop the Imperial Library. At least 15,000 new books were published, including translations of Western works, particularly of mathematics, science, and cartography. In East Asia, too, collecting books—especially rarities and beautifully made volumes—was a favorite occupation of the well-to-do citizens.

In fourteenth-century Korea, libraries mainly belonged to royalty and Buddhist temples. In response to the destructive Mongol invasions, the government resolved to preserve Korea's literary heritage, establishing four major "storehouses for history." There, books were copied so that duplicates could be archived and protected in different locations.

◀ Promulgated in the fifteenth century as new script for the Korean people, the *Hunminjeongeum* (*The Correct/Proper Sounds for the Instruction of the People*) was created so that common people could read and write in the Korean language.

The fifteenth-century Yi dynasty established the Korean alphabet, *Hangul*, expressly for teaching, and it was a key contribution to the growth of libraries and archives in the country. The Korean royal libraries classified titles as classics, history, philosophy, and encyclopedias.

Since the late twelfth century, Japan had been dominated by a feudal system, with the noble *samurai* warrior class at the apex of society. From the fifteenth to the early seventeenth centuries, the island was divided into many kingdoms that were in a constant state of conflict; these wars also involved Korea at times.

This warring era called on the military skill and leadership of the samurai, whose personal libraries held closely guarded texts on strategy, the science of warfare, military records, and other practical works useful to a feudal elite. One of these "warrior libraries" (*buke bunko*) had 20,000 books and continued to operate into modern times.

The Japanese read in Chinese, the literary language of the upper class. Private, family libraries (*kuge bunko*) contained classics, Buddhist sacred works, family histories, and genealogical records. Local rulers established schools and libraries for the benefit and education of their own, and for the use of Buddhist priests and scholars. Borrowing books was prohibited, and copying required permission.

The Tokugawa family came to power in 1603, beginning a more peaceful age in which the country was governed by a *shogun*, meaning "commander of the armies." With Japan at peace, warriors and warlords often turned to reading for intellectual development. Book learning increased and libraries grew, especially those of the exclusive schools for children of leading families. Japanese libraries were, regretfully, not for the people.

By now, several seaports of Japan, China, and Korea were trading profitably with European merchant vessels, as were the ports of South Asia, Africa, and the East Indies. Much like the Mughal Akbar, people of the seventeenth century were becoming intellectually restless. A new age of European colonialism and of navigation and commerce brought peoples around the world into contact—and conflict—as never before. Christian missionaries were usually the forerunners, armed with books with which to save lost souls.

WAR AND A GOLDEN AGE

A t the close of the sixteenth century, the first English "public" library appeared, although it offered little in the way of books to borrow. The books were chained to the stalls and could only be read in-house.

The Francis Trigge Chained Library in Grantham, Lincolnshire, is considered the ancestor of the public libraries that followed it, largely because its patrons were not required to be members of an institution, such as a college or a church. Trigge (c. 1547–1606), rector of Welbourne, established the library in 1598 in a room over St. Wulfram's Church, decreeing it should be open to the clergy and residents of the neighborhood. The borough provided furnishings, and Trigge provided a hundred pounds to buy books.

Through the seventeenth century, many a library routinely used chains to protect their titles from theft, especially the reference works. The chains were riveted to the front cover of Trigge's books, which numbered more than three hundred and fifty titles. Protestant and Catholic works were well represented in the library, considered a unique period collection that manifests the conflicting religious ideas of the Reformation.

◀ A nineteenth-century view of the circular library at Wolfenbüttel, built 1705–10, and said to have influenced the design of the British Museum Reading Room constructed in the 1850s.

▲ This engraving of a chained bookcase in Hereford, England, is from *The Book-Hunter in London,* 1895, by book collector William Roberts.

Europe of the sixteenth and seventeenth centuries engaged in flourishing worldwide trade, which was paralleled by growing traffic in ideas (mostly disseminated by the written word). A wave of intellectual vitality reached across the classes, thanks to the availability of books, whether inexpensive purchases in city shops or rare old tomes studied in a college library. The audience for books further increased by the growing practice of reading aloud.

This was also an era of almost-constant wars of religion, which raged for more than 120 years beginning in the 1530s. Europe was especially decimated during the final conflict, the Thirty Years' War of 1618–48. Her population declined from 21 million in 1618 to 13 million by war's end. Many of the deaths were caused by famine and disease. Much of Germany was devastated, from the Baltic Sea in the north, to Munich in the south.

In spite of this conflict, new European libraries arose in this era, as the wealth acquired by foreign trading ventures allowed aristocrats and merchant princes to buy books and house them in palatial splendor. The best books in a number of libraries, however, were not purchased but arrived in military wagons returning from the latest campaign. A significant factor in the growth of some libraries was the acquisition of books as spoils of war—largely from the scourged German states.

During the wars of religion, library looting was virtually legalized, as it had been by the dissolution of monasteries in England. At the outset of the Reformation, Martin Luther had encouraged the establishment of town libraries, many of which appeared in Germany. Their holdings, too, often came from plundered churches and monasteries.

Private and university libraries, both Protestant and Catholic, benefited from looted libraries, whether books were taken from captured castles or

▲ The illuminated twelfth-century manuscript *Große Heidelberger Liederhandschrift* is the most comprehensive source for texts of "courtly love songs" adapted into German from the Provençal troubadour tradition. This codex belonged to the Palatinate Library of Heidelberg.

from defenseless churches. Further, with book publishing prospering, there were more printed books than ever for armies to collect. The hauls from certain campaigns were rich. Grand libraries far from the fighting swelled to ever-grander proportions. Historians termed them "treasure houses of books," but much of that treasure was war booty.

Sweden's King Gustavus Adolphus (1594–1632), a Protestant, virtually emptied libraries in his army's path. The king donated these books to many a budding Swedish library, and he improved the Royal Library; but the largest consignment came to rest in the university library at Uppsala, founded during this age of upheaval. Specially targeted by Gustavus Adolphus's raiders were the schools, seminaries, and colleges of the Jesuit order. Devoted to intellectual pursuits, including education and preaching, the Jesuits possessed fine book collections that became valuable prizes.

France, Austria, Italy, and parts of southern Germany were spared the intense suffering of northern lands, and for the most part their libraries remained intact. Although the Thirty Years' War did not reach Italy's superlative Renaissance libraries, plundered German books did. The Vatican acquired the Palatine Library of Heidelberg University in 1623, spoils won

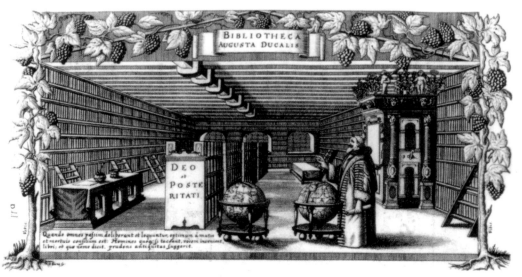

▲ Duke August is shown in this 1650 engraving while surveying his library at Wolfenbüttel; under pseudonyms, the duke wrote books on chess and cryptography (in those days, concealing information within written text).

by a Bavarian noble who had each book rebound, making sure to include an inscription that announced he had taken it "as a prize of war from captured Heidelberg" and sent "as a trophy" to the pope.

At Wolfenbüttel, in Lower Saxony—a German region laid waste by the Thirty Years' War—August, Duke of Brunswick (1579–1666), set out to build a larger library for his own collection, which he had preserved during the conflict. Starting with 10,000 volumes (some of which had been confiscated from monasteries and nunneries and acquired by his forbears), Duke August developed the library and, with dedication, he eventually collected more than 100,000 titles.

The 1648 Peace of Westphalia brought the worst conflicts to a close. France emerged as the strongest country in Europe, along with Austria, as new, definite borders were agreed upon. Disciplined national armies were being created to replace the volunteer forces that had been paid with whatever booty they could take. At the same time, national libraries were developing— from Scandinavia to France and Italy, from England to Prussia and Austria.

This era is termed the "golden age of libraries," with millions of printed books available and widespread interest growing in both classical and national literature. National libraries would eventually become objects of pride. In that same spirit, most Europeans considered themselves as belonging to a nation first and a religion second. Wars of religion would give way to wars of nationalism, as fierce and widespread as ever.

Even in times of relative peace, books were lost, whether to water damage from leaky roofs, neglect, mold, bookworms, or to that most dreaded disaster of all—fire.

Library collections were always at risk, and many succumbed to fires, both accidental and suspicious. Untold numbers of books were burned up in the 1666 Great Fire of London, which destroyed 13,000 houses and 87 parish churches, as well as old St. Paul's Cathedral with its venerable ecclesiastical library.

With the upsurge in book printing, there was a need for accurate catalogs that described available titles, telling who held what books, old and new,

▲ The 1666 Great Fire of London destroyed Ludgate in the London Wall and Old St. Paul's Cathedral, as seen in this 1670 painting by an unknown artist.

and listing prices. Not enough catalogs were available to provide information on recently published books, so book fairs were important to the trade. Book-buying agents, book collectors, scholars, writers, printers, and publishers made their way to the fairs to buy and sell and learn what was new. Frankfurt and Leipzig held the most prominent book fairs, followed by Basel, Geneva, Paris, and Antwerp.

Descriptive catalogs from publishers and sellers began to be printed and distributed, sometimes by the thousands, to the book trade. Likewise, ever-growing libraries

▲ Portrayed in his palace in 1659, Cardinal Jules Mazarin was a leading collector of art, diamonds, and books.

needed efficient organization—catalogs that went beyond the usual few categories of: the Scriptures, classical writings, law, and astrology. Emerging categories included the sciences, philosophy—divine and natural—mathematics, medicine, the arts, architecture, linguistics, commerce, economics, biography, industry, maps, and contemporary works in history and exploration.

The larger the library's collection, the more it needed a thorough catalog. These catalogs were essential for aiding the librarian in finding and shelving books. Since the stacks were closed to the public, the library staff was required to locate requested titles.

The line of eminent figures essential to the development and administration of libraries continued with French scholar and physician Gabriel Naudé (1600–53). Author of the seminal work on library science, *Advice on Establishing a Library*, Naudé instructed private collectors on how many books were practical (which depended on the collector's wealth and ability to maintain them), how to select and acquire titles, and how to create catalogs.

Naudé advised collectors to first acquire works considered important by the leading experts in a given field, and then to add others that interpreted or commented on the first. He also favored acquiring books in their original languages and purchasing entire libraries when possible. He opposed censorship, and encouraged library owners to allow others to use their books, a practice he considered a great honor for the owner—an honor equal to that of having the opportunity to build a fine library.

An avid patron of secondhand booksellers, print shops, and bookbinders, Naudé encouraged collectors to do the same in search of valuable works. He used his vast experience building and organizing libraries for princes of the church, including France's Cardinal Jules Mazarin (1602–61). Mazarin's first library, built with Naudé's help, was dispersed when political upheaval forced the cardinal to flee Paris.

Mazarin eventually returned and set to work on a second library, which by the 1660s had 25,000 volumes and was, he said, "open to everybody without exception." The Bibliothèque Mazarine collection was bequeathed to a college that became part of the Palais de l'Institut de France. In the following century, Mazarin's model, shaped by Naudé, influenced the creation of at least 50 public libraries in France.

Arranging a library well is essential, Naudé said, quoting ancient Rome's Cicero: "It is order that gives light to memory."

Gabriel Naudé was followed as a leading library administrator by the brilliant mathematician, scientist, philosopher, and jurist, Gottfried Wilhelm Leibniz (1646–1716). Born in Leipzig, Saxony, Leibniz was a multitalented contributor to several sciences. He wrote on scores of subjects, producing tens of thousands of letters and manuscripts. His special talent of possessing extensive knowledge in many fields was shared by several founders of library science, including Naudé.

As did Naudé, Leibniz found employment overseeing libraries for aristocrats—in his case, the German dukes who built the Wolfenbüttel library, known as the Herzog August Bibliothek, or the Duke August Library. Leibniz helped design a building to house the Wolfenbüttel collection, one of the first European structures built exclusively as a library. There, Leibniz created a cataloging system that became the guide for other major European libraries.

Even though he administered the mighty Herzog August Bibliothek, Leibniz advised bibliophiles to be extremely selective when building a collection, stating that he preferred "a small, well-chosen library . . . to a great mass of books" that is "only for show."

Sir Robert Bruce Cotton (1571–1631), one of England's leading bibliophiles, used busts of famous Romans to organize the library he built. The collection of books, artifacts, and coins that became the Cottonian Library at Westminster, London, was first organized around 1585. A scholar, a Member of Parliament, and an enthusiastic antiquarian, Sir Robert was a founder of England's Society of Antiquaries, which investigates relics, legends, and books from the distant past. The flowering spirit of nationalism took root early in England, and with it came a passion for ancient books that represented the people's heritage—titles essential to any substantial library, institutional or private.

Among the Cottonian's treasures was the original manuscript, bound in codex form, of *Beowulf,* the Old English heroic epic believed to have been penned around the year 1000. It is not known how the previous owner acquired the manuscript before selling it to Cotton. A significant portion of his manuscripts, codices, drawings, maps, and prints came from monastery libraries dispersed during the reign of Henry VIII.

▲ English bibliophile Sir Robert Bruce Cotton sat for this 1626 portrait after spending a lifetime building one of the finest private libraries of the day.

Also in the Cottonian were the *Lindisfarne Gospels,* an illuminated Latin manuscript produced in the seventh or eighth century at Lindisfarne monastery in northern England. The *Gospels* had been taken by Henry's official looters from Durham Cathedral. Cotton also owned the works of the fourteenth-century poet who composed *Pearl* and *Sir Gawain and the Green Knight.* One of the most significant and rarest books was the *Codex Alexandrinus,* a fifth-century manuscript of the Greek Bible. The Cottonian had the most valuable collection of manuscripts in Britain, perhaps in all of Europe.

With regard to the library's distinctive finding system, the Cottonian was housed in a room twenty-six feet long and six wide, furnished with book presses and cabinets, each topped with the bust of a famous Roman,

◀ The *Cotton Genesis*, a fifth- or sixth-century Greek copy of the Book of Genesis, was destroyed in a 1731 fire. Of more than 440 book pages, with approximately 340 illustrations, only 18 scraps of vellum remain.

emperors and ladies, such as Augustus Caesar, Cleopatra, and Julius Caesar. The library's catalog located a title by giving the name (by first letter) of one of the fourteen busts (N for Nero, O for Otho, V for Vespasian, and so on). Next came the shelf, indicated by a letter, starting at the top shelf with A; then came the title's number (in Roman numerals) when counting across the shelf from the left.

The *Battle of Maldon,* another epic, which relates the story of a tenth-century Viking victory over the Anglo-Saxons, was to be found under Otho, O, on the top shelf, A, in the twelfth (xii) position across.

Suspected of anti-Royalist sympathies at a time when monarch and parliament were at odds, Cotton was punished by having his library confiscated by the government in 1630. This event illustrates the power of the written word, for the Royalists feared the ideas in some of Cotton's books might support Parliament's cause. Upon Cotton's death the following year, the collection was returned to his heirs.

In 1702, Cotton's grandson, Sir John Cotton, donated the collection to the nation. Subsequently moved several times to different lodgings, the library was maintained in Ashburnham House, part of St. Peter's College. Ashburnham House was also the residence of the librarian Richard Bentley (1662–1742), a theologian and classical scholar.

On an October night in 1731, a fire started in the library. Bentley struggled out of the blaze with the *Codex Alexandrinus* clutched in his arms. Staff members broke open locked bookcases and hurled the contents out of the windows. The blaze was put out, but there were serious losses. The *Lindisfarne* manuscript was undamaged, as were the *Pearl* poems. Other titles were not so fortunate. The *Battle of Maldon* was destroyed, and the *Beowulf* was partly burned, although it would remain—smoke-stained and brittle—available to future scholars and translators.

In the 1750s, the British Museum and Library took charge of the Cottonian collection. Some items, including the *Codex Alexandrinus* and the *Beowulf*, became prized properties of the museum. The British Library, now separate from the museum, continues to organize its Cottonian books according to the famous heads.

In the early 1600s, English statesman and scholar, Thomas Bodley (1545–1613), realized the old library above the Divinity School at Oxford University had been emptied by the royal commissioners as part of the "reformation of the university." The original six hundred manuscript titles—largely Roman Catholic, and therefore disagreeable to Henry Tudor's England—had been dispersed. Even the original furniture and book presses had been sold off.

A former Oxford student, Bodley was widely traveled and had been employed as a diplomat to foreign courts. At the turn of the seventeenth century, disenchanted with ministerial intrigues, he gave up government service:

Whereupon, examining exactly for the rest of my life what course I might take . . . I concluded at the last to set up my staff at the Library door in Oxford, being thoroughly persuaded that in my solitude and surcease from the Commonwealth affairs I could not busy myself to better

Sir Thomas Bodley's retirement years and personal fortune were spent on building a library for the university at Oxford. ▶

purpose than by reducing that place (which then in every
part lay ruined waste) to the publick use of students.

The notion of "publick use" did not equate with the future meaning of
"public library." In Bodley's case, it meant Oxford men could use the library
freely, although no one (except in rare cases, and then usually only a prospective donor) would be permitted to borrow books.

Bodley described his qualifications to undertake the building of a library:
First, he possessed knowledge of ancient and modern tongues, and of "sundry
other sorts of scholastical literature"; second, he maintained the financial
wherewithal; third, he enjoyed the company of a number of worthy friends;
and fourth, he had the time. He was also familiar with major cities and with
their libraries, book fairs, booksellers, and purchasing agents.

Although Bodley was well-to-do, he had to sell, pawn, and borrow to
build a collection. By the time his library opened in 1602, there were more
than 2,000 books (299 of them manuscripts). As with other devoted library
builders of the age, he took great care to record every book purchased or

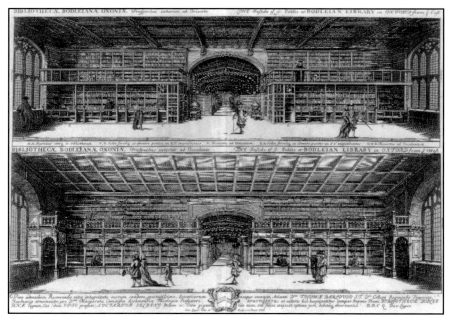

▲ These eastern (top) and western views of the Bodleian are titled, "The Interior of the Public or Bodleian Library
in Oxford," although the library was mainly for the university community.

donated. He printed a catalog that detailed how the collection was established, and he kept track of donors, whose names and contributions were maintained on an honor roll. Bodley conveyed his own fortune, land, and houses to endow the library.

The Bodleian Library, as it came to be known, was the first of its kind officially designated to receive "legal deposit" copies of every recently published title, a means of maintaining accurate government records on book publishing. The library was open six hours a day (except Sundays). The first librarian, Thomas James (c. 1573–1629), wrote, "The like Librarie is no where to be found."

Indeed, the Bodleian was unique and soon became prominent, attracting valuable gifts and donations, including bequests of several of the finest private libraries. Robert Cotton generously donated titles from his own extensive collection. The original library was expanded, and the Bodleian—or "The Bod," as students came to call it—took its place as one of the world's leading university libraries, and also one of the most beautiful.

Bodley worked daily at his chosen life's task despite persistent weak health. He saw to it that the library would have one of the best catalogs of the day. He was knighted by the scholarly King James I, who remarked on a visit in 1605 that the library founder should have been named "Godly" rather than Bodley.

For the most part, Sir Thomas was open-minded in the selection of books for his new library, and many a contemporary author was honored by having his or her work accepted. Increasingly published were poetry, fiction, and memoirs of explorers (sometimes exaggerated reports of seeking mythical cities of gold). Adventurer Sir Walter Raleigh (1554–1618) personally donated his published books to the Bodleian. Raleigh's 1595 memoir, *The Discovery of Guiana,* recounted, with a good deal of myth, his own quest for the city of gold:

> And I have been assured by such of the Spaniards as have seen Manoa, the imperial city of Guiana, which the Spaniards call El Dorado, that for the greatness, for the riches . . . it far exceedeth any of the world. . . .

Raleigh's riches were more likely to be found in the hold of a captured Spanish silver fleet galleon than in the jungles of Guiana, but such literature sold well. One outstanding best-seller was *Practice of Godliness*, or *Brief rules directing Christians how to keep their hearts in a constant holy frame and how to order their conversation aright*, by Puritan minister Henry Lukin (1628–1719). This title had a printing of 10,000 copies in 1659.

Raleigh's fanciful memoir notwithstanding, Sir Thomas was dead set against accepting certain types of popular literature. Many a future scholar would wish he had never declared:

> I can see no good reason to alter my rule for excluding such books as Almanacks, Plays, and an infinite number that are daily printed of very unworthy matters. . . . Haply some plays may be worthy the keeping—but hardly one in forty. . . . This is my opinion, wherein if I err I shall err with infinite others; and the more I think upon it, the more it doth distaste me that such kinds of books should be vouchsafed room in so noble a library.

Francis Bacon (1561–1626), English jurist, philosopher, and scientist, was a patron of the Bodleian and Cottonian. Bacon expressed the veneration he felt for noble libraries, which he considered sanctified places: "Libraries are as the shrines where all the relics of saints, full of true virtue, and that without delusion or imposture, are preserved and reposed."

Bacon did more than praise libraries; he also conceptualized a practical system for cataloging their holdings. He divided knowledge, and therefore books, into three categories:

> The parts of human learning have reference to the three parts of man's understanding, which is the seat of learning: history to his memory, poesy to his imagination, and philosophy to his reason.

Each category—history, poesy, and philosophy—was subdivided into narrower subjects. History, for example, was arranged under the subheadings of natural, civil, ecclesiastical, and literary.

Toward the close of the seventeenth century, increased literacy had altered the standing of books and libraries. Book learning was no longer the exclusive domain of aristocrats and clerical scholars. The middle class emerging in Europe could be defined as much by its ability to read as by its newfound wealth.

One result of the era's commercial and intellectual progress was that radical social theories—and the philosophers who articulated them—gained influence in the university and the government. Among the issues linked to those radical ideas were the meaning of natural rights and natural law, and the desire of common people for more freedom. Also hotly discussed was the significance of reason (rational thinking).

Social theories were favorite fare at the many public coffeehouses, where debate thrived and wits were keen. Considered more respectable than the "beer-seller's fireside," coffeehouses became popular in the mid-seventeenth century. The house was usually open to everyone, generally without deference to rank, as attested to by one set of "Rules and Orders of the Coffee-House":

The seventeenth-century English coffeehouse was a congenial haven for camaraderie as well as a lively setting for sharp and witty debate of issues of the day. ▶

First, gentry, tradesmen, all are welcome hither,
And may without affront sit down together:
Pre-eminence of place none here should mind,
But take the next fit seat that he can find. . . .

Periodicals (printed weekly newspapers, sometimes from foreign lands) were the most popular reading matter. New books, many of them brief monographs on a specific subject, were also discussed around the tables. Wars, politics, economics, scientific and social developments, and the concept of nationhood were brooded about and analyzed over penny bowls of coffee.

Opinions were plentiful and given readily and confidently, as if the customers were experts in world affairs—and in many cases they were. Alongside coachmen, farmers, and mechanics sat college professors, hangers-on at the royal court, government clerks, and military officers. One versifier said:

They know all that is good or hurt,
To bless ye, or to save ye;
There is the college and the court,
The country, camp, and navy;
So great a university,
I think there ne'er was any,
In which you may a scholar be
For spending of a penny.

In the spirit of the coffeehouse, avid readers joined subscription libraries and social libraries where, for a fee, they could borrow books. Some of these libraries offered judiciously selected titles in keeping with specific interests and tastes of the membership. Others offered a wide array of subjects for a broader reading public. These libraries, also found on the Continent and in the British colonies, were an interim stage between the libraries of the wealthy elite—private and institutional—and the public libraries yet to appear in any number.

As educated and wealthy commoners rose in society, the hidebound supremacy of nobility was being eroded. The library in its various forms was an outlet for a flood of newly printed books and spurred social unrest. Reading, or being read to, offered new horizons of knowledge (and of hope) for the lower classes. An additional benefit of reading was the pleasure and entertainment offered by the written word.

The heartfelt sentiments of Samuel Johnson (1709–84), eighteenth-century English author, were just as relevant to Europeans and colonials a century before: "Books that you may carry to the fireside, and hold readily in your hand, are the most useful, after all."

One significant effect of typesetting and large-scale printing was that authorship of specific works could be more surely ascertained. Previously, texts were often copied and recopied and incorporated, without attribution, into other works. This obscured the original authorship. Identical typeset editions, however, bore the author's name and were printed by the thousands—establishing for posterity the original author.

Further, in the whirlwind of religious controversy that characterized the period, it was desirable to know who had written what: Was his work Calvinist, Lutheran, or Catholic? In England, which erupted into civil war in 1642–51, it also became vital to know who was Royalist and who Puritan.

The British civil conflicts between the forces of the monarchy and Parliament exacted their own price in library destruction. Yet, Puritan champion Oliver Cromwell was a benefactor of libraries after the Royalists were defeated, and he came to power in 1653 as Lord Protector. At the death of James Ussher (1581–1656), Anglo-Irish book collector and Archbishop of Armagh, his library was about to be sold to the king of Denmark, or to Cardinal Mazarin—that is, until Cromwell stepped in and forbade it.

Instead, Ussher's collection was acquired by the parliamentary army in Ireland and, in 1661, became part of the library of Trinity College, Dublin. Trinity's library was immediately elevated in stature and was destined to become one of the world's finest.

▲ An eighteenth-century engraving of the Trinity College Library, Dublin.

Publishing and bookselling continued to grow, as did the size of the literate public. Criticism arose too, for books were seen as entertainment, not just some sacred source of education, religion, and instruction in sobriety. An Italian proverb asserted: "There is no worse robber than a bad book."

English satirist and translator Tom Brown (1663–1704) put similar criticism in somewhat harsher terms: "Some books, like the City of London, fare the better for being burned."

Brown's quip would not have gone over well with anyone who had lost books to fire, but then again, he wrote the sort of popular works genteel bibliophiles disdained. Literary historians described Brown's prolific work as "the comedy of the age translated into a light-fingered prose." Enemies claimed Brown had more the "spirit of a scholar" than of a gentleman.

Another controversial English author, Jonathan Swift (1667–1745), contributed mightily to the deluge of popular literature. Swift's 1726 satirical novel, *Gulliver's Travels*, was "universally read, from the cabinet council to the nursery," according to a friend. Sensing an immediate best-seller—and determined to keep ahead of book pirates—Swift's publisher had five printing

A woodcut illustrating Jonathan Swift's eighteenth-century work, "Battel [*sic*] of the Books," represents authors as knights warring over the respective merits of classical and contemporary books. ▶

houses produce the first edition simultaneously. Since then, *Gulliver's Travels* has always remained in print, although governments and religions, skewered by his wit, would have preferred banning it.

Swift rankled scholars and book collectors alike with his 1704 essay, *Battle of the Books*, depicting a pitched battle in the King's Library between classical and contemporary books. They fight over whether modern ideas—"enlightened" by rational and scientific thinking—were superior to classical Greek and Roman ideas, criticized as superstitious.

Those who believed that it was an "age of reason" contended that knowledge had surpassed the ancients. Opponents claimed contemporary knowledge was simply standing on the shoulders of the likes of Homer and Aristotle, whose works contained all that was necessary to know. Sir William Temple (1628–99), an English statesman and essayist who championed the ancients' position, said, "Books, like proverbs, receive their chief value from the stamp and esteem of the ages through which they have passed."

The Cottonian Library's Richard Bentley, not yet the rescuer of the ancient *Codex Alexandrinus* from the flames, was lampooned by Swift. Bentley is depicted as unable to catalog his book collection because "a great heap of learned dust," blowing from a shelf of contemporary books, is blinding him. Swift, who had been Temple's secretary, made sport of both camps, deriding those champions of reason who believed their age was superior to all that had come before.

▲ New England Puritans of the seventeenth century walk to church, the husband with his musket and the wife with a prayer book or Psalter.

THE LIBRARY IN COLONIAL NORTH AMERICA

As European colonists began arriving in the New World in the 1500s, they brought with them their ambitions, firearms, faiths, and books.

In this vast and alien land, books were precious, cherished by explorers, pilgrims, adventurers, settlers, merchants, and missionaries alike. In search of new lands and profit, Europeans planted colonies along the coasts and penetrated into the uncharted interior, at times making war with native peoples. Often, the only link with their home countries was the printed word. Many had an old Bible, perhaps a book of hymns, or occasionally the recently published memoirs of pioneers and travelers who had gone before them.

From New Spain to New England and New France, the wealthier colonists and clergymen built up their libraries. Sometimes, these private collections would be combined for the benefit of other readers, or were bequeathed to become the cornerstone of a new seminary or college.

A hunger for knowledge and education was common to many North American colonists, and books were essential to their intellectual and spiritual health. Reading often helped shape and define their quest for a better life and a better society, one founded on liberty, knowledge, and political independence.

Soon after Spain's first colonies were established in the New World, there were printing presses, accomplished colonial authors, and a stimulating intellectual life, especially in Mexico City—the heart of the empire. Yet, long before the coming of Europeans, Mesoamerica had its own book tradition, one the Catholic conquerors tried to stamp out.

Awaiting Spain's Hernán Cortés and his six hundred conquistadors when they landed on the east coast of Aztec-ruled Mexico in 1519 was a people who possessed ancient writing in a form of hieroglyphics. The Aztecs had many beautifully bound books, published on sheets made from stretched deerskin or from the fibers of the agave plant. The writing was Mayan and was comparable in complexity and sophistication with ancient Egyptian hieroglyphs. These books told the history of a great Aztec empire, with minute details of community life, biographies, important events, and religion. They were proof that Mesoamerican culture was as venerable as that of the Europeans.

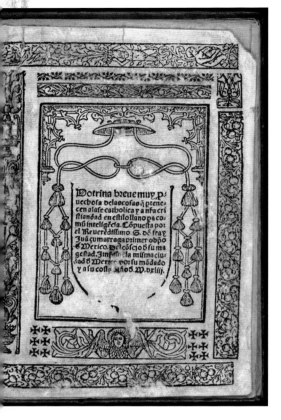

▲ The first archbishop of Mexico, Juan de Zumárraga (1468–1548), wrote *Doctrina breve*, the first book published in the Western hemisphere, printed in Tenochtitlan (Mexico City) in 1539. This page is from the 1544 edition, held in the Rare Book Division of the Library of Congress.

Although Cortés soon defeated the Aztecs, the native books were seen as a threat by the Catholic priests, who wanted the people to forget their history and accept Spanish rule. Most priests, with the exception of Bartolomé de las Casas, sought out and destroyed all the texts they could find, whether religious tomes or simply record books of local governance. Ironically, what the Spanish were eradicating was, in fact, a biased Aztec version of history. The Aztecs, themselves, had tried to wipe out Mayan culture and traditions previous to the Spaniards' arrival.

By the time Cortés arrived, the Aztecs had dominated the Mayans and Mesoamerica for about a century. In those, years the Aztecs had destroyed Mayan books and documents and replaced them with new works and a false

▲ In this 1876 oil painting, Spanish Dominican priest Bartolomé de las Casas gazes through a window at the Mesoamerican native peoples whose enslavement he denounced.

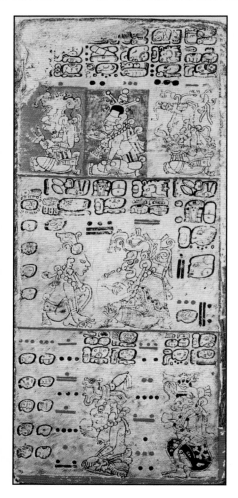

▲ The earliest known book written in the Americas, *The Dresden Codex* dates to the eleventh or twelfth centuries. Named for the Royal Library at Dresden, Germany, which acquired it in 1739, the work is attributed to Yucatan Mayas and is one of the few pre-Columbian codices to survive eradication by Spanish conquistadors.

history that portrayed the Aztecs as rightful rulers. Now, the Aztec books were, in turn, destroyed by Cortés and his priests.

Within a few years, the Spanish realized the immense value of these books, which were filled with precolonial history, genealogies, land claims, astronomy, poetry, and medicine. The surviving volumes were collected and copied, and Spanish priests and scholars collaborated with native scribes, who were taught the Roman alphabet in order to translate them. New books were published in both Spanish and Nahuatl, the native language. These translations included a massive encyclopedia that delved deeply into the culture and nearly forgotten ancient history of Mesoamerica.

As New Spain developed, its rapidly growing printing industry turned out pamphlets and monographs by colonial intellects. Among these writers was Sister Juana Inés de la Cruz, a Carmelite nun who dared to challenge the opinions of leading priests.

Born in 1648 into a prosperous family near Mexico City, Sister Juana was a favorite at the colonial viceroy's court, where she had been a lady-in-waiting before joining the Carmelites. Her library consisted of more than four thousand books, mostly inherited from a grandfather. In this library, Sister Juana educated herself at a time when young women were not permitted to attend college. Intellectual pursuits were not considered appropriate for women, but nevertheless she became a playwright, poet, and composer. She was also a student of scientific thought and experiment, and corresponded with English scientist Isaac Newton.

Priests and even bishops admired and respected Sister Juana, but in 1690 she fell afoul of church politics. A

Caulino tom. 2.

FIEL COPIA
De la insigne Muger, que lo fue ad-
mirable de todas las Ciencias, Facultades, Artes, vari-
s Ydiomas, con toda perfection, y de el Coro de los pri-
ores Poetas Latinos, y Castellanos, de el Orbe, por lo q.
singular, y Egregio numen produxo en sus excelentes
lebradas obras: LA M: IUANA YNES DE LA CRUZ,
enis de la America, Glorioso desempeño de su sexo, Honra
e la nacion de este nuebo Orbe, y Argumento de las admira-
ones, y elogios de la antigua, Nacio el dia 12 de Noujembre a
s 11 horas de la noche año de 1651 en vna piesa que llamaban la
eida de la hazienda de labor nombrada S. Miguel Nepantla In-
dicion de Chimalhuacan, Provincia de Chalco, Recivio el Sa

▲ Sister Juana Inés de la Cruz, the "Mexican Phoenix," at the writing desk in her beloved library.

private letter of criticism she had written to a Jesuit priest was discovered and published by a bishop, who wished to use it to his advantage against the priest. The bishop agreed with the contents of Sister Juana's letter, but since she was a woman, he admonished her to stop writing and instead to devote herself to prayer. She wrote an eloquent rejection, asserting the right of women to education, declaring that the original church fathers had been in accord with schooling women.

Sister Juana wrote: "Oh, how much harm would be avoided in our country" if there were women to teach women rather than risking the hazards of male instructors being placed in intimate settings with girl students. Many fathers refused their daughters an education for just this reason. Sister Juana said that such risks "would be eliminated if there were older women of learning, as Saint Paul desires, and instruction were passed down from one group to another, as in the case with needlework and other traditional activities."

For her outspoken defiance, Sister Juana was punished, commanded in 1691 to stop writing, and forbidden to use her beloved library. Next, her books and her musical and scientific instruments were confiscated. She died four years later. Hispanic literary tradition ranks Sister Juana as a major figure, known even in her own time as the "Mexican Phoenix," a flame rising from the ashes of religious authoritarianism.

Spanish America led the way in book publishing, as the New World's first printing press was set up in Mexico, where in 1539 the first North American title was printed. This was a book of religious instruction, written in both Spanish and native Nahuatl.

No British colonial titles were published until the mid-1600s. The first printing press in the English-speaking colonies arrived in Massachusetts in 1638, and was set up in the home of Henry Dunster, first president of Harvard College in Cambridge. In 1663 this shop produced the earliest Bible published in British North America. As with the first Spanish book, it was intended for native readers and was the first book printed wholly in a Native American language—Algonquian.

◀ *The Whole Booke of Psalmes Faithfully Translated into English Metre* is a 1640 hymnal printed in Cambridge, Massachusetts, by Stephen Daye. Also known as *The Bay Psalm Book*, it was the first book printed in what became the United States.

A large number of the bound books in the colonies were official ledgers and court dockets kept by government offices. The practice of manufacturing blank books for the use of clerks and secretaries became common in the 1700s. Their volumes of public records made up the first reference libraries, used by officials, legislators, and lawyers.

To the north, New France possessed no printing presses, its culture and economy tightly controlled by a dictatorial governor based in Quebec. Canada's small population of native peoples and French colonials were mainly employed in producing furs and lumber for the profit of the crown. There were only 2,200 Europeans in New France in 1663, when Quebec's Jesuit seminary, Laval College, established the first Canadian library—one of the oldest in North America.

Although no books were printed in New France, some wealthy Canadians had impressive private libraries. According to Peter Kalm, eighteenth-century Swedish traveler and botanist, Canadians seemed more interested in science and literature than were colonials in British America.

The first Canadian printing press arrived in 1752, brought to Nova Scotia by British settlers. The first Canadian newspaper appeared in Quebec in 1764, soon after the fall of New France to the British after the French and Indian War. By then, printers in British America had, for decades, been producing books, stationery, business handbills, and legal documents, as well as local newspapers. These periodicals were filled with classified advertising and announcements of the arrival and departure of merchant ships with lists of cargoes and goods for sale. As colonial unrest brought about a "continental" spirit of resistance to British colonial policies, newspapers began to report the latest political developments in the colonies and Britain.

More than ever before, the printed word was a force for change in British America, where by 1770, a well-read middle class had come to power.

It was one thing to set type and run a printing press, but the casting of individual letters of type in lead was a specialized process dominated by Great Britain. Although Americans produced skilled metalworkers, including gunsmiths and artisans in pewter ware, there was no American-produced type until 1769, when the first colonial type foundry was established in New Haven, Connecticut.

By then, English engraver and type caster William Caslon had designed the typeface that became the most popular in North America. Widely used in books and newspapers, Caslon type was used for the Declaration of Independence in 1776.

Locally manufactured paper was also essential for a successful printing industry. The first North American paper mill was established in Mexico City in 1575. It was not until 1690 that the first British-American paper mill began operations near Philadelphia. As more skilled papermakers immigrated to the British colonies in the 1700s, new mills were established, usually near population centers that had dynamic printing operations.

British-Americans of the 1700s believed education should not be exclusively for the wealthy or the clergy. New England Puritans were the best educated in the colonies, with a literacy rate above 70 percent among white adult males. This was comparable to England's literacy rate in towns and cities. Later in the century, it was estimated that 90 percent of white New England women and virtually all white males could read and write. In the other colonies, literacy levels rose steadily to compare favorably with England's.

Although books might have been scarce and expensive in America, most households of the rising middle class possessed four or five titles, including the Bible and books of religious instruction. Other commonly owned volumes were on medicine, animal husbandry, agriculture, and child rearing. Such practicality often gave way to the memoirs of adventurers and explorers, and even to collections of poetry. Benjamin Franklin's eclectic *Poor Richard's Almanack* was among the most popular American publications of the era.

American-produced pamphlets (or monographs) concerned with current issues were widely read by the 1750s. Newspapers—"colonial rags," they were often termed—steadily increased in number. Through books and periodicals, Americans were addressing other Americans in print, stimulating intercolonial communication that fostered a growing sense of unity. That unity, often spurred on by antigovernment ideas, was not appreciated by the established authorities. Some colonies forbade the operation of printing presses or the publishing of newspapers. One Virginia governor railed against "free schools and printing," claiming them to be the root of "learning," which in turn promoted "disobedience and heresy."

Printing prospered in colonial America, however, as reading and education brought about new ideas, including a new sense of what it meant to be American. In 1775, an appetite for book learning contributed to a spirit of disobedience that led directly to the demand for independence from Great Britain. The result was the establishment of the United States, a republic with a constitution founded on the "natural right" of the individual to equality, liberty, and the pursuit of happiness.

The histories of several institutions of learning in colonial times begin with prominent individuals contributing books to create a library. In 1638 British America's first institutional library was established in Massachusetts as the foundation of Harvard University.

Harvard's library was founded by a donation of books from a clergyman intent on propagating his faith. Puritan minister John Harvard left his estate and four hundred volumes to a seminary starting up in Newtowne, a village near Boston. Harvard's library consisted mostly of theological titles, with some Greek and Roman classics. The collection was invaluable to the school, which immediately attained credibility as a place of learning. The seminary was named in Harvard's honor, and Newtowne was renamed after Cambridge, England, where he had earned his degree before immigrating to the colony in 1637.

Harvard College prospered throughout the seventeenth century, and by 1720 its library had some 3,500 books. By 1764 it was the largest library in British America, with 5,000 volumes, but disaster struck that year when the library was destroyed by fire. The task of rebuilding began immediately, and the collection soon grew to 15,000 titles. By the time the Revolutionary War ended in 1783, Harvard's library had been increased by the addition of hundreds of books confiscated from Loyalists forced to flee from Massachusetts.

Harvard allowed patrons to borrow or return books only on Friday mornings, when three titles could be taken and kept for up to six weeks. In those times, an education depended more on textbooks and lectures than on the library. For those who tried to read in the library, no candles or lamps were

A 1726 view of Harvard College in Cambridge, Massachusetts, which already possessed one of the largest libraries in North America.

allowed, in order to minimize the danger of another fire. Whenever a fire was burning in the hearth, the librarian or an assistant had to be present at all times.

For all its success, Harvard's library grew relatively slowly, with only 20,000 titles at the close of the eighteenth century. Major European university libraries of this era had 200,000 titles. This shortcoming was cause for complaint among contemporary students and graduates, who would eventually see to it that Harvard Library grew to become the largest private collection in America by the late nineteenth century, with almost 230,000 books.

In 1699, Church of England clergyman Thomas Bray was sent to the colony of Maryland to report on the condition of the Anglican Church in America. In his mid-forties, Bray was a highly regarded intellectual with a special interest in Anglican missions in the colonies. Anglicanism was the official religion of England and several of her colonies. Since Anglican ministers could be ordained only in England, they were invariably English-born, and therefore were a strong link between church members in America and the mother country.

Bray worked tirelessly to establish Anglican parish libraries in America and England. By the time he left America, after a year's work, Bray had founded 39 lending libraries and a number of schools. His efforts would eventually lead to the establishment of almost 100 libraries in America. He was also instrumental in the founding of more than 200 libraries in England.

▲ English clergyman Thomas Bray, depicted by an unknown artist, was instrumental in establishing and maintaining libraries in the central colonies of British North America.

While visiting Maryland, Bray became particularly concerned about the subjugation of Indians and the enslavement of Africans. He was inspired to establish a missionary organization, the Society for the Propagation of the Gospel, to minister to these peoples. The society was founded in England in 1701, a year after he left America. In the thirty years of his life following the visit to the colonies, Bray preached and wrote vigorously against slavery and the oppression of Indians.

Bray's work in America is recognized as the first major coordinated effort to establish libraries in the New World.

But it was a former Boston printer, Benjamin Franklin, who led in the founding of the first American subscription library.

In 1723, the eighteen-year-old Franklin abandoned his duties as a print-shop apprentice and left for Philadelphia, where he established his

▲ Scottish portraitist David Martin (1737–97) was known for depicting his subjects in their most natural settings—Benjamin Franklin is reading a book in this 1767 painting.

own printing and publishing operation. Just a few years after arriving in Philadelphia, Franklin was part of a circle of like-minded intellectuals and book lovers. In 1727, he and some friends formed "a club of mutual improvement," as he wrote in his autobiography.

Calling themselves the "Junto"—meaning a council or a combination of individuals organized for a specific purpose—they met on Friday evenings to discuss politics, morals, and natural philosophy, as science was then termed. Once every three months, a different member would write an essay to be discussed and debated. Members often brought in books to consult in order to prove or clarify a point. As men of moderate means, few could afford to purchase enough titles to constitute a library, but they shared what books they possessed.

Franklin wrote:

A proposition was made by me that since our books were often referr'd to in our disquisitions upon the inquiries, it might be convenient for us to have them altogether where we met, that upon occasion they might be consulted; and by thus clubbing our books to a common library, we should, while we lik'd to keep them together, have each of us the advantage of using the books of all the other members, which would be nearly as beneficial as if each owned the whole.

▲ This 1815 Library Company of Philadelphia subscription receipt includes a hefty library fine for the patron "neglecting to make" a payment due to the company.

Franklin's proposition for a library "was lik'd and agreed to, and we fill'd one end of the room with such books as we could best spare."

This library, set up in the home of one of the members, inspired Franklin to draw up a proposal for a subscription library. In 1731, fifty founding members contributed funds to establish the Library Company of Philadelphia, which, for Franklin, was "[his] first project of a public nature." Membership increased to one hundred subscribers, who paid an initial fee and annual dues. The idea caught on across the colonies, and by the 1750s a dozen new subscription libraries had appeared, established in Pennsylvania, Rhode Island, South Carolina, Massachusetts, New York, Connecticut, and Maine. By contrast, the first British subscription library was not established until 1756.

Franklin later referred to the Library Company as "the mother of all the North American subscription libraries, now so numerous." The Library Company soon was prosperous enough to begin publishing its own titles. In addition to a growing number of books, its holdings began to include maps, collections of fossils, antique coins, minerals, and scientific instruments such as telescopes and microscopes, which were loaned out. Needing more space, the company rented the second floor of Philadelphia's Carpenters' Hall in 1773. The following year, the First Continental Congress convened in the meeting hall downstairs to discuss the future of the colonies and relations with Great Britain.

Congressional delegates were allowed library members' privileges, as were attendees of future congresses, which declared independence, fought the Revolutionary War, and established the United States of America.

Permanent library quarters were built in 1791, when Philadelphia was temporarily the nation's capital. The Library Company served as the library for members of Congress until the establishment, in 1800, of the new capital at Washington, D.C.

New York Society Library bookplate, a copper and steel engraving by Peter R. Maverick (1755–1811) ▶

Payment receipt issued in 1796 to a subscriber to the New York Society Library, founded in 1754.

The foundation of the New York Society Library was laid in 1700, when Reverend John Sharp, chaplain of the British Army in New York, bequeathed his library to the city. As a later historian put it, Reverend Sharp manifested:

> a kindly care for those who should come after him, and, at his death, left those books which had been his solace and his strength, for the use of the public, to whisper words of wisdom and of warning to those who might turn for a moment from the pursuits of trade to listen to their teachings.

The chaplain's library was augmented by additional contributions, typically religious works. According to the historian, another minister

> bequeathed his library to the Society for the Propagation of the Gospel in Foreign Parts, and they presented it to the City of New York "for the use of the Clergy and Gentry of New York and the neighboring provinces."

The library was decisively enlarged in 1754 by a "society" of prominent New York gentlemen who combined to establish a library for their own use. In this case, "society" does not refer to an upper class but means a group, much as Franklin's "Junto" meant an organization with a specific purpose—sometimes referred to as "a set of gentlemen." These New York gentlemen bought seven hundred new books.

Following the example of the Junto, the seventy founders of the New York Society Library opened their membership to the public, by subscription.

▲ The Loganian Library in Philadelphia was absorbed by the Library Company in 1792. The foundation of the Loganian was the library of Pennsylvania Quaker and statesman James Logan (1674–1751), one of the three largest private libraries in the colonies.

They announced the hope that "a Scheme of this Nature, so well calculated for promoting Literature, will meet with due Encouragement from all who wish the Happiness of the rising Generation."

In 1775, that coming generation was met with the crisis of the Revolutionary War, with New York City becoming an armed camp occupied by British forces. The conflict brought desolation and fire to the city and to the library, which was then affiliated with King's College, later to become Columbia University. Plundering British troops made off with any book they could steal. Soldiers would conceal books in their knapsacks, often bartering them for rum.

By the time the city was liberated in 1783, the library had lost track of most of its collection. It was a miracle when six hundred missing books were discovered in a local church, although no one seemed to know how they had come to be there.

After the war, the library grew to several thousand volumes and was housed in City Hall before moving to Federal Hall, where in 1784 Congress met to deliberate the writing of the Constitution. As in Philadelphia, the delegates had borrowing privileges, and the New York Society Library served as the Library of Congress.

▲ Washington, D.C., was captured and torched by British forces in August 1814; the Capitol, which housed the Library of Congress, burns in the distance.

THE LIBRARY IN THE YOUNG UNITED STATES

As British America thrived and grew, so did its many private libraries, which were broadened to contain titles on colonial history, European politics, and economics. Military leaders acquired their own specialized set of books, as in the case of New England's Miles Standish, who owned a handbook for artillery.

Prosperous colonials had an appetite for the latest books on science, natural history, philosophy, and human rights. Titles on astronomy, metaphysics, geography, surveying, and the "art of thinking" were shelved beside the works of political philosopher, John Locke, and poet, John Milton.

Private libraries were bequeathed to schools and colleges, and a Boston merchant left his collection, along with sufficient funds, to establish the first town library for public use.

Many colonists who settled British America handed down a solid educational foundation to the following generations. This tradition of education and self-improvement led to a wider movement to defend the rights of the individual, a basis for the American Revolution and subsequent independence. The urge for learning also led to the creation of public libraries across the country.

When, in 1800, the United States established its capital city at Washington, D.C., the government also established the Library of Congress. This library was soon destroyed by the British during the War of 1812, but

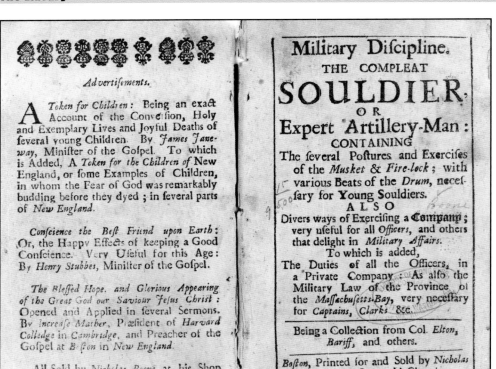

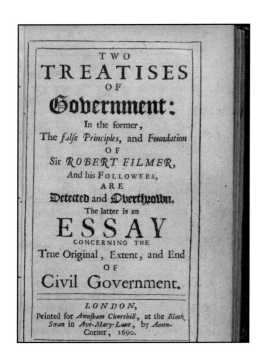

▲ Title page of a 1701 military manual for training in the use of artillery, a self-taught skill later employed fighting British troops in the American Revolution.

◄ The 1690 edition of English philosopher John Locke's *Treatises of Government*. Thomas Jefferson considered Locke one of "the three greatest men that have ever lived," along with Locke's countrymen, Francis Bacon and Isaac Newton.

rebuilding began immediately. Even as the Library of Congress was literally rising from the ashes, a vision of what it could be was expressed in an 1815 editorial in the *National Intelligencer*: "In a country of such general intelligence as this, the Congressional or National Library of the United States [should] become the great repository of the literature of the world."

The Continental Congress found itself on the run in 1783, the final year of the Revolutionary War. Although victory was imminent after Washington's resounding triumph at Yorktown in late 1781, Congress had endless financial difficulties and usually neglected to pay the troops. The result was mutiny.

In the course of the war more than one unpaid regiment mutinied and had to be punished with harsh discipline. The most dangerous uprising, as far as members of Congress were concerned, occurred early in the summer of 1783 when recently recruited Pennsylvania troops marched into Philadelphia. The furious mutineers surrounded Independence Hall, where Congress was in session, and demanded their pay—in some cases pointing bayonets at the chests of the delegates. The mutineers, who numbered three hundred, were at last convinced to desist or face firing squads, and the mutiny ended. Congress, however, felt unsafe in Philadelphia and set off for Princeton, New Jersey, and later for Annapolis, Maryland.

With the Library Company of Philadelphia collection no longer available, Congress member James Madison proposed that three hundred books be purchased for a congressional library. One of the best-read and most intellectual members, Madison was a good friend of fellow Virginian Thomas Jefferson, sharing a love of books and the conviction that liberty and education went hand in hand.

Madison's proposal was not carried through, but it was the first substantial attempt to create a library for Congress. During the next seventeen years after the Revolutionary War, the Philadelphia Library Company and New York Society Library alternated as congressional libraries whenever delegates held sessions in those cities (each for a time serving as the capital of the new United States).

▲ Thomas Jefferson, known as the "Father of the Library of Congress," was empowered as president in 1802 to appoint the first Librarian of Congress.

In April 1800, president John Adams approved legislation to transfer the government from Philadelphia to Washington, D.C., which now officially became the nation's capital. In this same act was the authorization to establish the Library of Congress.

The act called for a library containing "such books as may be necessary for the use of Congress—and for putting up a suitable apartment for containing them therein. . . ." The congressional Joint Committee on the Library was created by this act, and, in 1811, the committee was officially made permanent. It is Congress's oldest continuing joint committee.

With the 1800 legislation, a fund of five thousand dollars was appropriated to purchase books, which were kept in the Senate, or north, wing of the Capitol building. The congressional library was designated as a reference library for the use of members of Congress only.

Thomas Jefferson became president in 1801 and took great interest in the library, often recommending books to acquire. Jefferson had a large library of his own and was known for buying books on his visits to Europe. In 1802, an act of Congress authorized the president to name the first Librarian of Congress, and gave itself power to establish library rules and regulations. This act also granted the president and vice president the right to use the library.

John J. Beckley, the first Librarian of Congress, was paid two dollars per day and was also required to serve as clerk to the House of Representatives.

Within a few years, there were three thousand titles in the Library of Congress, which was housed in a timber-framed room with a double row of windows. Then, in August 1814, during the War of 1812, a British invasion force captured Washington and torched the Capitol building. The Library of Congress was destroyed in the conflagration.

The following January Congress authorized the acquisition of Thomas Jefferson's private library to "recommence" the operations of the Library of Congress. In office at the time was president James Madison, who, back in 1783, had been an early proponent of establishing a permanent Library of Congress.

The War of 1812 between the United States and Great Britain was brought on by a small number of powerful congressmen known as "war hawks." Most Americans did not want a war, nor did the British, who were embroiled in a

▲ William Russell Birch (1755–1834) painted this view of the Capitol building in Washington before it was burned down in 1814 by the British.

worldwide conflict with Napoleonic France. The war hawks envisioned territorial gain, especially in the possible capture of Canadian lands.

Citing frequent British violations of American sovereignty on the high seas, the United States declared war in June of 1812. The first invasions into Canada were repulsed, but in 1813 the towns of York (later Toronto) and Niagara-on-the-Lake were burned by the Americans. Destroyed with Niagara was a small subscription library, Canada's first.

The land engagements of the War of 1812—which lasted until early 1815—were mostly minor, but the British destruction of Washington, D.C. in 1814 was a national disaster and embarrassment.

In August of that year, the British invaded Maryland, sweeping aside disorganized volunteer defenders, and marched on Washington. As the enemy approached the undefended capital, the government and Washington's eight thousand residents fled, except for a handful of intrepid clerks and assistants who managed to load a wagon and escape with irreplaceable congressional documents and archives, including the Declaration of Independence.

President James Madison's first lady, Dolley, is reputed to have courageously rescued precious pictures and furnishings from the White House before the British arrived, but the three thousand books of the congressional library were left behind in the Senate wing of the Capitol. There the British took revenge for the burning of Niagara and York.

▲ The account book that survived the 1814 destruction of Congress's library was taken as a souvenir by the British commander, whose family later returned it to the United States government.

The facts are in dispute, but legend has it that the invaders plundered the library and used books to set the Capitol building ablaze. Several other public buildings, including the White House, were set afire, as some Americans looked on helplessly. When one despaired of the "elegant library" being destroyed, he was overheard by the British commander, Admiral George Cockburn, who expressed regret, saying, "I do not make war against Letters nor Ladies." Even Cockburn's own officers objected to wantonly destroying buildings that had surprised them with

▲ The Capitol building after burning in the War of 1812, shown in ink and watercolor, c.1814, by Connecticut-born miniaturist George Munger (1783–1824).

their quality and grace. The admiral was not swayed, however, for he was resolved to humiliate the United States.

Only a torrential downpour saved the burning Capitol building from complete ruin. The Senate wing suffered such devastation that even marble columns were destroyed. Walls still stood at the Capitol and White House, but the once-beautiful interiors were ravaged and charred. One of the only congressional volumes to have survived was a government account book of receipts and expenditures for the year 1810, taken as a souvenir by Cockburn himself. In 1940, a benefactor donated this book to the Library of Congress, and in it was the notation: "Taken in the President's room in the Capitol, at the destruction of that building by the British, on the capture of Washington 24th, August 1814."

The British invasion force soon was forced to withdraw, and the American government and residents returned to a melancholy, devastated Washington. Congress took up temporary quarters at the nearby Blodgett's Hotel, and one of its first resolutions was to restore the library.

Peace terms were arrived at by December, although fighting continued until the news reached North America. The British suffered a bloody defeat at

▲ The first of two pages of Jefferson's catalog which listed the books in his library.

New Orleans in January 1815, though the war officially was over. In that same month, Congress purchased Jefferson's own private library as the foundation for what would become a great national library: the Library of Congress.

Soon after the first Library of Congress was destroyed in 1814, retired president Thomas Jefferson (1801–1809) offered to sell Congress his personal library as a replacement.

The seventy-one-year-old Jefferson knew something of library fires because a few years previous he had lost part of his own library in this very way. He had reconstituted the collection and for some years had hoped Congress would purchase his library. This was an appropriate moment, for he was in dire need of cash.

Jefferson wrote to Congress about his library:

> I have been fifty years in making it, and have spared no pains, opportunity or expense, to make it what it now is. While residing in Paris I devoted every afternoon . . . in examining all the principal bookstores, turning over every book with my own hands, and putting by everything which related to America. . . .

In January 1815, Congress purchased Jefferson's 6,487 volumes appraised at $23,950, more than doubling the congressional library's original size. Further, the Library of Congress was transformed from a special library of books on law, economics, and history to become a general library, the result of Jefferson's personal interests being so broad. One of the most influential political philosophers of the age, Jefferson was fluent in several languages and a skilled architect. Mainly self-educated, his education had come from his books, which composed one of the finest private libraries in North America. He described his library as containing everything "chiefly valuable in science and literature."

As president, Jefferson had been a key advisor in the selection of the Library of Congress's first books. Now it was Jefferson who again determined the content of the library. Unlike the first Library of Congress, the books would not be limited to "those branches of science which belong to the deliberations of members as statesmen," as he once had advised.

In October 1814, the Senate voted unanimously to make the purchase. Many members of the House of Representatives, however, objected that Jefferson's library included subjects that seemed extraneous or inappropriate for a legislative library. Opponents of an outright purchase included New Hampshire's Daniel Webster, who preferred to acquire the entire collection and then return to Jefferson "all books of an atheistical, irreligious, and immoral tendency."

Anticipating such difficulties, Jefferson said about his library, "I do not know that it contains any branch of science which Congress would wish to exclude from their collection; there is, in fact, no subject to which a Member of Congress may not have occasion to refer." His library included philosophy, history, law, religion, architecture, travel, natural sciences, mathematics, studies of classical Greece and Rome, modern inventions, hot-air balloons, music, submarines, fossils, agriculture, and meteorology.

Jefferson was the ultimate example of a great thinker in that "Age of Reason," a man who believed in practical application of abstract theories. He sought to operate Monticello by scientific farming methods, and was always after some new seed or plant for experimentation. During most of his life (until injured in a fall from horseback) he played the violin, regularly ordering the latest compositions published in Paris and London. He was known as a connoisseur of fine wines, especially those from France, as he loved French culture.

Author of the Declaration of Independence, a former governor of Virginia, and

◀ In the late nineteenth century, the Library of Congress acquired a collection of Benjamin Franklin's papers and books, among them this volume, with Franklin's hand-written notations in the margins.

United States ambassador to France, Jefferson pursued wide-ranging intellectual interests, which could be seen in his books. He organized them into broad classifications, according to three aspects of the human mind: memory, reason, and imagination, with forty-four subdivisions.

Of supreme importance to Thomas Jefferson was individual freedom, especially freedom of thought and self-expression: "I have sworn upon the altar of God eternal hostility against every form of tyranny over the mind of man."

Early in 1815, after much debate, the House at last voted by a slim margin to make the purchase. When shipped to the Library of Congress, the books were packed into specially made pine boxes and carried in ten wagonloads to Blodgett's Hotel, where Congress was temporarily housed during the rebuilding of the Capitol. There they were placed in a library room in the charge of George Watterson, the third Librarian of Congress, but the first to work full-time in that position.

Watterson gave the books bookplates and labels, keeping them organized according to the classifications Jefferson had used. These books remained at the heart of the library's collection until 1851, when a disastrous fire engulfed the main reading room and destroyed more than half of them.

Thomas Jefferson died on July 4, 1826, the fiftieth anniversary of Independence Day. He chose the epitaph inscribed on his tombstone:

> Here was buried Thomas Jefferson,
> Author of the declaration of American independence,
> of the statute of Virginia for religious freedom,
> and father of the university of Virginia.

Jefferson did not refer to himself as the father of the Library of Congress, but in 1980 an act of Congress named the library's main structure the Thomas Jefferson Building.

New England's remarkable literacy began at the very outset of the Massachusetts Bay Colony, established in 1620 by the English Pilgrims. The earliest colonists brought books with them and immediately ordered more to be sent from England. Every ship arriving in the colony had consignments of books to augment private libraries that eventually would compare with the best of their kind in the world.

An English visitor to the prominent Cotton Mather family residence in 1686 was astounded by the library:

> He shew'd me his Study: And I do think he has one of the best (for a Private Library) that I ever saw: Nay, I may go farther, and affirm, That as the Famous Bodleian Library at Oxford, is the Glory of that University, if not of all Europe . . . so I may say, That Mr. Mather's Library is the Glory of New-England.

Booksellers became numerous in the colony, especially in Boston, where the town library had been established by 1653. In that year, merchant Robert Keayne left his collection to the community, along with a bequest for it to be used for the construction of a building that would serve as a public library and town hall.

Through the 1600s, the library at the Boston Town Hall continued in operation in "the library room at the east end of the town house." It grew steadily, usually with donated books both from the deceased and from individuals who returned to England. The colony's records of wills often refer to books left to the "Towne Lybrary," and many books were inscribed "for the Publike Library at Boston."

Like so many libraries before, there were losses of books, including those damaged by a fire at the town house in 1711, as noted in the diary of Judge Samuel Sewall:

> In our Boston Library several valuable Books were lost, as the Polyglott Bible, the London Criticks, Thuanus's History, a Manuscript in two Folios left by Capt: Reyn [Keyn] the Founder; &c.

A public announcement requested anyone who possessed, as a result of the fire, any "books, carry'd away at that time, or any other Goods, are desired to bring them to the Post Office, that the true Owners may have them again."

▲ The Boston Atheneum in the 1850s, from *Ballou's Pictorial Drawing-Room Companion.*

▲ Interior view of the Boston Atheneum in the mid-nineteenth century, from
Ballou's Pictorial Drawing-Room Companion.

Boston's Puritans had a penchant for immediately burning any unacceptable books that arrived from England, including those that criticized the dominant faith or otherwise were "blasphemous & hæretticall bookes."

Through the 1700s and into the 1800s, the Boston Town Library thrived, organized as in other colonies as a "subscription" or "society" library for individuals who paid dues for membership. A new type of library, known as an "athenaeum," issued shares to members and spent its capital not only to purchase books but also periodicals, and to present cultural events.

In 1807, the Boston Athenaeum was founded by fourteen gentlemen who were members of the Anthology Club, which published literary periodicals. The club was originally founded in 1804 by Reverend William Emerson, father of poet Ralph Waldo Emerson. Fashioning their institution on the Athenaeum and Lyceum in Liverpool, England, the objective was to combine the "advantages of a public library containing the works of learning and science in all languages" with an art gallery.

Throughout the next fifty years, the Boston Athenaeum was the premier center of Boston's intellectual and cultural life. By 1851 it was one of the five largest libraries in the United States. Meanwhile, the original Boston Town Library was superceded by the Boston Public Library, established in 1848 as the first publicly supported municipal library in the United States.

Boston Public Library became a leading model for the modern urban public library. Following European library policy, Boston Public had noncirculating, "reserved" scholarly books that were not to be borrowed, but patrons were permitted to take out popular titles at no charge. This "reference books" policy soon became a widely followed standard in the United States and Canada.

English-born Robert Keayne was a successful businessman in the Massachusetts Bay Colony in the mid-1600s. According to Puritan standards, Keayne was sometimes too successful, too eager to make a profit, and he was fined for avarice by the colony's government.

Financial success, however, did allow Keayne to collect books and build a fine private library, which he left to Boston upon his death in 1653. His wife and son were given first choice of books, except for the "Lattine and Greeke" titles, which, with the rest, were bequeathed to the future town library. Thus, the year 1653 is considered the date of the establishment of the first public library in America.

Keayne also left funds, subsequently augmented by later colonists, to build a structure that would serve as a market, library, and gallery. Construction of this "Boston Town House" began in 1657, laying a cornerstone for a municipal library system and eventually the Boston Public Library, the third largest library in the United States.

In the late 1800s, young Amy Lowell, future Massachusetts poet, educated herself by reading from the seven thousand books in the family library and in the Boston Athenaeum.

Lowell later wrote a poem titled "The Boston Athenaeum," about spending so many hours in that library. Some verses are excerpted below.

> Thou dear and well-loved haunt of happy hours,
> How often in some distant gallery,
> Gained by a little painful spiral stair,
> Far from the halls and corridors where throng
> The crowd of casual readers, have I passed
> Long, peaceful hours seated on the floor
> Of some retired nook, all lined with books,
> Where reverie and quiet reign supreme!
>
> And as we sit long hours quietly,
> Reading at times, and at times simply dreaming,
> The very room itself becomes a friend,
> The confidant of intimate hopes and fears;
> A place where are engendered pleasant thoughts,
> And possibilities before unguessed
> Come to fruition born of sympathy.
>
> And as in some gay garden stretched upon
> A genial southern slope, warmed by the sun,
> The flowers give their fragrance joyously

To the caressing touch of the hot noon;
So books give up the all of what they mean
Only in a congenial atmosphere,
Only when touched by reverent hands, and read
By those who love and feel as well as think.

Our fathers' fathers, slowly and carefully
Gathered them, one by one, when they were new
And a delighted world received their thoughts
Hungrily; while we but love the more,
Because they are so old and grown so dear!

In 1831, French nobleman and politician Alexis de Tocqueville journeyed through the United States on an assignment from his government to study the American prison system. Part of de Tocqueville's travel journal was published in 1835 (the first of two volumes), entitled *Democracy in America.*

An anecdotal study of American culture, de Tocqueville's journal noted that pioneers living on the frontier often originally came from "civilized" regions and had a high degree of book learning. He wrote, "The Americans never use the word peasant, because they have no idea of the class which that term denotes; the ignorance of more remote ages, the simplicity of rural life, and the rusticity of the villager have not been preserved among them. . . ."

Although it first appeared, upon meeting a frontiersman, that "everything about him is primitive and wild," de Tocqueville observed: "He wears the dress and speaks the language of cities; he is acquainted with the past, curious about the future, and ready for argument about the present; he is, in short, a highly civilized being, who consents for a time to inhabit the backwoods, and who penetrates into the wilds of the New World with the Bible, an axe, and some newspapers."

In a typical backwoods cabin, de Tocqueville often found on one wall the map of the United States, near which were, "upon a shelf formed of a roughly hewn plank, a few volumes of books—a Bible, the six first books of Milton, and two of Shakespeare's plays. . . ."

▲ Eastman Johnson's 1868 portrayal of a young Abraham Lincoln reading by the fireplace in his log cabin home captured the image of the literate frontier settler.

Newspapers, wrote de Tocqueville, were to be found in virtually every hamlet and town he passed through. Had de Tocqueville returned to America in the next few decades, he would have seen that community libraries had started to appear in frontier settlements.

By the first decades of the 1800s, several types of "public" libraries had developed, including subscription and athenaeum libraries formed by organized societies. There were also mercantile libraries for members of trade groups and employees working in various industries—libraries intended for the improvement of their education and skills. All these various libraries were broadly referred to as "society libraries."

As a strong middle class developed in the United States, the demand for public education took on unstoppable momentum nationwide. Urban areas were attracting great numbers of newcomers, both immigrants from abroad and rural folk from the country. A movement developed to educate them, with the focus being on achieving universal literacy and mandatory public education. Democracy, it was asserted, required educated, informed citizens. Public libraries, supported by the government, became an essential institution for the education of the masses.

APPRENTICES' LIBRARY.

Every Book must be returned to the Library, or renewed, within two weeks The fine for keeping beyond that period.

WILL BE THREE CENTS PER WEEK.

For returning a book with leaves turned down, one cent.

For Scribbling, or any other injury done to the book, fines are to be fixed by the Committee of Attendance.

₊ Boys are requested to learn the number on the Card.

▲ Borrowing rules for an apprentice library were applicable everywhere.

Libraries would not, however, be limited to urban areas. Communities across the country offered some municipal support to improve and fund existing society libraries, and in 1816 mainly rural Indiana authorized the establishment of county library systems. Peterborough, New Hampshire then led the way by founding the first wholly tax-supported local public library in the United States.

The Peterborough Town Library was founded during a town meeting in April 1833 and became the model for the modern community library—open to all and free of charge. Two years later, New York State took the innovative step of authorizing school districts to raise taxes for supporting libraries that were to be managed by local schools and open to the public. This arrangement developed rapidly, and by 1850, libraries in the state's public schools contained more than 1.5 million books. The following year, Canada passed its own school district library legislation modeled on New York's system.

Within a few decades, however, school-based public libraries suffered from inadequate funding, and they eventually were changed to serve only the school's students and teachers. Yet, this school-library concept served as a basis for the future public library system in America.

Shown in the mid-twentieth century, the Peterborough Town Library, Peterborough, New Hampshire, is considered the first taxpayer-funded public library in the United States. ▶

▲ An 1898 scene in the Reading Room of all-women Smith College, Northampton, Massachusetts, by Walter Appleton Clark (1876–1906) illustrated a *Scribner's Magazine* article, "Undergraduate life at Smith College."

THE LIBRARY MOVEMENT

A merican community libraries were thriving throughout the first half of the nineteenth century, whether as social libraries with paid membership or general libraries established by a benefactor. New England, alone, had more than a thousand such libraries in this period, and thousands more—some in institutions, others in bookshops, fire companies, and public reading rooms—were scattered across the country.

Massachusetts poet and essayist, Ralph Waldo Emerson (1803–83), voiced the feeling of American intellectuals when he praised libraries:

> Consider what you have in the smallest chosen library. A company of the wisest and wittiest men that could be picked out of all civil countries, in a thousand years, have set in best order the results of their learning and wisdom.

Too often local libraries flared up but died out, subject to the enthusiasm or resources of the benefactor.

One such benefactor was Jesse Torrey Jr. (b. 1787) of New Lebanon, New York, who, in 1804, established a "free juvenile library" for both boys and girls in New Lebanon. Torrey, champion of education and human rights (he was a staunch abolitionist), campaigned for governments to establish free libraries funded by taxation of "wines and spirituous liquors which shall be imported." Such taxation would also "discourage intemperance."

How long Torrey's juvenile library lasted is not known, but he wrote prodigiously on the need for libraries. His major work, published in 1817, was *The Intellectual Torch*, subtitled "Developing an original, economical and expeditious plan for the universal dissemination of knowledge and virtue by means of free public libraries."

In a few decades, the efforts of the likes of Torrey (not bibliophiles, necessarily, but those extremely passionate about libraries) would bring about the "library movement" that swept America, and also parts of Europe. With readership rising in all social classes, the need for libraries ceaselessly increased from decade to decade. Sunday schools established book collections for children, as did temperance and religious organizations. Fiction became more acceptable in such libraries—even desirable, in the hope that interesting stories would stimulate reading among young people.

Not only was there a deep-seated urge among many in the wealthier classes to educate Americans, and thereby make them better citizens, but there was also the need to inform the flood of immigrants, who would have a better chance of integrating into American society if they could read American publications. Newspapers and magazines were stocked alongside fiction, scientific works, and manuals for training "mechanics," as skilled laborers were called.

▲ The Mercantile Library Association of Philadelphia, pictured in 1869 by *Frank Leslie's Illustrated* weekly newspaper.

Along with the athenaeums and literary societies, mechanics' libraries (also known as "apprentice libraries") continued to be established. So, too, were mercantile libraries for the edification and, increasingly, the entertainment of clerks, who could study economics as well as enjoy novels and short stories. These working-class libraries were joined by a wave of new college libraries being founded in the newly opening western territories, where immigrants set up communities that reflected their original homes back east.

Most college libraries served their school's curriculum for educating clergy, and the collections were small and limited. There were virtually no separate library facilities, for the books were usually housed in rooms and overseen by a faculty member. The University of South Carolina was a forerunner in 1841 when it erected a separate library building.

A special library for physicians had its origins in the 1830s when the army's surgeon general's office collected medical books, which eventually became the foundation of the National Library of Medicine.

▲ Architectural perspectives of a "Building for the Library and Philosophical Apparatus of the Military Academy" at West Point, New York. Military libraries fell under the category "special libraries."

Before the Civil War (1861–65), volunteer associations and "institutes" bore much of the burden of creating and operating circulating libraries. One of the most dynamic was the Hartford Young Men's Institute, organized in 1838 in Hartford, Connecticut. The Institute loaned books and scheduled lectures while developing its collection, eventually merging with the Hartford Library Company, begun in 1774 as one of America's earliest private subscription libraries.

In 1844, the Institute moved into the newly constructed Wadsworth Athenaeum, a leading art museum that served as the library's home for more than a century. One of the prominent librarians was Henry M. Bailey, who served from 1846–68. Bailey was an essayist whose work, published in the 1850s,

▲ Lewis Wickes Hine (1874–1940) photographed older children reading in New York City's Henry Street Settlement library in 1910. This was one of the first "settlement homes" established to help families escape miserable urban living conditions.

captured the mood of the Young Men's Institute library. Bailey's *Thoughts in a Library* was a sentimental ode to librarians, patrons, and library reading rooms alike:

> It is a stormy evening: the rain patters on the roof and beats against the windows. All without is cold and cheerless, all within is pleasant and cheerful. The gas burns brightly, and an air of comfort is diffused over everything, in striking contrast to the dreariness of the night without. The table is crowded with readers, and just now there is a momentary stillness: a hush, so deep, that nothing is heard but the ticking of the Library clock, as it measures off the fleeting time.
>
> I look around me and think, what a blessing are these books! . . . Books are friends who never desert us. Is the world cold?—Here is a retreat where the mind can revel in beauty and sweetness. Here the cares of life can be forgotten for a time, and the "soul find rest" . . .

Bailey observes how the children grow, sees the young men who "have given up Robinson Crusoe and the Lives of the Pirates, and have taken to Hawker on Shooting and . . . who sometimes come back fragrant with the perfume of a mild cigar" and cologne. Yet, even in 1852 there was more to the library than books and book learning. He describes one of these young men

> in the Reading Room, deep in the Merchants' Magazine, but his eyes frequently wander over the cover towards the Librarian's table, where a young lady is waiting for a book. The young lady after some difficulty is suited, and on leaving, happens to look over to the young gentleman, who, by the merest accident, raises his eyes at the same time. The young lady hurries away, and as the door closes after her, the young gentleman comes forward, and with a slight hesitation in his manner, says "He does not wish to be inquisitive, but he would like to know the name of that very pretty young lady who has just gone down stairs!" O happy spring-time of life, when the dawn of young love first rises in the soul!

In his writings, Bailey mused on how so many library patrons have departed for the West or for "the metropolis," but the "Library is the same."

As with many who stayed behind, Bailey was active and productive, taking part in the country's first Librarians' Convention, held in New York City in 1853. The eighty-two attendees were all men who had been "called" by an announcement:

> The undersigned, believing that the knowledge of books, and the foundation and management of collections of them for public use, may be promoted by consultation and concert among librarians and others interested in bibliography, respectfully invite such persons to meet IN CONVENTION AT NEW YORK, ON THURSDAY, THE FIFTEENTH DAY OF SEPTEMBER, for the purpose of conferring together upon the means of advancing the prosperity and usefulness of public libraries, and for the suggestion and discussion of topics of importance to book collectors and readers.

▲ New York's Astor Library, pictured in the mid-nineteenth century, held approximately 200,000 volumes, which were read on the premises, since the library did not lend books.

Meeting at a New York University chapel on Washington Square, the convention chose Charles Coffin Jewett, librarian of the recently established Smithsonian Institution, as president. This was not only the first convention of librarians in the United States, but was also probably the first of its kind in the world. For three days, the delegates "ground out an astonishingly large grist of library and bibliographic business," according to a 1952 article published by the American Library Association:

> They made speeches, some prepared, others apparently extemporaneous, on various aspects of their common interests, read papers on cataloging, classifying and indexing, on exchanges between libraries, on the proper selection of books, on better distribution of government documents, and adopted over a score of resolutions.

Although few of these resolutions were put into effect and memories of this convention faded into the mists of time, the work done at the meetings "had an important even though indirect influence on libraries and librarians for many years," according to the article:

> This first convention began a new era in American librarianship, and the effects and impetus had not been entirely dissipated when librarians met in Philadelphia in 1876, nearly a quarter century later, and formed the permanent organization, the American Library Association.

By 1853, Henry Bailey's *Thoughts in a Library* was likely well known to his fellow librarians, who would have appreciated his closing to the reading room essay:

> But the evening has worn away, the readers are gone, the deep-toned Center bell strikes ten, and it is time to close the Library.

State libraries began to appear in the 1800s, often as collections of reference books for their legislative bodies. These libraries grew slowly, supported inadequately at first. Pennsylvania's was the first true state library, established in 1816, soon followed by Ohio, New Hampshire, Illinois, and New York (all created by 1818). The U.S. Bureau of Education produced a national survey in 1876 that reported every state and territory as having an official library, though these were made up of mainly law collections.

It was the New York State Library that took the lead in expanding the services and activities of the state institutions. State Librarian Melvil Dewey (1851–1931), who served from 1888 to 1905, created the position of reference librarian and also founded a children's department within the library. Dewey asserted that state libraries were the best agencies for supporting the development of public and school libraries. He also initiated a program of traveling libraries—collections of one hundred books sent to communities without public libraries.

Dewey's traveling libraries were met with the "missionary zeal" (as it has been described) that gripped hundreds of thousands of Americans determined to establish libraries and improve the lot of the people. Traveling libraries, essential to their mission, began to appear in state after state, sometimes government-sponsored, sometimes private. New York's system often served as a model. This enthusiasm also led to the founding of state library commissions tasked with aiding small communities to establish library services.

The zealous aspirations of the library movement can be heard in the words of New York City clergyman Henry Ward Beecher (1813–87):

> Let us congratulate the poor that, in our day, books are so cheap that a man may every year add a hundred volumes to his library for the price of what his tobacco and beer would cost him. Among the earliest ambitions to be excited in clerks, workmen, journeymen, and, indeed among all that are struggling up from nothing to something, is that of owning, and constantly adding to a library of good books. A little

library, growing larger every year, is an honorable part of a young man's history. It is a man's duty to have books. A library is not a luxury, but one of the necessities of life.

▲ New York State Library in Albany, around 1900.

As the nation expanded westward, laying railroads and telegraph lines, recovering from the Civil War of the 1860s, which transformed the nation forever, Americans came to believe in the power of self-improvement through education. The popular hunger for learning could only be satisfied with books. Everywhere, civic-minded citizens created public libraries with private gifts of books and funds from benefactors.

Despite all the efforts of volunteers, however, there was always a shortage of money, and few local governments were willing to spend public funds to build libraries. At the same time, libraries in larger cities were growing in size and patronage. By the 1870s, virtually every large city had a public library, usually established by consolidating smaller collections and incorporating disparate libraries, and invariably supported by private wealth.

Henry Bailey's Hartford offers an appropriate example of how public libraries developed in cities during the late nineteenth

This 1874 view of the Cincinnati Public Library's main hall shows the decorated glass ceiling, designed to let in light that even illuminated the alcoves. ▶

181

century. In 1878, the Hartford Young Men's Institute became the Hartford Library Association, with more than 640 members of both genders. In 1893, a special act of the Connecticut General Assembly changed its name to the Hartford Public Library. Former Boston Athenaeum staff librarian, Caroline M. Hewins (1846–1926), originally hired by the Institute in 1875, became the first librarian.

Hewins soon was active in the newly formed American Library Association, and in 1891 helped found the Connecticut State Library Association. In 1904, she led in opening one of the first children's libraries in the United States (she also wrote children's books). Her career of fifty-one years at the library earned Hewins an honorary master of arts degree in 1911 from Hartford's Trinity College—the first woman so honored by the college.

The last decades of the nineteenth century and the first of the twentieth comprised an era that saw the rise of librarianship and of women as librarians. These were peak years of American library growth. Crucial to that growth was industrialist and philanthropist Andrew Carnegie (1835–1919).

By 1875, 188 public libraries had been established in the United States, thanks to the library movement. More than 600 were operating in 1886, the

year Carnegie began dispersing his personal fortune for the construction of free public libraries in the United States. No other individual before or since has made a greater single impact on American public libraries, which already had made a great impact on Carnegie.

In the 1850 industrial town of Allegheny, Pennsylvania, fourteen-year-old Carnegie, a Scottish immigrant, spent as long as he could in the personal library of Colonel James Anderson, who had opened his 400-book collection to the

◀ Industrialist and philanthropist Andrew Carnegie, photographed at his desk in 1913, near the end of his library-funding era, which helped build more than 2,500 libraries.

working boys of the city. Carnegie's own father had organized a library in the old country for fellow workers in the weaving trade. Every Saturday afternoon, young Andy waited eagerly for the library to open, and he sat and read for hours on end.

Carnegie said he was so grateful to Anderson that, as a young man, he "resolved, if ever wealth came to me, [to see to it] that other poor boys might receive opportunities similar to those for which we were indebted to this noble man."

Thirty-six years later, now one of the richest men in the world, Carnegie gave more than $330,000 for a library and community center in Allegheny. It was the first of more than 1,600 American free public library buildings Carnegie would donate.

Carnegie made his fortune in the Allegheny-Pittsburgh region, largely from steel producing and construction. By 1870, at the age of thirty-three, he had resolved to keep only $50,000 a year from his earnings, and to "make no effort to increase fortune but spend the surplus each year for benevolent purposes. Cast aside business forever except for others."

This was Carnegie's "Gospel of Wealth," and in his lifetime, he gave away more than $333 million—90 percent of his fortune. He believed the rich should live without extravagance, provide moderately for the needs of their dependents, and distribute their "surplus" funds for the benefit of the common man—especially to help those who endeavored to educate themselves. Library construction was part of his vision for "the improvement of mankind."

Carnegie believed cultural organizations, such as libraries, helped raise up the working class. He enumerated seven areas to which the wealthy should devote "surplus" funds (in order of importance): universities, libraries, medical centers, public parks, meeting and concert halls, public baths, and churches. In 1881, Carnegie began his library philanthropy by donating funds for his hometown, Dunfermline, Scotland, to build a public library.

The best gift a community could receive was a free public library, but he gave only on the condition that "the community will accept and maintain it as a public institution, as much a part of the city property as the public schools, and, indeed, an adjunct to these."

▲ Even before Oklahoma became a state (in 1907) the Carnegie Library in Guthrie was in operation, funded by a $25,000 Carnegie grant. The library officially opened in 1903.

The strings attached to the Carnegie gift were that the community provide the site, and that the elected officials—the local government—promise to pay to staff and maintain the library, guaranteeing to spend annually at least 10 percent of the amount of the original Carnegie gift. The community was required to draw from public funds to run the library—not use only private donations. Carnegie wanted these libraries to be part of the fabric of public life and the responsibility of the community. Only those determined to sustain them and make them grow would receive a Carnegie gift:

> I do not think that the community which is not willing to maintain a Library had better possess it. It is only the feeling that the Library belongs to every citizen, richest and poorest alike, that gives it a soul. . . .

Carnegie continued funding new libraries until shortly before his death in 1919. Libraries were given to Great Britain and much of the English-speaking world: Almost $56.2 million went for construction of 2,509 libraries world-

CARNEGIE PUBLIC LIBRARY, AUSTIN, MINN.

.O.WOLD

Hand-Colored

▲ The Carnegie Public Library built in 1904 in Austin, Minnesota, was severely damaged by a major tornado in 1928.

wide. Of that, $40 million was given for construction of 1,670 public library buildings in 1,412 American communities.

Since Carnegie had made his fortune in part by the labor of workers, who often fought bloody pitched battles against his companies during strikes, he had enemies among those who despised all wealthy industrialists. He was accused of donating libraries only because he was an egotist who wanted monuments to himself. One railway workers' union official objected to Carnegie's offering Detroit a library grant, saying, "Carnegie ought to have distributed his money among his employees while he was making it. No man can accumulate such wealth honorably. It may be legally honest, but it's not morally honest."

Others considered Carnegie's offer an insult: "We ought to be able to take care of ourselves, I should think," said a Detroit newspaper editor, adding, "Who told Mr. Carnegie that we were worthy objects of charity, I wonder? It doesn't seem to me that anybody was ever given authority to go begging for a city as big and as prosperous as this one is. . . ."

185

▲ The 1906 Carnegie Library in Teddington, England, on the north bank of the Thames River, was built in the contemporary Edwardian Baroque style.

Samuel Gompers (1850–1924), president of the American Federation of Labor, and the country's most powerful union leader, did not object to Carnegie's library grants: "Yes, accept his library, organize the workers, secure better conditions, and particularly reduction in hours of labor, and then workers will have some chance and leisure in which to read books."

Others thought the 10 percent maintenance requirement an unwanted increase in the tax burden and objected on these grounds. Of course, many more enthusiastically urged local governments to apply for a Carnegie grant. Some communities flatly turned down offers of grants, which always disappointed Carnegie. He wanted the working man or woman to enter public libraries and think, "Behold, all this is mine. I support it, and am proud to support it. I am joint proprietor here."

Carnegie also contributed to the construction of more than a hundred large academic libraries, donating his millions in various ways. His larger benefactions included the creation of the Carnegie Institute in Pittsburgh, the Carnegie Institution in Washington, the Foundation for the Advancement of Teaching, and the Carnegie Endowment for International Peace.

For more than a century, Andrew Carnegie's community libraries have directly touched the lives of millions of Americans in almost every state. Most of those public libraries were still in operation at the start of the twenty-first century. While many Carnegie library buildings have been converted into museums, offices, and community centers, and others demolished, more than 1,300 of the original 1,412 American buildings are in use as libraries, and 1,137 have essentially the same exteriors. Carnegie libraries are still essential to New York City's public library systems, with 31 of the original 39 still in operation. The main library of Pittsburgh's public library system—named the Carnegie Library of Pittsburgh—and 7 of its branches are Carnegie libraries.

Without Andrew Carnegie's gospel, it is unlikely so many community libraries would ever have been established. One aspect of his philosophy that still endures is Carnegie's determination that libraries should have open stacks so readers can freely browse. Before then, most library collections were in closed stacks and requests were fetched by staff as patrons waited outside a gate.

Carnegie's open-stack approach was in keeping with the latest American library thinking, as expressed by John Cotton Dana (1856–1929) in his 1899 *A Library Primer*, written to teach "library management for the small library, and to show how large it is and how much librarians have yet to learn and to do." Cotton was emphatic about patrons being permitted to browse stacks:

> Let the shelves be open, and the public admitted to them, and let the open shelves strike the keynote of the whole administration. The whole library should be permeated with a cheerful and accommodating atmosphere.

Cotton's *Primer* discusses library architecture, interior (comes first) and exterior, stack layout and height (not too high), decoration (simple), light (natural, as much as possible), and furniture ("Arm-chairs are not often desirable," because they are heavy to move and appeal to loafers). Cotton struck another keynote in his *Primer*, with a succinct description of an ideal librarian (using "he" in the generic fashion of the times):

> The librarian should have culture, scholarship, and executive ability. He should keep always in advance of his community, and constantly educate it to make greater demands upon him. He should be a leader and a teacher, earnest, enthusiastic, and intelligent. He should be able to win the confidence of children, and wise to lead them by easy steps from good books to the best. He has the greatest opportunity of any teacher in the community. He should be the teacher of teachers. He should make the library a school for the young, a college for adults, and the constant center of such educational activity as will make wholesome and inspiring themes the burden of the common thought. He should be enough of a bookworm to have a decided taste and fondness for books, and at the same time not enough to be such a recluse as loses sight of the point of view of those who know little of books.

The profession of trained librarianship was well in the making by now, fostered by Melvil Dewey, who in 1884 founded the Columbia School of Library Economy in New York City, the first American institution for the instruction of librarians. Linked to all-male Columbia University—until objections arose that too many women were in Dewey's classes—the school moved to Albany, New York, a few years later. It became the New York State Library School, which Dewey directed while also serving as state librarian.

His rigorous curricula and his many library-development innovations (including his Dewey Decimal Classification system) established him as a prominent pioneer in library science.

Most of Dewey's library students continued to be women, reflecting and reinforcing the profile of librarianship as it developed into the twentieth century.

Librarians were faced with a persistent challenge as the number of books increased in the United States through the nineteenth and early twentieth centuries: An ever-present current to ban controversial books flowed steadily through society.

The usual charges leveled were broad and subjective: obscenity, indecency, or threats to public morals. The list is long and diverse, ranging from John Cleland's 1748 *Fanny Hill*, a novel about an English "woman of pleasure" banned in 1821, to Theodore Dreiser's 1925 *An American Tragedy*, a tale of a Missouri religious backslider.

In between, Mark Twain's 1884 *Huckleberry Finn* was banned by the Concord, Massachusetts, public library for what one critic said was "coarse language." Twain's use of slang was characterized as demeaning and damaging, "the veriest trash . . . more suited to the slums than to intelligent, respectable people."

Leading these banning campaigns, generally, were religious organizations or individuals in positions of influence—not so much working librarians, who had been instilled with that American "library spirit" which honored intellectual freedom (within bounds, of course).

Yet, in 1905, the Brooklyn Public Library banned both *The Adventures of Huckleberry Finn* and *The Adventures of Tom Sawyer* from the children's department when the young woman in charge of the section objected to the "coarseness, deceitfulness and mischievous practices" of the characters. Furthermore, "Huck not only itched but scratched," and said "sweat" instead of "perspiration."

◀ Melvil Dewey, (center) is pictured in 1888 with the pioneering library-science class of the program he founded at (otherwise all-male) Columbia University in New York City.

Objecting, Asa Don Dickinson (1876–1960), head librarian at Brooklyn College, wrote to ask Samuel Clemens (1835–1910), creator of Tom and Huck, to defend his work to the Brooklyn library. Clemens replied to Dickinson:

> I am greatly troubled by what you say. I wrote Tom Sawyer & Huck Finn for adults exclusively, & it always distressed me when I find that boys and girls have been allowed access to them. The mind that becomes soiled in youth can never again be washed clean. I know this by my own experience, & to this day I cherish an unappeased bitterness against the unfaithful guardians of my young life, who not only permitted but compelled me to read an unexpurgated Bible through before I was 15 years old. None can do that and ever draw a clean sweet breath again on this side of the grave. Ask that young lady—she will tell you so.
>
> Most honestly do I wish I could say a softening word or two in defense of Huck's character, since you wish it, but really in my opinion it is no better than God's (in the Ahab & 97 others), & the rest of the sacred brotherhood.
>
> If there is an Unexpurgated [Bible] in the Children's Department, won't you please help that young woman remove Tom & Huck from that questionable companionship?

After reading Clemens's letter—and after much rancor among the staff—the library compromised by placing the titles on shelves accessible to both adults and children. Word of the controversy got out, however, and Brooklyn's "literary prudery" was widely criticized in editorials and newspaper articles across the nation.

Hartford Public's Caroline Hewins refused to ban Tom and Huck from the newly opened children's library that meant so much to her—which was good, especially since Sam Clemens had lived several blocks away in Hartford until a few years earlier.

Librarians, prudish and progressive, were essential and almost ubiquitous fixtures in twentieth-century American communities, as important as schoolteachers, and even more strict. In his 1957 Broadway hit, *The Music*

◀ The Children's Room of the Pratt
Institute Free Library in Brooklyn,
New York, is seen in 1910. The print
was taken from a negative made
by photographer Levin C. Handy
(1855–1932), nephew and protégé
of famed photographer Mathew
Brady (1822–1896).

Man, composer Meredith Willson (1902–84) recalled women librarians of his Midwest youth—and one in particular from farther west, Marian Seeley of Provo, Utah. The musical features Marian Paroo, the pretty and spunky librarian of River City, Iowa.

Itinerant musical instrument salesman, Harold Hill, woos "Marian the Librarian" with an assortment of "civilized world" clichés about maintaining silence in a library:

> Madam Librarian.
>
> What can I do, my dear, to catch your ear?
> I love you madly, madly Madam Librarian . . . Marian
> Heaven help us if the library caught on fire
> And the Volunteer Hose Brigademen
> Had to whisper the news to Marian . . . Madam Librarian!
> What can I say, my dear, to make it clear
> I need you badly, badly, Madam Librarian . . . Marian
> If I stumbled and I busted my what-you-may-call-it
> I could lie on your floor
> Till my body had turned to carrion . . . Madam Librarian. . . .
> But when I try in here to tell you, dear
> I love you madly, madly, Madam Librarian . . . Marian
> It's a long-lost cause I can never win
> For the civilized world accepts as unforgivable sin
> Any talking out loud with any librarian
> Such as Marian . . . Madam Librarian.

ORGANIZING KNOWLEDGE

U niversity and college libraries proliferated in Europe and America from the eighteenth to twentieth centuries. So, too, did national libraries.

The Elector of Brandenburg, Friedrich Wilhelm (1620–88), had developed a private library in Berlin, though there had been few monastic libraries left to confiscate. The Great Elector, as Friedrich Wilhelm was known, personally provided the funds and saw to it that a collection was built, eventually reaching 20,000 printed books and 1,600 manuscripts. The Elector drew up catalogs and developed classifications that remained serviceable for another century. He also decreed the collection should be open to the public.

Friedrich Wilhelm's library, later named the Royal Library, was a prime example of "royal solicitude" with regard to book collections. His successors, unfortunately, were not so solicitous, and the library was allowed to languish. Frederick the Great (1712–86), however, provided ample resources and also a new building for the Royal Library's growth. With the abdication of the royal German House of Hohenzollern after World War I (1914–18), the Royal Library would become the Prussian State Library.

◀ A sectional view of the New York Public Library, from *Scientific American*, 1911, shows seven levels of stacks where books are shelved. Elevators transfer books to the appropriate levels.

In the eighteenth and nineteenth centuries, despite almost constant warfare, great libraries prospered throughout Europe. Yet many private aristocratic and ecclesiastical collections were destroyed or dispersed during the chaos of the French Revolution that began in 1789, and the subsequent worldwide conflicts waged with Napoleonic France until 1815.

From the start of the Revolution, French church libraries were declared national property, and the libraries of émigrés who fled the country were also confiscated. Eight million books changed hands, and, as had happened before, plundered libraries usually went to supplement collections of the victors and their associates. The Bibliothèque Nationale in Paris acquired at least 300,000 books and thousands of manuscripts as the seized collections of Germany, the Netherlands, Austria, and Italy flowed into France.

There were so many books, however, that most were merely stored, and it required decades to organize a national system that put library collections, including those in universities, in manageable orderliness. Many titles taken as war booty were eventually returned, but many more remained in France.

The suppression of the Jesuit Order in the late eighteenth and early nineteenth centuries released another stream of books, as their learned libraries were dissolved. The order's restoration in 1814 brought about rapid growth, and libraries developed in newly founded Jesuit institutions of higher learning around the world. In the United States alone, twenty-two universities were founded or taken over by the Jesuits during this era.

One of the most notable and exciting cultural developments of the mid-nine-

◀ Lambeth Palace Library, shown in a nineteenth-century image from *The Book Hunter*, was founded as a public library in 1610 and is the principal repository of historical records for the Church of England.

teenth century was the discovery and excavation of lost Mesopotamian and Syrian cities, such as Nineveh and Babylon. Assurbanipal's library at Nineveh was discovered and, for the most part, the tablets (many in pieces) were brought to the British Museum. Although tablets from different sites were inadvertently mixed up and often impossible to precisely identify, they certainly offered archaeologists and cuneiform translators a close view of ancient libraries. Those discovered libraries, in turn, served as windows into an unknown age, which could be examined, studied, and revealed to a wider public.

Following a less high-minded British tradition when it came to antiquaries, the empire went to war with Ethiopia in 1868, formerly the Aksum—the land at world's end—with the Biblical-era books and treasures. At the time, Ethiopia was ruled by Tewodros II (c. 1818–1868), an independent-minded and proud monarch, whose personal letter to Queen Victoria was dismissively shunted aside by Foreign Office bureaucrats and never delivered. In response, Victoria sent an emissary—none other than Hormuzd Rassam, discoverer of Assurbanipal's library.

Rassam also was taken hostage and remained imprisoned for two years, until freed in 1868 by a British expedition that defeated the Ethiopians. It is reported that the defeated Tewodros committed suicide using a pistol Queen Victoria had sent him as a gift in happier times.

A portion of subdued Ethiopia's ecclesiastical and antiquarian treasures was looted and fetched off to Europe, where the items would bring a good price at the bustling new museums and libraries.

In many countries, art museums and museums of natural history and science were being established, most with special libraries. The Victoria and Albert Museum (V&A) was founded in London in 1852, inspired by the Great Exhibition of 1851 which showed the "works of all nations" at London's Crystal Palace exhibition center. Honoring Queen Victoria and her consort, Prince Albert, the V&A would grow to be the world's largest museum of decorative arts and design, with a permanent collection of 4.5 million objects.

The V&A would also come to house the National Art Library, which would have 750,000 books, specializing in the study of fine and decorative arts. The library's treasures include the notebooks of Leonardo da Vinci.

Circulating libraries were important cultural institutions in Britain and America during the nineteenth century, affording the rising middle class access to a broad range of reading material—poetry, plays, histories, biography, philosophy, travels, and especially fiction (now immensely popular). The first known circulating library that loaned books for a fee was most likely that of Scottish poet Allan Ramsay, who rented titles from his Edinburgh shop early in the eighteenth century.

Circulating libraries were of three major types: specialist libraries; book clubs, which were flourishing; and commercial libraries, which developed in major cities and most notably offered a wide collection of novels. Although university and college libraries flourished, as did special libraries for governments, associations, and businesses, these were still not open to the general public.

Commercial libraries were the largest circulating libraries, with the most diverse stock and clientele. For-profit circulating libraries and nonprofit social libraries paved the way for the free public library—one supported by taxes and open to all people. Circulating libraries in Britain, America, and parts of Europe were crucial to the spread of literacy and the love of books and reading, as expressed by English essayist Charles Lamb (1775–1834): "I love to lose myself in other men's minds. When I am not walking, I am reading. I cannot sit and think; books think for me."

This was fine for those who had access to libraries or could buy books. Thomas Carlyle (1795–1881), English philosopher, biographer, and historian, succinctly challenged the government to make the creation of local public libraries a national duty, when he asked, "Why is there not a Majesty's Library in every county town? There is a Majesty's gaol and gallows in every one."

In 1850, the process of founding public libraries was initiated by the British Parliament, which passed the Public Libraries Act. This act authorized municipalities with a population of 100,000 or more to levy a tax to build a public library—although they could not buy books with that money. Norwich, England, was the first city to adopt the act, and the eleventh in the country to open a public library (the first was in Winchester, England).

As major British cities established free public libraries, American states were authorizing municipalities to levy taxes for libraries. The Boston

Public Library, which opened in 1854, became a model for the rest of the country as the concept of public libraries spread across the continent. The library movement reached around the world to peoples linked to Europe or the United States by cultural or imperial ties. The Australians were certainly inspired, and the Melbourne Public Library (a reference library) opened in 1856, followed by Sydney's Free Public Library, established in 1869.

In general, American public libraries were authorized and maintained locally, whether by municipalities or school districts. State library commissions or the state library itself were usually the supervisory agencies. In most other countries, public libraries were authorized and maintained by a national governmental or provincial authority.

A crucial responsibility of the supervisory authorities in America, and elsewhere, was to educate and train librarians, now so widely needed. The establishment of the American Library Association in 1876 was soon followed by a British organization (and others internationally). These associations afforded new opportunities for librarians to cooperate on a national basis. Persuading elected officials to support libraries with public funds became proportionately easier as the library movement grew and libraries proliferated.

By the late 1920s, national library organizations, encompassing various associations for academic, public, research, school, and special libraries, were dynamic enough to convene in Rome to discuss international communication and cooperation. Among the fundamental issues were cataloging standards, borrowing and lending between libraries, censorship, and how to promote library development. This convention led to the establishment, in 1927, of the International Federation of Library Associations and Institutions (IFLA) in Edinburgh, Scotland. There were fourteen European associations involved, as well as the American Library Association.

IFLA defined its mission as the representation of librarians in matters of international interest, the promotion of continuing education for library personnel, and the development, maintenance, and promotion of guidelines for library services. IFLA membership grew in number, representing 155 countries by the twenty-first century. More than 1,700 library associations, from every type of library, are currently IFLA members.

In nineteenth-century Stockholm, the Swedish Royal Library, established in 1661, had been rebuilt despite two major losses: the 1654 abdication of Queen Christina (1626–89), who converted to Catholicism and carried many books to Rome; and a 1697 fire that destroyed 18,000 bound volumes and manuscripts. The royal library, now the National Library of Sweden, had obtained 40,000 books.

The National Library moved into new, dedicated premises in Humlegården in 1877, and proved to be progressive ten years later when it began installing electric lighting. Natural gas was the most common institutional lighting source in modernized countries, but its volatility was always a fire risk, especially in libraries—and there was also the increased potential for carbon dioxide poisoning. Most libraries preferred daylight and thus closed their doors by dark.

The coming of the electric light in the late nineteenth century would rapidly change library operations, which now could continue to stay open in the evenings. Working people, especially, benefited from these longer library hours.

By this time, libraries were certainly safer repositories for books than they ever had been. In 1906, Augustine Birrell wrote of how much better cared for books were than just thirty years earlier, when water from leaky roofs and the broken windows of neglected collegiate and cathedral libraries would soak forgotten stacks of stored volumes. In some cases "the ivy had pushed through and crept over a row of books, each of which was worth hundreds of pounds."

Even the ravages of determined bookworms could not compare with the consequences of such neglect. Birrell described a bookworm eating its way through a fifteenth-century vellum tome, reaching the eighty-seventh page before giving out. In the twentieth century, however, bookworms were failing because they were repelled by the new chemicals used to make paper:

> Worms have fallen upon evil days, for, whether modern books are readable or not, they have long since ceased to be edible. The worm's instinct forbids him to "eat the china clay,

the bleaches, the plaster of Paris, the sulphate of barytes, the scores of adulterants now used to mix with the fibre." Alas, poor worm! Alas, poor author! . . . [W]hat chance is there of anyone, man or beast, a hundred years hence reaching his eighty-seventh page!

In the United States, the topics of collection maintenance and bookbinding were often on the mind of Ainsworth Rand Spofford (1825–1908), former librarian of the Library of Congress. The Library of Congress's sixth librarian served from 1864 to 1897, directing the expansion of the library from a congressional collection to a national one—from 60,000 items to more than a million.

In his retirement, Spofford published *A Book for All Readers*, which in 1908 the *New York Times* described as "written from the fullness of knowledge and experience of a veteran librarian for the guidance of younger members of his chosen profession." Understanding bookbinding was one of the many prerequisites for Spofford's "librarian"—not to mention "a wide knowledge of books," "an acquaintance with ancient and modern literature," proficiency in foreign languages, a solid education in history, and "familiarity with what constitutes condition in library books, and with binding and repairing processes, for the restoration of imperfect volumes for use."

Despite, as the *Times* put it, the "drawbacks and discomforts of library work, small salaries, the peculiar trials and vexations" of the profession, Spofford waxed eloquent on the "advantages" of

Librarian of Congress Ainsworth Rand Spofford, pictured around the turn of the twentieth century. ▶

the profession, which included satiating the appetites of "those who are hungering and thirsting for knowledge," and serving as "a guide, philosopher, and friend" to these information seekers.

Spofford wrote (using the generic "he"):

> To learn continually for oneself is a noble ambition, but to learn for the sake of communicating to others is a far nobler one. In fact, the librarian becomes more widely useful by effacing himself, as it were, in seeking to promote the intelligence of the community in which he lives. One of the best librarians in the country said that such were the privileges and opportunities of the profession that one might well afford to live on bread and water for the sake of being a librarian, provided one had no family to support.

The books the librarian maintained, however, deserved royal treatment according to Spofford, who called for the finest Morocco leather covers, the redder the better. Red bindings lit up the shelves and made the library a more cheerful place. This practice, he said, was the policy of the National Library of France, which had bound most of its great collection in the finest red Moroccan leather.

—✳—

To the majority of librarians and staffers around the world, however, the daily issues and decisions that arose from the tasks of classifying, abstracting, and organizing books were

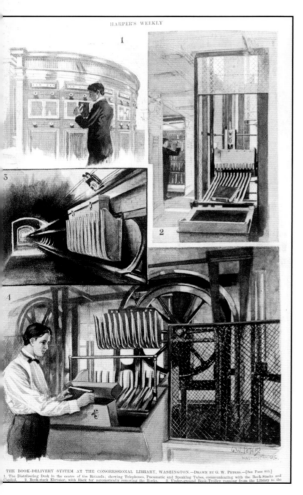

◀ Operating the automated book-delivery system was one of many daily 1897 tasks at the Library of Congress.

THE BOOK-DELIVERY SYSTEM AT THE CONGRESSIONAL LIBRARY, WASHINGTON.—DRAWN BY G. W. PETERS.—[SEE PAGE 815.]
1. The Distributing Desk in the centre of the Rotunda, showing Telephones, Pneumatic and Speaking Tubes, communicating with the Book Stacks and Capitol.   2. Book-stack Elevator, with Rack for automatically removing the Books.   3. Underground Book Trolley running from the Library to the

▲ An 1897 *Harper's Weekly* illustration in the "Congressional Library" in Washington stresses the "present congested condition" in the reading room.

◀ The Library of Congress in the nineteenth century.

far more immediate than worrying about fine bindings. Increasingly, libraries were growing so large and acquiring titles on such vastly diverse subjects that librarians had to spend endless hours organizing and cataloging the collection.

Faced with an ever-multiplying array of titles to acquire, catalog, and shelve, librarians needed efficient and accurate catalogs. Creating them became the life's work of many catalogers, who often were compulsive, passionate, and fastidious. Birrell told of a Bodleian "sub-librarian" who was the chief compiler of the most up-to-date catalog. The fellow was a stickler, seeking out every stray volume to be sure it was accounted for in his lists. He was ideal for the tremendous task at hand, which wore on day after day.

Throughout much of his obsessive thirty-six-year career, this Bodleian cataloger used an old vellum-bound folio as a cushion for his desk chair, where it remained, well-dented, until the librarian's career ended. For the first time, his associates looked at the folio he had been sitting on and checked it against the fellow's meticulous catalog. It was not there. Of all the titles in the library, it was the only one the devoted cataloger had missed.

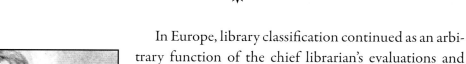

In Europe, library classification continued as an arbitrary function of the chief librarian's evaluations and opinions. One of the most controversial librarians was Antonio Panizzi (1797–1879), the Italian-born head of the British Museum Library. Panizzi's career at the library began in 1831, where he served as chief librarian from 1856 to 1866. In this time, he oversaw and helped design the spectacular Round Reading Room, constructed in the museum's quadrangle and opened in 1857. Panizzi was knighted for his services, but many a

◀ Italian-born Chief Librarian of the British Library, Sir Anthony Panizzi, pictured in this 1874 engraving, was knighted in 1869 for his service to the library from 1831 to 1866.

▲ The British Library Reading Room, which opened in 1857, has been the British Museum Reading Room since 1997, when the library opened new quarters.

researcher considered his extremely complex (some said unusable and capricious) bibliographic cataloging system as benighted.

There were ample complaints about Panizzi's stewardship; he was described as uncooperative, vindictive, and arrogant by disgruntled patrons such as Thomas Carlyle, who had the backing of none other than Prince

Albert. Yet, Panizzi was supported by the museum trustees, and his 1841 "Ninety-one Cataloguing Rules" remained in use into the twenty-first century as the basis for digitized library cataloging.

Panizzi's iron-fisted librarianship is credited with prompting the disgusted Carlyle and friends to establish, also in 1841, the London Library, which became the world's largest independent lending library.

In the United States, library-science innovator Melvil Dewey was also developing a system of bibliographical classification. What became known as the Dewey Decimal System was drastically needed in this booming era of library building, since current classification standards were inadequate for the task of organizing books—let alone managing the inundation of periodicals and archival materials increasingly housed and maintained in libraries.

▲ Librarians work with the Library of Congress card catalog between 1900–20.

Since the first libraries, organization and classification of collections were usually based on current cultural concepts of how knowledge was divided into fields such as religion, science, philosophy, history, and mechanics; or, as in first-century China, the arts, poetry, philosophy, military sciences, technology, and medicine.

Medieval and Renaissance philosophies had laid the basis for nineteenth-century bibliographical classification. Secular writing was still subdivided into the *trivium*—grammar, rhetoric, and logic—and the *quadrivium*—arithmetic, geometry, music, and astronomy. As knowledge and book collections broadened, classifications multiplied. By the late nineteenth century, the book, and its information, had become essential for society to function and progress; thus, it was also essential that libraries be organized and easy to search.

Dewey organized knowledge into ten main classes, represented by numbers (as decimals). These classes were each subdivided into ten divisions, and each division into ten sections, and so on, until a thousand topics were classified. The Dewey Decimal Classification (DDC) is generally used for nonfiction titles, while fiction titles (which do not have DDC numbers) are usually organized under genre and the author's name.

Working in the same field as Dewey, Northampton, Massachusetts, town librarian Charles A. Cutter (1837–1903) devised an "expansive classification system" which uses letters to classify the main categories of books. Cutter had been head librarian at the Boston Atheneum, but it was while founding the Northampton library that he developed his system, which influenced the Library of Congress classification.

Cutter's classification system is as follows: A, general works (encyclopedias, periodicals, society publications); B–D, Philosophy, Psychology, Religion; E–G, Biography, History, Geography, and Travels; H–K, Social Sciences, Law; L–T, Science and Technology; X, Philology; Z, Book Arts, Bibliography.

Numbers are added to further subdivide categories, as are periods, slashes, and symbols, as well as the first letter of an author's last name. Other numbers and letters can be added—"expanding" the classifications; while this is required in large libraries, small libraries need not be so specific.

The Library of Congress has its own classification system, developed early in the twentieth century and mainly used by research and academic libraries, but

Dewey's DDC is simpler and serves public libraries well. Dewey and Cutter were also among the first founders of the American Library Association.

In the century-old United States, a great coming-of-age celebration was staged in the 1893 World's Columbian Exposition held in Chicago. Twenty-seven million people visited this six-month-long world's fair of international exhibition halls. The Exposition showcased America's wealth, technology, culture, and genius alongside the best that nineteen other guest nations had to offer. The fair was lauded as a commemoration of "the nearness of man to man, the Fatherhood of God and the brotherhood of the human race," according to its American director general.

Yet women had to organize and protest until they were permitted their own "Board of Lady Managers," and African Americans were restricted

▲ Women read in the library of a Washington, D.C., normal school in 1899.

in their presentations, forbidden to have a dedicated exhibition hall, and required to be housed in their own states' facility. There was, however, a "Colored People's Day" that honored African American cultural contributions, with music and poetry and presentations by three mostly black colleges and universities. Also, books by several black women authors were included in the Woman's Building Library exhibit, which had seven thousand books— all by women.

The Woman's Building was a statement of female cultural and civic accomplishments, with sixty-five "different categories of women's creative productions ranging from the fine arts to the liberal arts to manufactures to horticulture." The Woman's Building Library was meant to show the cumulative contribution of the world's women to literature. This "landmark collection," as one historian termed it, not only made a statement about the cultural and intellectual force of women writers, but also expressed solidarity among women of diverse cultural and racial origins—including the African American women writers whose memoirs, short stories, novels, poetry, and juvenile fiction were displayed on the shelves as equals to their white peers.

The southern United States remained segregated through the first half of the twentieth century, and libraries mirrored the social conditions. African Americans were kept out of most public libraries in the South, although there were libraries designated for blacks. Those institutions, of course, were invariably inferior in collections and facilities. In his collected *Essays on Art, Race, Politics, and World Affairs*, black author and playwright Langston Hughes (1902–67) included his "Books and the Negro Child."

Hughes wrote about the importance of finding books that were uplifting to black children. He mentioned several titles that were particularly valuable, then observed:

> But there is a need for many more books still unwritten in this field; and after the books are written a need for Negro library facilities throughout the South, where most dark people still live.

◀ The title of this late nineteenth-century photograph of a young cavalryman and family is "Son reading the Bible to his parents."

◀ A scene in the library of Fisk University, Nashville, Tennessee, around 1900.

The main public libraries in the cities of the South are not open to Negro readers. Some of the larger towns (but far too few) have branch libraries for their colored citizens, but these branches are understaffed, often with only a single librarian who sometimes is janitress as well, and usually poorly supplied with books, perhaps a collection of dog-eared volumes turned over to the Negro branch when too badly worn for further use by the whites. Few of these Negro branch libraries in the South can afford or have the books or space to allow separate children's departments. Many of the libraries in the Negro schools and colleges are pitifully lacking in books, too. Fortunately, [certain charities have] done something to remedy this for the schools—but more needs to be done, in both schools and cities, for through the written word a people may find themselves. Faced too often with the segregation and scorn of a surrounding white world, America's Negro children are in pressing need of books that will give them back their souls. They do not know the beauty they possess.

Some major American libraries outside of the South also remained segregated until the 1950s.

In Asia and Africa—largely colonized by 1900—library organization followed the pattern of aristocratic institutions for the elite, missionary libraries for proselytizing, and colonial libraries to serve governance—and sometimes to help educate indigenous populations. Foreign professional librarians usually were the guiding hands in colonial societies, building public and university libraries.

Serving as librarian at the Punjab University library in Lahore, India, in 1915–16, former Brooklyn College librarian Asa Dickinson founded the Punjab Library Association. Dickinson also organized library-training classes at the university—a course that did not even exist in British universities at that time. Another difference from Britain in some parts of India was that trained librarians were preferred over professors to head academic libraries. In Britain, the head of an academic library was required to have certain scholarly qualifications. In Calcutta (Kolkata) University, the priority was to select a professional librarian for the head position.

This influence came, in part, from American librarians such as Dickinson, who were employed by South Asian institutions. Dickinson had a law degree from Columbia University, had studied under Melvil Dewey, and had spent ten years at several libraries, including Brooklyn Public. The training program developed at Punjab was the first formal library school in "the East," as South and East Asia were termed. The second library was founded in 1920 at Boon University in China.

One of Dickinson's students, Khalifa Mohammad Asadullah (1890–1949), became a leading proponent of South Asian library development. A native of Lahore, Asadullah was the first qualified librarian of the Government College in that city. He rose through the governmental library bureaucracy to become librarian of the Imperial Library, later the National Library of India, in Calcutta. Asadullah was a founding member of the Indian Library Association in 1933, and was its first secretary, from 1943 to 1947. He founded a library training program in Calcutta, but departed in 1947 to reside in Pakistan.

Another leader of South Asia's public library movement, Shri Iyyanki Venkata Ramanayya (b. 1888), is known as the "Father of the People's Library Movement in India." Shri Iyyanki, as he was known, established several library associations, city and state, as well as helped found the Indian national association. He established literary journals as well as journals on library science—usually at his own cost, in order to elevate the profession of Indian librarianship.

Shri Iyyanki worked to establish public libraries in rural regions less accessible to government services and education. His many honors included a national award as a distinguished citizen—indicated by the honorific, Shri.

In other and completely separate Asian library developments, the world's largest book was literally "built" as part of the Kuthodaw pagoda in Mandalay, Myanmar (Burma).

Constructed between 1860 and 1868, the book consists of more than seven hundred marble tablets inscribed with Buddhist teachings—originally in gold, which has long since been removed. Each tablet, three and a half feet

 A view of the *stupas* that house stones inscribed with Buddhist teachings at the Kuthodaw pagoda in Myanmar.

wide by five tall and five inches thick, stands in its own *stupa*, or cave-like structure, containing Buddhist relics.

Burmese King Mindon Min (1808–78) directed the creation of the book, which stands at the foot of Mandalay Hill, intending it to be a religious and traditional symbol that would outlast British colonial forces encroaching on his kingdom.

———❋———

In the late nineteenth and early twentieth centuries, during the waning years of China's Qing Dynasty, access to Western learning was an important revitalizing force to many reformers and revolutionaries throughout the country. They considered Chinese imperial traditions and culture as a constraint on the progress of the Chinese people. They saw how other nations had broken free of many historical shackles and gained strength through modernization. One author described an allegorical iron house that imprisoned China.

Intellectuals and activists looked to the literature, philosophy, and political movements of Europe and America for guidance. The Russian revolution that began in 1917 was especially studied. The Treaty of Versailles, ending World War I, was both infuriating and energizing to Chinese reformers. Capitalizing on China's weakness and disunity, the treaty powers simply transferred German imperial holdings to China's neighbor, and newly emergent military power, Japan.

Japan's strength was both worrying and inspiring for China's intellectuals, particularly Japan's rapid military modernization along Western lines. Chinese access to Western learning had been limited to Christian missionary schools and their libraries until the turn of the century. At the time the Qing, and later, the early Republican governments, sent students to study abroad, mostly in Japan, but also in Europe and America.

The traditional imperial examination system, based on classical Chinese learning, was abolished in 1905, and the number of modern universities increased. Libraries increased in number in the first three decades, not only within new universities but also at the national, provincial, and munic-

◀ Students in the Nanking University library, mid-twentieth century.

Reading room
in the Shanghai
Library in the
mid-twentieth century. ▶

ipal levels. In spite of civil wars and regional hostilities, local and national funding fueled growth in modern libraries, which no longer restricted access to officials and examination candidates. Although the closed-stack design of these libraries made them less convenient than Western public libraries, improved access to their Chinese and translated Western materials was a major, and welcome, development.

During the social and political upheavals in China between 1910 and 1920, Peking (Beijing) University was China's cultural epicenter, and a magnet for political activists. Li Dazhao (1888–1927), who studied in Japan and in 1921 was co-founder of the Chinese Communist Party (CCP), was the university's head librarian for much of this period. In 1927, Li was executed for radicalism by a regional warlord. It was Li's assistant and intellectual adherent at the university library who would play the dominant role in China's mid-twentieth-century revolutionary history: Mao Zedong (1893–1976).

Destined to become chairman of the CCP and founder of the People's Republic of China, Mao was strongly influenced by Li Dazhao. Mao's mentor and fellow librarian advocated armed revolution, which would have to originate with the Chinese peasantry, who would be educated in the Communist doctrine found in books.

▲ New York Public Library in 1915, as seen from across the intersection of East 42nd Street and Fifth Avenue.

LIBRARIES, LIBRARIANS, AND MEDIA CENTERS

Library and library science development in twentieth-century Europe and North America influenced educational institutions throughout Asia, Africa, and the Americas. World War II in East and Southeast Asia brought unprecedented devastation to the peoples and infrastructure of many countries. Civil wars in Vietnam, Korea, China, and elsewhere continued this destruction.

In the second half of the twentieth century, decades of peace allowed for the reconstruction of archives and libraries, and promoted the building of new community and university libraries. Library systems in the formerly embattled East Asian nations of China, Japan, and Korea took giant steps in growth and use, as major libraries developed in urban centers such as Beijing, Tokyo, Seoul, and Taipei.

The Japanese invasion of China in the 1930s, however, dealt a crushing blow to the progress of Chinese libraries. More than 2.7 million books were lost during the years of Japanese occupation, almost half of China's total stock of books. After the Japanese surrender in 1945, libraries continued to suffer in the almost five years of civil war between the Communists and Nationalists. There were only fifty-five public libraries of any size in China when the People's Republic was established in 1949.

▲ Children borrow books from a 1960s street library in Loyang, the People's Republic of China.

The anti-intellectual movements of the late 1950s and the following Cultural Revolution (1966–76) restricted the usefulness of libraries to scientific materials and Communist writings exclusively. Since the death of Mao in 1976, and because of the opening and reform movement launched in 1978—largely by Deng Xiaoping (1904–97)—Chinese libraries have boomed. They have added materials on economics and finance, and are no longer restricted to the writings of approved Communist theorists.

By 1986, China had more than 200,000 libraries: national, university, scientific, and educational. There were 2,300 small public libraries, and more than 53,000 cultural center reading rooms with book collections. Library science, or information science, departments operated in more than 40 institutions of higher learning. By 2004, China had more than 2,700 public libraries.

▲ Emerging from forty years of war and civil war, the Peking University campus, situated on a former royal garden, reputedly rivals the loveliest of Beijing's formal gardens.

Ever since the nineteenth century, Japan's quest for modernism and technological knowledge stimulated the adoption of Western-style public libraries. An extensive nationwide system was in place by World War II, but Japan's militarism and its totalitarian government brought on war as it sought to militarily dominate East and South Asia. The resulting devastation, wrought by Allied bombing, cost Japan heavily in the loss of many libraries.

The National Diet Library was established in 1948, its facilities divided between Tokyo and Kyoto. The library was originally founded for the policy and legislation research of Japan's parliamentary body, much like the American Library of Congress. The National Diet Library was the result of merging several libraries established in the late nineteenth century. Founding the National Diet Library corresponded with reconstruction efforts in postwar Japan, under American occupation. The library was one method of strengthening the authority of the popularly elected Diet within Japan's governmental system.

Japan's public libraries grew rapidly in number, from approximately 700 in 1958 to almost 1,900 in the 1990s. Today, 91 percent of Japanese cities have libraries, compared to only 70 percent in 1970.

In a paper presented to the 1996 annual conference of the International Federation of Library Associations, Japanese scholars described the crucial importance of library development to their newly democratic society:

> In Japan public libraries used to be frequented only by antiquarians engaged in research or students who needed to study there. The library was a place for limited use, and often as a study room. Since the mid-1960s, however, a new attitude has been introduced toward the public library, using such catchwords as "to guard the people's right to know"; "to ensure free and equal access to information for all people."

In 2002, the National Diet Library opened a separate International Library of Children's Literature.

Japanese colonial occupation of Korea throughout the first half of the twentieth century brought modern library concepts to the peninsula; however, among the Koreans, a long tradition of librarianship, writing, and libraries was already established. In a presentation to that same 1996 IFLA conference, Korean scholars expressed the ethnic pride of many Asian peoples when they noted:

> With a written history dated back more than 2,000 years, Korea, a country with ancient roots, has developed an advanced culture. . . . Korean librarianship evolved as part of Korean culture.

The National Library of Korea was established in the South Korean capital, Seoul, in 1945, only two months after the Japanese surrender in World War II. Within a year, an affiliated library school was opened in order to staff the National Library.

The Korean Peninsula endured yet another destructive war between 1950 and 1953, when North Korea invaded South Korea and drew in forces of the United Nations and the People's Republic of China (PRC). Library and librarianship losses were again heavy. A number of prominent library leaders were captured and taken to North Korea. Afterward, the IFLA and the United Nations Educational, Scientific, and Cultural Organization (UNESCO) were instrumental in aiding South Korea's library systems to rebuild and prosper.

Established under the Ministry of Education, the Korean National Library is currently administered by the Ministry of Culture. In 2006, the National Library opened a separate branch called the National Library for Children and Young Adults, also in Seoul. As of 2009, the National Library held more than 7 million volumes, with approximately 15 percent of the collection consisting of foreign books and materials.

▲ Patrons browse the bookshelves of the Bibliothèque de l'Institut islamique (Islamic Institute Library) in Dakar, the capital city of Senegal.

Since the Thirty Years' War of the seventeenth century, few decades have seen the immense destruction of libraries that occurred between 1914 and 1945, an era of two world wars. Germany and much of Europe were spared library losses in World War I—northern France, Belgium, Russia, and the Italian-Austrian border were the most populated European theaters of war. In World War II, however, heavy aerial bombardment destroyed many libraries in many regions of the world.

These two great conflicts opened in 1914 with the methodical destruction of an eighteenth-century library by German troops, news of which shocked the world. The Belgian university town of Louvain was burned when its people resisted the German invasion. The university library was bombarded and set ablaze, with more than 300,000 books and many manuscripts lost. Such wanton destruction dismayed and saddened a world not yet used to total war, but by the time Germany and her allies were defeated in 1918, reports of such catastrophes were commonplace.

Rebuilding the Louvain university library became an immediate *cause célèbre* in the United States, and donations poured in to see it through reconstruction. By 1928, construction was completed and books were being donated, increasing the collection to 900,000 volumes. Then in 1940, soon after the start of World War II, the new library was again in ruins, intentionally bombarded by Nazi commanders who saw it as a symbol of Belgian and Allied defiance. Nevertheless, after the war, reconstruction began once more and was finally completed by the year 2000.

Louvain presented an extreme example of twentieth-century nationalist pride, so often the spark for destruction but also for reconstruction. The ashes and ruins of destroyed libraries during World War II, private and public, from London to Berlin, Warsaw to Milan, Manila to Shanghai and Hiroshima, were tremendous. Yet, after each firestorm, there came a concentrated rebuilding.

Too often, however, the next generation took its turn eradicating libraries that were the pride and cultural repository of a people. In 1981, civil strife between Sri Lanka's ruling majority and the Tamil minority that asserted its cultural identity and political rights brought on riots and mob attacks. The Jaffna Public Library, with its rich collection of Tamil literary heritage, was burned down. Soon after, in 1984, Indian government troops attacked armed Sikh separatists occupying the Golden Temple in Amritsar, India. Hundreds died, and the Sikh library with irreplaceable books and manuscripts was destroyed.

In 1992, as Yugoslavia disintegrated, the newly founded Serbian Republic of Bosnia and Herzegovina sent forces to lay siege to Sarajevo, stronghold of the independent Republic of Bosnia-Herzegovina. The National University Library, a prominent symbol of Bosnia-Herzegovina's identity, was targeted by Serb artillery in a three-day bombardment that reduced 90 percent of its

▲ As seen in this World War I poster, collecting books for the services was a priority of organizations concerned with the welfare of the off-duty military.

1.5 million books to ashes. As the fire raged, hundreds of Sarajevans struggled to rescue what they could, saving 100,000 volumes.

And the twentieth century saw many library fires, large and small, caused by accident and arson. In 1911, a fire, cause unknown, in the New York State Capitol in Albany destroyed almost half a million books and 270,000 manuscripts that included historical records documenting New York's colonial history.

In 1966, the Jewish Theological Seminary in New York suffered a loss of some 70,000 volumes and damage to many more from heat, smoke, and water. Fortunately, the rare books and manuscripts were stored off the premises.

Between April and September 1986, the Los Angeles Central Library suffered two frightening blazes set by arsonists and costing 400,000 volumes and the contents of the Music Department Reading Room. Major fires struck the Academy of Sciences Library in Leningrad in 1988 and England's Norwich University Library in 1994.

The American-led invasion of Iraq in 2003 unleashed destruction that damaged the archive department of the Iraqi National Library and Archive in Baghdad. The fire was followed by looting as United States troops stood by, ordered not to intervene. Rare volumes and documents, including one of the oldest copies of the Qur'an, were lost. Yet, the main book collection was not damaged. Investigators observed that the main destruction was to records from the government of Saddam Hussein (1937–2003), as if the arsonist had purposely torched them to eradicate what they contained.

Cellist Vedran Smailovic plays in the rubble of the National Library of besieged Sarajevo in 1992, despite the library being a favorite target of Serbian artillery. ▶

▲ Patrons at the reading room of the Library of Congress, Division for the Blind read with various methods of "tactile type," such as Braille (c.1920).

The 1761 Duchess Anna Amalia Library in Weimar, Germany—with a research collection of more than a million books, 10,000 maps, and many rare books and historic documents—lost 50,000 volumes in a 2004 fire. As in similar library disasters, much of what was saved was rescued by staff and volunteers hand-passing whatever they could through open windows and doors.

Library architecture of the nineteenth century often contributed to a fire's devastating power, as its previous emphasis had been on promoting air flow inside a building in order to inhibit the growth of mold. The result, if a fire started, was its rapid spread throughout the library. Sprinkler systems and smoke detectors, combined with policies of converting older libraries into spaces that can be closed off with fire doors, became safety priorities.

In most cases, libraries were reconstructed, but Sarajevo's library re-builders suffered from a shortage of funds, as did Iraq's. What could feasibly be done in the way of restoration, salvage, and repair was completed. Wherever there were people who had once used those libraries, there was support and hope for renewal.

Even the many angry book burnings which lasted into the twenty-first century—whether for supposed blasphemy or sedition—did not intimidate those dedicated to freedom of thought and the liberty of libraries. In 1953, at the height of an American anti-Communist book burning and censorship campaign, president Dwight D. Eisenhower (1890–1969) expressed the feelings of many in his Dartmouth College commencement address:

> Don't join the book burners. Don't think you are going to conceal faults by concealing evidence that they ever existed. Don't be afraid to go in your library and read every book, as long as that document does not offend our own ideas of decency. That should be the only censorship.
>
> How will we defeat communism unless we know what it is, and what it teaches, and why does it have such an appeal for men, why are so many people swearing allegiance to it? . . .
>
> And we have got to fight it with something better, not try to conceal the thinking of our own people. They are part of America. And even if they think ideas that are contrary to ours, their right to say them, their right to record them, and their right to have them at places where they are accessible to others is unquestioned, or it isn't America.

Luis Soriano (center) and one ▶ of his two "biblioburros," the prime movers of "Biblioburro," a traveling library in La Gloria, Colombia. Soriano, who started the service in the 1990s, named his means of transport Alfa and Beto.

▲ A panorama at dusk of the Getty Center below the center's Exhibition Pavilion.

With all the destruction of great libraries during the twentieth century, institutions in the United States were mercifully spared the ravages of war and flourished.

Among the most unique libraries in the world are certain private collections, unaffiliated with public or university libraries, which open their doors for research. These include the Newberry Library in Chicago; the Folger Shakespeare Library in Washington, D.C.; the Huntington Library in San Marino, California; the Research Library at the Getty Research Institute in Los Angeles; and the Morgan Library and Museum in New York. All were established by benefactors who bequeathed to posterity their beloved personal collections of books and treasures.

The Morgan Library was founded on the personal collection of financier J. Pierpont Morgan (1837–1913), which, in 1924, was donated to the public by son J. P. Morgan Jr. (1867–1943). According to library documents, Pierpont Morgan was a "voracious collector" who "bought on an astonishing scale, collecting art objects in virtually every medium," including rare books, manuscripts, drawings, prints, and antiquaries. The museum's mission is to be an educational institute fostering the study of mainly Western history and culture:

> The Morgan is one of the very few institutions in the United States that collects, exhibits, and sponsors research in the areas of illuminated manuscripts, master drawings, rare books, fine bindings, and literary, historical, and music manuscripts.

The library's rarities include ancient seals and tablets as well as papyrus fragments. There are Old Testament miniatures, Mozart manuscripts, and a fifteenth-century Gutenberg Bible. The reference department is especially strong in medieval and Renaissance manuscripts, incunabula (books printed before 1501), early printed books, bookbinding, and books on books.

Few American libraries can compare with the Morgan's holdings, but no library anywhere can compare with the holdings of the Library of Congress (LoC), the largest library in all the world.

In July of 1815, as the United States government salvaged the burned-out remains of Congress's library building destroyed by the British, an editorial in Washington, D.C.'s daily *National Intelligencer* asserted:

> In all civilized nations of Europe there are national libraries.... In a country of such general intelligence as this, the Congressional or National Library of the United States [should] become the great repository of the literature of the world.

It was precisely this attitude that led to a collection of more than 32 million books and more than 138 million total items. The LoC has a draft copy of the Declaration of Independence, a Gutenberg Bible, and at least two Stradivarius violins. Many rare items are linked with America's past (although two-thirds of Jefferson's original collection was destroyed in an 1851 fire that burned 55,000 books).

◀ The Great Hall of the Library of Congress's Jefferson Building in Washington, D.C.

As the national library of the United States, the LoC receives copies of every book, pamphlet, map, print, and piece of music registered in the country. Its holdings are for research only—legislators and other high-ranking government officials are the only ones allowed to borrow.

Although the LoC's central mission is to research inquiries from members of Congress, it is open to the public. Two million scholars and tourists visit annually, using the twenty-two reading rooms. Researchers and browsers are also able to access millions of digitized reproductions online from its holdings, many of which are presented on its American Memory site. In 2005, the LoC launched the World Digital Library, a program for digitally preserving books, maps, and documents from all cultures of the world.

In the second half of the nineteenth century, librarian Ainsworth Spofford steered the LoC into becoming a truly national library for all Americans. Yet its collections are not limited to Americana; rather, they are universal, encompassing some 450 languages.

The library grew to occupy three massive buildings in Washington, with 530 miles of shelf space—more than any other library. Such space is needed to accommodate the 22,000 items published in the United States, which arrive every workday. An average of 10,000 items is added daily. The rest are traded with other libraries, distributed throughout government agencies, or donated to schools.

By far, the world's most numerous type of library is the public school library. Of the more than 123,000 libraries in the United States, almost 100,000 are in schools.

Public school libraries in developed countries evolved at various rates in the nineteenth and twentieth centuries. In France, they were not prevalent until the mid-twentieth century, while in the United States and Canada, school libraries have been ongoing since the public school movement of the nineteenth century—although with varied success.

In 1835, New York State passed the first school-district library laws that provided government-supported library service for the entire population of a school district. Many other states, and Canada, followed suit. Growth continued, more often in high schools than in elementary schools, slowing in wartime, and accelerating by mid-century. Still, by 1962, one-half of all American public schools lacked libraries.

Federal legislation in the 1960s funded school libraries and supported the training and hiring of librarians. By 1978, 85 percent of the public schools in the United States had a library or the recently named "media center," which collects and circulates films and audio recordings. Libraries and media centers often were virtually one in the same, and by the first decade of the twenty-first century, most public schools had access to the Internet.

Public libraries and their branches number more than 9,000; there are 3,600 academic libraries, 9,000 special libraries, and almost 1,500 government and military libraries.

Although reading time has fallen steadily in the United States over the last century (down 50 percent between 1925 and 1995), audiovisual circulation grew to become 25 percent of total library circulation by 2007. And circulation from public libraries has risen steadily: 425 million in 1939, 1.3 billion in 1990, and more than 2 billion in 2004.

Young people are a major segment of the population using public libraries. In 2004, juvenile borrowers accounted for 35 percent of total circulation. As for gauging public library use, estimating quantities of materials loaned falls short as an accurate measurement of the business of a library. Many come in to spend some time but do not necessarily leave with a borrowed book, CD, or DVD.

—※—

The future of libraries and librarians is often discussed in the context of computers and the Internet, of digital information read on a screen

This 1966 newspaper photograph of a librarian working with an early computer was captioned: "To the rescue; many librarians believe computers are the only means to effectively cope with their bulging bookshelves."

and printed information read from a page. Librarians and libraries are redefining their roles and functions to meet the swiftly moving developments and changes brought about by the World Wide Web and developing technologies.

Far from being a threat to librarians and librarianship, however, computers and the Internet are valuable instruments that enhance the librarian's abilities and importance to patrons. More than ever, librarians are expected to provide "information services," related to computers and the Internet. Sorting through the vast amount of electronic data, and understanding how to access it, requires knowledgeable, trained individuals in the library or media center.

The librarian also benefits from the power of the computer, as inter-library loan searches are easier than ever before—and so is maintaining the catalog.

▲ "Inquiring Minds," a 1999 grand prize photograph by eighteen-year-old Kirsten Baker, was taken in the public library of Liverpool, New York. The photo contest "Beyond Words: Celebrating America's Libraries," is sponsored by the Library of Congress and the American Library Association and underwritten by Ingram Library Services.

Librarians are reportedly experiencing increased job satisfaction thanks to the work they can get done with computers. Particularly in local libraries, the role of the librarian as "technology provider and community educator" is more essential than ever.

The Internet can stimulate a reader's interest in digging deeper into a subject, but even though many books will be available on desktop or handheld screens, far more printed materials will never be digitized. They will, however, be found in library stacks managed by a librarian who can guide patrons to what they are searching for. As one Smithsonian librarian put it, "The search engine has not replaced the librarian wholesale."

A librarian consulted in 2004 by a Smithsonian Institution study team said, "Librarians are needed to help patrons distinguish between authoritative sources of information and the vast quantities of unmediated materials available on the Net."

Or, as the Smithsonian's Ainsworth Spofford put it a hundred years earlier, the librarian must be able to "lead inquirers in the way they should go, and to be to all who seek . . . assistance a guide, philosopher, and friend."

LIBRARIES OF THE WORLD

The following selection of libraries is (almost) a random one, guided by the need to include certain institutions that must be on any survey of libraries, and by the wish to include a few others that are significant or outstanding in unique ways.

The great, important, and interesting libraries of the world are very numerous—and it could be said that every institutional library, large or small, deserves to be in such a survey. This selection is representative of certain types of libraries, though it can only introduce them.

The reader may one day take a closer, personal, look at some—and perhaps, also, at some of the others which are not here.

Bibliothèque Nationale de France

The National Library of France, in Paris, has its origins in the royal library of Charles V (1338–80), founded at the Louvre castle in 1368. Known as "The Wise," Charles built a library of 1,200 volumes, including classical works translated into French by royal commission. The collection was sold to an English duke in 1425, but Charles VIII (1470–98) reestablished the royal library, building on the libraries of previous kings.

This library developed steadily with each royal house until it was opened to the public in 1692. Among the major acquisitions of the seventeenth and

▲ Bibliothèque Nationale de France, Paris.

eighteenth centuries was the purchase of 120,000 engravings, supplemented by bequests of engravings—cornerstone of the Department of Prints. During the French Revolution, when the new government seized the private collections of aristocrats and clerics, the library received the confiscated books. Officially called the Bibliothèque Nationale in 1792, its holdings grew to 300,000 volumes.

The Napoleonic Wars, ending in 1815, saw the addition of spoils of war to the library. Conquest and confiscation brought in another quarter million books, 15,000 manuscripts, and several thousand prints. A good deal of the spoils, however, were returned to their original countries by peace treaties.

In 1868, the French government erected new buildings to house the collection, which by then had been renamed the Imperial National Library. Over the next hundred years, various organizational changes and governmental decrees changed the library's status—it belonged to the education ministry, then was part of a consortium of libraries, then fell under the ministry of universities, and then the ministry of culture, and at last, in 1983, became a division of the national government.

In the final decades of the century, new library facilities expanded and updated the Bibliothèque Nationale to make it one of the largest and most modern in the world. The library's cultural mission includes conserving and making available books published in France. Restoration studios offer advice and technical assistance, and a reproduction department converts books, images, and documents to microform and digital formats. The library also exhibits paintings and antiques of French culture, including the world globes made for Louis XIV.

A staff of 2,700 manages more than 13 million books, including 5,000 Greek manuscripts and 200,000 rare and precious titles—one-third from foreign lands. There are more than 350,000 periodical titles; 650,000 maps; 10,000 atlases; and 15 million images, including drawings, engravings, photographs, and posters. The manuscripts department has 350,000 volumes, and there is also a collection of 300,000 coins.

The Bibliothèque Nationale holds 1.5 million musical scores, archives, and reference works, and 1.1 million records and videotapes. Its digital library, available online, is steadily growing, with more than 200,000 scanned volumes and images.

British Library

Established by Parliament in 1753 as an afterthought to the newly opened British Museum, the national library was essentially a division of printed books and manuscripts—even though the head of the museum held the title "Principal Librarian."

The first library collections included the Cottonian Library holdings, owned by the government since 1700. Other private collections bequeathed or purchased were also part of the first collection, and were known as "foundation collections." They included the books, manuscripts, antiquities, and curios of the prosperous physician, Sir Hans Sloane. Managing the Sloane collection was one of the key reasons for establishing the museum and library.

In 1759, King George II (1683–1760) presented the collection of the Old Royal Library (that of the kings and queens of England). In this library were nine thousand printed books and many important manuscripts. Further royal and private donations built up the library, which had little in the way

▲ British Library Reading Room, London.

of capital for acquisitions. The thrifty trustees did, however, find the funds to acquire the private papers of an important Elizabethan minister in 1807.

Adding to the "foundation collections," George III's library was donated by the Crown, expanding by half the collection of printed books, and the library continued to count on aristocratic donations for its growth. The library's true expansion came in 1837 after Antonio Panizzi was appointed Keeper of Printed Books. Panizzi's first task was to move the book collection (235,000 volumes) to a new building, and he also undertook the enormous task of developing a new cataloging system.

Panizzi obtained acquisition funds and convinced Parliament to enforce the law that required legal deposit titles to be sent by publishers to the library. He also planned the massive circular Reading Room, opened in the quadrangle of the museum in 1857. Made of cast iron, concrete, and glass, the Reading Room opened in 1857, with twenty-five miles of shelves. Patrons had to apply in writing for a reader's ticket from the principal librarian.

Another professional, Sir Frederic Madden, developed the library's manuscript collection, acquiring valuable documents that became national

treasures. He also labored with the burned remnants of books from the Cottonian fire, identifying and reconstituting many works.

The library grew rapidly, and by 1875 held 1.25 million printed volumes. The catalog, which had been handwritten, had grown to 2,250 volumes—so large that it threatened to crowd patrons out of the Reading Room. The task of printing the *General Catalogue* was completed in 1905, a labor of almost twenty-five years. One of the most significant categories is maintained by the Oriental Department, which now has 40,000 manuscripts and more than 400,000 printed books. In this department is the only known copy of the first dated printed book, the *Diamond Sutra*, from ninth-century China. The library possesses two Gutenberg Bibles and two copies of the 1215 Magna Carta, as well as working manuscripts from famed composers, from Bach to Britten.

The library was expanded with new construction early in the twentieth century, and its sections included the Copyright Receipt Office, the Music Library, Map Library, Official Publications, and the Newspaper Library.

In the early 1940s, World War II brought immense damage to the library as bombing attacks destroyed major portions of the structure. In one 1941 air raid, approximately 225,000 volumes were lost. A number of irreplaceable items were, thankfully, evacuated to a safe haven.

As with many national libraries, despite additions throughout the century, there was ever a shortage of space. And new collections, such as scientific and technical works, were being sought after. Plans for a new library were debated for decades until building began in 1983. By now, the government had formally established the British Library, with the British Library Act of 1973.

After three decades of planning and debate, a new building for the library was opened in the mid-1990s, the largest public building erected in the United Kingdom in the twentieth century. The Reading Room was restored—without its former books, but with a modern information center—and is open to all patrons. The books are stored underground on 185 miles of shelves, well away from sunlight which is deleterious for them. An automated system retrieves books as quickly as twenty minutes after being requested.

Now one of the world's largest libraries, and one of the most prominent for research, the British Library holds more than 150 million items, including 25 million books and collections of music recordings, patents, stamps, manuscripts, maps, databases, periodicals, prints, and drawings. Extensive digitalized holdings are also available online.

Austrian National Library

The largest library in Austria, located in Vienna's Hofburg Palace, the interior of the national library is one of the most beautiful in the world. Aptly named the *Prunksaal*—ceremonial or "splendor" hall—the heart of the library has been described by library historians as "incomparable" and "astonishing." Its lavish eighteenth-century splendor is considered a masterpiece of baroque Austrian architecture.

It was not always so grand. When Emperor Maximilian II (1527–76) engaged a knowledgeable professional librarian to sort out his collection—then held in a local convent—the library was disorganized and dirty. Library administrator Hugo Blotius (1575–1608), of Holland, was shocked in 1575 when he arrived to take charge of the family library of the Habsburgs, rulers of the Holy Roman Empire, Spain, and other domains:

▲ Austrian National Library, Vienna.

How neglected and desolate everything looked! There was moldiness and rot everywhere, the debris of moths and book-worms, and a thick covering of cobwebs. . . . The windows had not been opened for months and not a ray of sunshine had penetrated through them to brighten the unfortunate books, which were slowly pining away. . . .

Blotius set to work airing and cataloging the collection of more than seven thousand volumes, gathered over the centuries by Habsburgs. As far back as the thirteen century, the royal house was collecting books, eventually including works with exquisite fourteenth-century Bohemian illustration; the writings of Greek, Latin, Hebrew, and Arab authors; and Latin translations of Aesop and Aristotle. Although much of the collection was sold off, some of these books survived to be organized by Blotius, and for that reason the library's historians claim its origins to be as early as the thirteenth century.

The Prunksaal was built, starting in the 1720s, as the *Hofbibliothek* (court library), and completed in 1732. Its art and ornamentation are divided into "war" and "peace," in keeping with the original list of books. The dome is painted with allegorical figures and is designed to praise the Habsburgs, who ruled Austria until the twentieth century.

The collection eventually became the Imperial and Royal Court Library, enduring revolution and war throughout the nineteenth and twentieth centuries. In 1920, it was named the Austrian National Library. New accommodations were built, and in 1966 the library expanded to the Heldenplatz, the outer plaza of the Hofburg Imperial Palace. It continued to grow in size and volume. By the first decade of the twenty-first century, the library held 7.4 million items in its collections.

Digital scanning of thousands of works continues, including holdings from the 330,000 broadsheets, posters, and Ex Libris (items from books). Manuscripts date from the fourth century, and there are collections of pre-1850 scientific instruments and globes, a papyrus museum with examples from the collection of more than 137,000 papyri, and 50,000 archaeological documents. The library contains Austria's music archives, including the national archive of Austrian folk songs, and also a department of "planned languages," including the Esperanto Museum.

National Library of Russia

Established in 1795 as the Imperial Public Library at the direction of Empress Catherine II (the Great), the National Library of Russia was constructed in the heart of St. Petersburg, capital of the empire. As with aristocrats around the world, Russia's wealthy in the eighteenth century were passionate about book collecting, and many had private libraries. In this era of surging nationalism, a Russian national library was intended to glorify the might of the state and to become one of Europe's finest libraries.

Yet, as much as the Russians intended to build a library with a literary and art collection that would be second to none, the founders also sought to make the collection open to the public. Few major European libraries sought to serve readers in this age, but the Russian library, said third director Alexei Olenin (1763–1843), was "for the benefit of lovers of learning and enlightenment." This sentiment was later to be asserted in efforts—at all social levels—to reform Russia's feudalistic society. This movement, which came to fruition in the mid-nineteenth century, led to freeing and educating the serfs. In keeping with this policy, the library was open to all readers, including women and peasants.

The new library would have the aim of "social enlightenment of Russian subjects," Olenin asserted. St. Petersburg's public library was instrumental in educating many of Russia's future leaders in science, literature, and art. The original library building, located on the Nevsky Prospekt and completed by 1801, had a neoclassical design.

The first foundation of the collection was the confiscated Zaluski Library, built in Warsaw by Polish brothers Jozef and Andrzej Zaluski. More than 400,000 printed items, maps, and manuscripts were looted from the library by Russian troops during a Polish uprising against imperial rule. Catherine, herself, directed the confiscation. In the following centuries, thousands of Zaluski items were returned according to terms of various treaties, but war and dispersion reduced the original collection to approximately 30,000 items. The Imperial Public Library was officially opened in 1814, shortly after a destructive war with Napoleonic France.

The National Library in St. Petersburg continued to grow and to acquire ancient and modern materials published in Russia, or by Russians residing abroad, termed *Rossika*. Among these is the *Ostromir Gospel*, the earliest book in Russian. The library owns the breviary of Mary Stuart (1542–87), Queen of Scots, and the personal libraries of French revolutionary-era authors Voltaire (1694–1778) and Denis Diderot (1713–84), both donated from Catherine's own library. The library owns early manuscripts of the New Testament, Old Testament, and Qur'an, and a tenth-century illuminated Greek Gospel on parchment.

Through world wars, the Communist revolution, a civil war, and the dissolution of the Union of Soviet Socialist Republics, the National Library of Russia has endured and usually remained open. In the twentieth century, book and art exhibits celebrated Russia's cultural heritage, while the collection of the National Library of Russia continues to be rich in books and artifacts of many nations, with a collection totaling 35 million items. In the early twenty-first century, with a new library complex under construction, the library calls itself "The pride of Russian culture."

Russian State Library, Moscow

The largest library in Russia, with 42 million items, the Russian State Library in Moscow is also one of the largest in the world. A national library founded in 1862 as the city's first free public library, it has an extensive numismatic and art collection, including 20,000 prints selected from the imperial collection at the Hermitage Palace in St. Petersburg.

The library was named The Library of the Moscow Public Museum and Rumiantsev Museum, honoring its founding patron, Count Nikolai Petrovich Rumyantsev (1754–1826), former chancellor of the empire. It is also known as the Rumiantsev Library. The first collections were kept in the eighteenth-century Pashkov House palace, one of Moscow's most splendid buildings. The palace had been damaged in the 1812 fire brought on by the Napoleonic invasion, then restored and used by the state as a boarding school for children of the nobility.

Donations developed the holdings, most notably an important collection of European paintings, an antiques collection, and a large number of religious icons. Additional facilities were constructed to contain the holdings. In the twentieth century, other institutions began to assume the role of museum, so the Rumiantsev was dissolved in 1925 and many of its holdings dispersed around the country. A large number of books were brought to join the library collection, and the complex was renamed the Lenin State Library of the USSR, honoring Communist revolutionary and founder of the Soviet Union, Vladimir I. Lenin (1870–1924).

Construction began on a new library building in 1930, in a "modernized neoclassic" style. After World War II, the building's last stage was completed; a reading hall for 250 persons. New construction continued as the holdings grew, and in 1992 the library was renamed the Russian State Library.

Exhibitions and projects have included "Russian Literary Heritage Online,"

◀ The Pashkov House palace in Moscow was the first site for the Russian State Library.

a mission to develop an online catalog offering access to all the library's bibliographic records, and a selection of its digital resources relating to author Leo Tolstoy (1828–1910), whose literary estate is a collaborative partner.

The State Library takes pride in its specialized collections of maps (150,000), musical scores, records, rare books, printed art, newspapers, and dissertations. The collections are "unique in terms of completeness and universality," with documents in 247 languages: "There is no field of science or practice, which would not be reflected in the sources stored here. The library is indeed the memory of Russia."

Library and Archives of Canada

Established by the Canadian government in 2004 for the collection and preservation of the documentary heritage of Canada, the Library and Archives of Canada (in French, Bibliothèque et Archives Canada) is located in the capital, Ottawa.

The director has the title Librarian and Archivist of Canada. The library and archive merged the Public Archives, founded in 1872, and the National Library, founded in 1953. Its building was constructed in 1967 with an original collection of 400,000 items. Since then, the holdings have grown to more than 18 million. A preservation center opened in Quebec province in 1997, with laboratories, vaults, and offices.

The collection of Canadiana—a special collection of publications and manuscripts concerning the country's literary heritage—ranges from art and artifacts to newspapers, globes, maps, microfilms, rare books, sound recordings, and videos.

◀ Library and Archives of Canada, Ottawa.

Toronto Public Library, Canada

In 2001, the Toronto Public Library (TPL) was the world's second-most-used library system, after Hong Kong. TPL has the largest circulation in North America, with 30.4 million books, CDs, and videos loaned annually. This is one-third larger than the Queens Borough Public Library in New York City, the library with the largest U.S. circulation, at 21 million. Toronto's system is Canada's largest, with 99 libraries and more than 11 million items to borrow or access.

The library's origins date back to 1830, when Toronto was known as York, and members of its Mechanics' Institute resolved "for the mutual improvement of its members in useful Scientific knowledge" that a "library of reference and circulation will be formed." Four years later, when Toronto was officially founded, the Institute's library—which started with fewer than five hundred titles—was providing workers (mechanics) classes ranging from philosophy and music to science, electricity, and architectural drawing.

In the 1880s, state and federal government legislation to create free public libraries (the Free Libraries Act of 1882) promoted the development of library systems, and in 1884 the Toronto Public Library officially opened in the Mechanics' Institute. The system lent particular importance to stocking books in many languages—a reflection of Canada's large proportion of immigrants, and also, the fact that a quarter of the population is French-speaking. A substantial portion of the Province of Ontario's population is French-Canadian. The first chief librarian, former bookseller and publisher James Bain (1842–1908), served for twenty-five years.

Soon after being established, the Toronto library also began acquiring Canadiana. Bain set out to acquire "every work of any consequence" in the fields of Canadian literature and history. Bain's goal was to establish the Toronto library as the repository of Canadiana, "unsurpassed by any other library in the country." That effort has continued, with the library publishing a catalog, updated annually, of Canadian works which reach back to the sixteenth century.

Funds from the Andrew Carnegie trust enabled the construction of ten libraries between 1907 and 1916, a number of which continued in operation into the twenty-first century. The original Central Reference Library is the student center at the St. George campus of the University of Toronto.

▲ A bookmobile operated by Toronto Public Library.

Prior to 1997, metropolitan Toronto's municipalities operated six public library systems, including Toronto Central Library. In that year, the government of Ontario amalgamated these municipalities, and their libraries merged with the Toronto Public Library. This created the largest library system in North America, which grew to contain 11 million items.

Toronto Public Library offers up-to-date computer and online facilities, with 1,500 public-access computers and public wireless Internet access at many branches. Online content is extensive, from books and periodicals to music, video, educational and literacy support, and research databases.

The systems also operate bookmobile buses that serve more than thirty neighborhoods throughout the metropolitan area. Bookmobiles have been in use since 1955, and are particularly valuable for children, elderly, and a number of communities without easy access to neighborhood branch libraries.

The Toronto Reference Library, opened in 1977, is a mostly noncirculating collection of 1.5 million volumes and 2.5 million other items, such as films, tapes, microforms, maps, and fine and performing arts.

Bibliothèque et Archives Nationales du Québec, Canada

The Bibliothèque et Archives Nationales du Québec (BAnQ), the library of the Province of Quebec, was created in 1967 and is the result of a merger of three major libraries: the Bibliothèque Nationale du Québec, the Archives Nationales du Québec, and the Grand Bibliothèque du Québec. The BAnQ collection includes the legal deposit copies of all works printed in Quebec or about Quebec, or by an author from the province.

The library's mission is "to assemble, preserve permanently, and disseminate Quebec's documentary heritage" and "to offer democratic access to Quebec's national documentary heritage, culture and knowledge . . . thus contributing to the personal development of citizens." The library also focuses on publishing bibliographies of relevant works.

The province's library heritage largely rested on church-controlled parish libraries, few of which developed into collections open to the public. A late-nineteenth-century movement to establish a public library for French-speaking Quebeckers was opposed by the church, which objected to its stocking of prohibited titles. This library went out of business in 1880. Furthermore, Quebec libraries refused to accept funds from the Carnegie endowment.

One foundation of the BAnQ was the Sulpician Library in Montreal, a Catholic library which had some 78,000 books. The St. Sulpice Library has titles dating back to the eighteenth century. Its quarters in the center of Montreal held a collection of reference works. In 1997, the BAnQ's general collection of 240,000 books were transferred to a central location in a newly renovated factory. Montreal also has a city public library system, the largest public French-language system in North America.

Subsequently, in 2005, the new facilities of the Grand Bibliothèque opened, with more than 4 million volumes that include the collec-

◀ Interior of the Grand Bibliothèque, Montreal.

tion of the Central Library of Montreal. There are 1.14 million books, 1.2 million other documents, and 1.66 million microfiches.

Approximately a million books in the Grand Bibliothèque are part of the Collection Nationale, considered the Quebec heritage collection. The library also has a large lending collection of multimedia items, with 70,000 music scores, 16,000 films, and computer software programs. There is also a collection of 50,000 documents for the visually impaired.

The Grand Bibliothèque officially opened in time for the 2005 World Book and Copyright Day, and Montreal was honored as the "World Book Capital" by UNESCO.

Royal Library of Belgium

Belgium's national library has roots in the fifteenth century, when the earliest known libraries belonged to monasteries and to the Dukes of Burgundy. The nine hundred manuscript titles of the Burgundian library were part of the Belgian royal library when it was established in 1837.

Belgium's diverse and rich cultural heritage includes more than 2,500 public libraries, although the country's population is less than 11 million. Its book heritage is also considerable, with Antwerp one of Europe's major printing centers since 1876.

The Royal Library is bilingual (Flemish and French) in keeping with Belgium's national composition. Its respective names are Koninklijke Bibliotheek and Bibliothèque Royale. It is a scientific institution belonging to the national government, and acquires information in every scientific discipline. Since 1966 it has been a legal deposit library responsible for cataloging and collecting every Belgian publication.

The library collects and conserves items from Belgium's national heritage, including books and periodicals, maps and engravings, and coins, medals, and printed music. Among the collections are many items from Belgium's musical heritage, including the Fétis archives, made up of the work and books of nineteenth-century Belgian musicologist, composer, and critic Francois-Joseph Fétis.

There are 4 million bound volumes, including a rare book collection numbering 45,000 works. The library has more than 700,000 engravings and drawings, and 150,000 maps and plans. There are more than 250,000 objects,

from coins to scales and monetary weights. The coin collection reputedly holds one of the most valuable coins in the entire field of numismatics: a fifth-century Sicilian tetradrachm.

The Royal Library is host to the Center for American Studies, which offers a master of arts degree program. The center was established by several Belgian universities as a new institute of higher learning, and has its own Library of American Studies (30,000 titles), Library of American Civilization (20,000 computerized volumes on pre–World War I United States), and the American Research Library (3,000 recent online periodicals).

Situated in Brussels, the capital, the Royal Library is open for reference only, and patrons must be eighteen years of age or older and pay an annual membership fee.

Royal Library of the Netherlands

The Koninklijke Bibliotheek, or Royal Library, is located in The Hague, seat of government for The Netherlands. Founded in 1798, the "KB" had its beginnings in the library of William V (1748–1806), Prince of Orange and head of the Dutch State, although revolutionaries forced him into exile from 1795 to 1806. It was named the Royal Library in 1806 by King Lodewijk Napoleon.

The Royal Library was named the National Library of the Netherlands upon the opening of its new quarters in 1982. As the national library, its main

An illuminated page from the fifteenth-century Cite de Dieu, held by the Royal Library Netherlands, The Hague. ▶

mission is to preserve the Dutch printed and written heritage. Virtually the entire known literature of the Netherlands is in the collection, dating from medieval times. As a legal deposit library, the KB accepts all publications issued by registered Dutch publishers. The library has 3.5 million items, more than 2.5 million being books.

The KB's special collections include incunabula, medieval and modern manuscripts, and early printed books. There are also important collections of songbooks, children's literature, sports books (e.g., falconry, mountaineering), books on games, books from private presses, and the largest collection of Dutch newspapers, both from the country and its colonies. The social sciences are not covered in depth, however, and scientific literature is not actively collected.

Yet, the library does have a collection of Dutch "gray" literature—documents which are conventionally disseminated through publishers and normal distribution systems but which have cultural or intellectual significance. Gray literature can include technical reports and working papers from a government or scientific research groups or committees. These documents are considered gray literature because authorship, publication date, and publisher may not be readily apparent.

Included among the library's "treasures" are works of art, such as *The Madonna with the Christ Child* by fifteenth-century French painter Jean Fouquet, considered one of the best of the era. Another valuable antiquity is a bound book by Christopher Plantin (1520–89), a sixteenth-century French printer and publisher. This binding of brown calfskin with gold tooling was dedicated to Emperor Charles V (1500–58) and produced at Plantin's workshop in Antwerp. Another distinctive item is eighteenth-century brocade paper from Augsburg, Germany.

An example of a rare book is the elaborately illustrated 1596 story of the travels of Jan Huygen van Linschoten (1563–1611), who journeyed to Spain, India, Indonesia, and East Asia.

KB patrons become members and must be at least sixteen years of age. Day passes for readers are also available. The reading room pass is free, while the online services have a small user-fee.

Hong Kong Public Libraries, China

The first public library in Hong Kong was the City Hall Library, opened in 1869. Hong Kong was a British colony from 1842 until sovereignty was transferred to the People's Republic of China in 1997. The Hong Kong Special Administrative Region, with only 400 square miles of territory on the south China coast, is one of the most populated metropolitan areas in the world, with 7 million people.

The public library system, with sixty-six libraries and ten mobile operations, was, according to visitations, the most-used library in the world in 2001. This year was an important landmark for the public library service in Hong Kong, with the construction of the twelve-story Hong Kong Central Library, the largest public library in Hong Kong with 2.3 million items. Equipped with state-of-the-art technologies, the library serves as the administrative headquarters and main library of the public library network, as well as the major information center for Hong Kong.

Unlike most public libraries, which are under a local jurisdiction, the HKPL is operated by the Leisure and Cultural Services Department, which operates similarly to a government ministry. The Hong Kong Public Libraries collection has 12.1 million items, including books, audiovisual materials, newspapers, periodicals, CD-ROM databases, microforms, and maps. Some may be borrowed, while others are for use in the libraries. The Hong Kong Collection is a comprehensive compilation of Hong Kong–related materials, which has grown to

◀ Hong Kong Central Library.

more than 70,000 items. One, the Hok Hoi Collection, consists of more than 34,000 volumes, with a large number of classical Chinese thread-sewn rare books.

The automated library system is one of the largest in the world, with Chinese and English capabilities.

Italian National Libraries

The Biblioteca Nazionale Centrale of Florence and the Biblioteca Nazionale Centrale Roma are Italy's two national libraries.

The Florentine library was founded in 1714, when the approximately 30,000 volumes of renowned scholar Antonio Magliabechi were bequeathed to the city. By 1743, it was required that a copy of every work published in Tuscany be submitted as legal deposit to the library, known as the Magliabechiana. The library was opened to the public in 1747.

Over the centuries, its holdings were combined with other important collections, and by 1885 it was renamed the National Central Library of Florence. The various collections were kept in rooms belonging to the Uffizi Gallery, one of the world's oldest and most famous art galleries. Since 1935, the collections have been housed in a building on the bank of the Arno River in Santa Croce.

In 1966, a disastrous flood of the Arno damaged nearly one-third of the library's holdings, most notably and regrettably its periodicals and rare books, including the Magliabechi collection. The Restoration Center was subsequently established and is credited with having saved many of these priceless artifacts, although much work remains to be done, and some items were lost forever.

The National Central Library of Rome was founded in 1876, providing Italy's new capital with a comprehensive book archive intended to preserve and express national culture. The library was originally located in the sixteenth-century college building of the Jesuit Bibliotheca Maior. It was from this library that the early collection of manuscripts and printed books came. Later sources included the libraries of religious orders that were suppressed after the 1861 creation of the Kingdom of Italy. The many states of the Italian peninsula were united during this time, and their various institutional libraries came under central government control.

▲ The National Central Library of Florence.

Some of those libraries are among the oldest in the world, dating to classical Roman times. During World War II, aerial bombing and ground combat heavily damaged many Italian libraries and book collections.

In 1975, the library moved to the Castro Pretorio archaeological area, its present location, where in ancient Roman times the military barracks of the imperial guard stood. Extensive refurbishment, upgrading, and expansion were completed in 2001, offering improved facilities and state-of-the-art technology.

The National Central Library of Rome is a research library and is entitled to receive one legal deposit copy of all publications printed in Italy. Its holdings also include a comprehensive collection of foreign books and publications, with particular emphasis on Italian culture abroad.

The Rome library holds more than 6 million volumes, plus about 8,000 manuscripts and approximately 2,000 incunabula. The collections contain more than 25,000 sixteenth-century publications; 20,000 maps; a collection of 10,000 prints and drawings—in addition to those collected in book form. There are more than 45,000 periodicals.

Italy's National Library System, administered from the Florence library, is responsible for the automation of library services and the indexing of national holdings.

New York City Public Libraries

New York's five boroughs have three separate and independent public library systems with more than 30 million book volumes. The New York Public Library, Queens Borough Public Library, and Brooklyn Public Library have more than 208 branches, and if considered as a single institution, would be the largest public library in the world. The three library systems had 37 million visitors and a total circulation of 35 million items in 2006. All public libraries in New York's three systems are used free of charge.

New York Public Library

The New York Public Library (NYPL) is one of the world's leading research libraries, the seventh-largest public library in the United States, and the country's twenty-sixth-largest library. The NYPL serves the boroughs of Manhattan, the Bronx, and Staten Island, with eighty-nine libraries: four non-lending research libraries, four main lending libraries, a library for the blind and physically handicapped, three specialized libraries, and seventy-seven neighborhood branch libraries.

The NYPL's research collections contain almost 44 million items—books (16 million), maps, videotapes, etc. The NYPL Branch Libraries contain 7.3 million items, including 4.4 million books. The collections together total more than 50 million items (20 million of them books). Only the Library of Congress in Washington, D.C., and the British Library have larger book holdings.

In 1886, the city received a bequest of $2.4 million from former governor Samuel J. Tilden (1814–86) to establish and maintain a free reading room. Already present in Manhattan were the Astor Library (opened in 1849) and the Lenox Library (opened in 1871). Both libraries, provided by wealthy benefactors, were open to the public and free of charge. By the late 1890s, these libraries were struggling financially. Using the Tilden bequest, they were consolidated into "The New York Public Library, Astor, Lenox, and Tilden Foundations."

Further consolidation took place in 1901, this time with the New York Free Circulating Library. Combined with a grant of $5.2 million from philanthropist Andrew Carnegie to build branch libraries, the library trustees were in a position to contract with the City of New York to operate the NYPL

◀ New York Public Library's lions—originally called Leo Astor and Leo Lenox, after the early benefactors, later Patience and Fortitude.

system. This private-public partnership, which continues into the twenty-first century, is unusual with regard to most great public libraries, typically created by government statute.

Construction began in 1902 to erect a central library in midtown Manhattan, and after nine years, the building was officially opened by president William Howard Taft. Several thousand New Yorkers attended the open house the next day, touring a library building with 1 million volumes. The Main Reading Room, lined with reference works, is 78 feet wide, almost 300 feet long, and its ceilings are 52 feet high.

The magnificent architecture, chandeliers, tall windows, and handsome furnishings combined over the years with rooms named for famous authors, but the spirit of the NYPL main library has been democratic, open to ordinary people working to improve themselves. In 1995, a Science, Industry, and Business Library opened, with 2 million volumes and 60,000 periodicals—America's largest public library devoted to science and business.

Two other research libraries are the Schomburg Center for Research in Black Culture and the New York Public Library for the Performing Arts. The NYPL's facilities are maintained to be state-of-the art, although its trademark stone lions at the entrance have remained the library's—and one of Midtown's—best-known symbols.

Queens Public Library, New York City

In 2007, the Queens Borough Public Library in New York City was the number-one library system in the United States in terms of circulation, loaning 21 million items. The Queens Library ranks twentieth nationally in the number of volumes held: 6.6 million.

Queens has sixty-two branches serving the borough, which has a population of 2.27 million. The borough has one of the largest immigrant populations in the United States—almost half the Queens population—and this is reflected in its collections, which have a considerable percentage of non-English books. Spanish is the main language other than English.

The first library in Queens was Flushing's subscription library, founded in 1858 and becoming a free circulation library in 1869. Queens was a county of New York until 1897, when it was established as a New York City borough. At this time, several local libraries were operating, including the Long Island City Public Library, which had several branches. The various libraries were consolidated early in the twentieth century, and additional branches appeared—some in storefronts—along with traveling libraries to better meet the public's growing appetite for reading.

An elegant four-story Central Library opened in 1930, built by Works Progress Administration funds, but it was replaced in 1966 by a larger facility. Growth continued, with seven local Carnegie-funded libraries erected—most of which continue in operation today. Including the Central Library, the Queens Library eventually had sixty-two locations, seven Adult Learning Centers, two Family Literacy Centers, and a bookmobile. One important program is designed to provide young students with homework materials, tutors, and monitors.

Among its resources is the Black Heritage Reference Center, which is New York State's largest collection dedicated solely to materials "written by, about, for, with and related to Black Culture."

Another facet is the International Resource Center, with books, magazines, CDs, and DVDs representing the world's cultures, including Bengali, Chinese, French, Gujarati, Hindi, Korean, Portuguese, Punjabi, Russian, Spanish, and Urdu.

Brooklyn Public Library, New York City

The library system of New York City's Borough of Brooklyn is the fifth-largest public library system in the United States in terms of visitation, and eleventh in volumes held, with almost 4.7 million books.

The Brooklyn Public Library (BPL), established in 1892, was originally planned as a network of libraries throughout the then-independent city of

Brooklyn. In 1898, Brooklyn was consolidated as a borough of the City of New York. The library system remained an independent nonprofit organization funded by the city, state, and federal governments, and also by private donors.

Construction of the Central Library at Grand Army Plaza began in 1912, and was finally completed in 1941. Between 1901 and 1923, the work was supported by Carnegie library philanthropy, which donated $1.6 million toward the development of twenty-one branch libraries. By the twenty-first century, the BPL system had fifty-eight branches located within a half-mile of every Brooklyn resident. The system includes a business library in Brooklyn Heights and a bookmobile. The Central Library, alone, has an annual visitation of 1 million patrons.

The BPL's local history division's Brooklyn Collection includes books, maps, photographs, newspapers, ephemera, prints, and newspaper clippings, as well as more than 10,000 photographs of Brooklyn.

Boston Public Library

Founded in 1848, the Boston Public Library (BPL) is the largest public library in the United States, and the third largest of all the libraries in the country. With 16 million volumes, Boston Public is surpassed only by the Library of Congress and the Harvard University library system.

Boston Public is credited with a number of American library firsts: It was the first publicly supported municipal library; the country's first large library opened to the public; and the first public library to loan out books and other materials. All adult residents of the Commonwealth of Massachusetts are entitled to borrowing and research privileges.

After more than twenty years of efforts to establish a public library—efforts supported by trustees of the 1807 Boston Atheneum, an independent library and museum—the Boston Public Library was established in a former schoolhouse. This first library, which opened in 1854, had 16,000 volumes—already too large a collection for its quarters. That same year plans, were initiated to build a new structure, which was erected at Copley Square in 1895 after seven years of planning and construction.

Named the McKim Building after the renowned architect Charles Follen McKim (1847–1909), the building's facade is based on sixteenth-century Italian architecture, although French designs also influenced McKim. The new library contained a children's room (another first in the United States) and a central courtyard in the style of a Renaissance cloister.

One of several inscriptions placed on the three facades reads THE COMMONWEALTH REQUIRES THE EDUCATION OF THE PEOPLE AS THE SAFEGUARD OF ORDER AND LIBERTY. Another inscription, above the entrance, reads FREE TO ALL.

As the library grew, so too did the public usage of the collections. Another first occurred in 1870, when the BPL opened the first branch library in the United States, located in East Boston. There were twenty-one more branches by 1900, and they would eventually number twenty-six.

In the 1970s, new facilities were erected for the circulating collection of the general library and for the BPL headquarters, while the McKim Building housed the research collection. By the twentieth century, the BPL could proudly state that:

▲ Boston Public Library, Bates Hall.

In addition to its 6.1 million books, the library boasts over 1.2 million rare books and manuscripts, a wealth of maps, musical scores and prints. Among its large collections, the BPL holds several first edition folios by William Shakespeare, original music scores from Mozart to Prokofiev's "Peter and the Wolf"; and, in its rare book collection, the personal library of John Adams.

Many items from the BPL collections are displayed in rotating exhibits. More than 2.2 million patrons visit the library annually, including scholars busy with research and Bostonians "looking for an afternoon's reading," as the BPL Web site puts it.

Across from the central entrance stands a monument to twentieth-century Lebanese-born poet and philosopher Kahlil Gibran, a generous benefactor who spent many hours in the library as a young man. The inscription reads: IT WAS IN MY HEART TO HELP A LITTLE, BECAUSE I WAS HELPED MUCH.

Chicago Public Library

The Chicago Public Library (CPL), which serves the city of Chicago's population of 2.8 million, is the largest library system in the Midwest, and one of the largest urban systems in the world, with 10.7 million volumes.

The library's beginnings were in an abandoned water tower after the Great Chicago Fire ravaged the city in 1871. The 3,000 volumes were augmented by a donation of 8,000 books from England. This foundation of a free public library grew steadily, with a circulation of 13,000 that first year. By the twenty-first century, the CPL had a circulation of 7.8 million annually.

The CPL's outreach to the population of this young and sprawling plains city began immediately, with a number of "outposts," or "stations"—sites with small book collections where patrons could order titles that were delivered by horse-drawn carriage. These stations were located in stores, churches, and factories. These deposit stations accounted for two-thirds of the circulation by 1900.

The library itself moved around for its first twenty-four years, at last finding a home in the Central Library, built in 1897. Demand for library books continued all over the city, and by the mid-twentieth century the traveling library, or bookmobile, was essential, circulating 100,000 books annually. The branch system speedily developed between 1960 and 1986, with 76 neighborhood branch libraries in operation in that time.

Although there were renovations and additions to the Central Library over the years, its space remained limited compared to the growing collection. In the late 1980s, a grassroots fund-raising campaign began, resulting in a new, state-of-the art central library building, which was opened in 1991 and named for former mayor Harold L. Washington (1922–87). Since then, great efforts have gone into renewing or rebuilding many branch libraries, some of which replaced rented storefronts.

One of the CPL's jewels is the Carter G. Woodson Regional Library, which opened in 1975. Named after the "Father of Modern Black Historiography," the library is home to one of the largest repositories of information on the black experience in the Midwest.

The library expresses its responsibility to the Chicago community as a mission "to provide equal access to information, ideas and knowledge through books, programs and other resources." The CPL asserts, "We believe in the freedom to read, to learn, to discover" and further adds:

> Since first opening its doors to the public in 1873, the Chicago Public Library has maintained its status of one of the City's most democratic of institutions—providing all Chicagoans with a free and open place to gather, learn, connect, read and be transformed.

In collaboration with the City of Chicago, the CPL opened fifty-two

Chicago Public Library. ▶

new or renovated neighborhood libraries between 1989 and 2009—extraordinary public library growth. The CPL has seventy-nine locations throughout the city, including the main library and two regional libraries. The system strives to provide:

> innovative library services, technologies and tools Chicagoans need to achieve their personal goals and to establish the City's role as a competitive force in the global marketplace.

As part of that policy, the CPL provided 3.6 million free computer sessions on nearly 2,000 public-access computers in 2007, while the library's Web site received more than 25 million hits per month.

Los Angeles Libraries

The most populous county in the United States, Los Angeles County, California, has almost 10 million residents served by two great public library systems: the County of Los Angeles Public Library, and the Los Angeles Public Library.

Together, these two libraries have approximately 14 million volumes and a combined circulation of almost 30 million. The county system serves most of the incorporated cities in the region, while the city system serves the Los Angeles metropolitan area. They operate a total of 156 libraries which serve a population of 16.5 million.

County of Los Angeles Public Library

The County of Los Angeles Public Library, established in 1912 by the County Free Library Act, operates under the authority of the County Board of Supervisors. It is the second-largest public library and thirteenth-largest library in the United States, with almost 7.9 million volumes. It serves more than 3.5 million residents, including those in 51 of the 88 incorporated cities of Los Angeles County—an area extending over 3,000 square miles. Visitation is 12.8 million, with 2.6 million online-usage sessions.

The mission of the library, which is headquartered in Downey, is to "provide our diverse communities with easy access to the information and knowledge they need to nurture their cultural exploration and lifelong learning."

To this end, the library provides many resources, including literacy services, programs for children and families, resource centers for patrons of several ethnic origins (American Indian, Asian, black, and Chicano), as well as business, government, and consumer-health information. Supplementing the book collection, the library also offers magazines, newspapers, microfilm, government publications, and many specialized reference materials, including online databases. There are special collections, Californiana collections, and local history collections.

The library runs eighty-four regional and community libraries, four bookmobiles, and seven special reference and resource centers.

Los Angeles Public Library

The sixth-largest public library in the United States, with 6.2 million volumes, the Los Angeles Public Library was established in 1872. One of the world's largest publicly funded libraries, the LAPL follows a mission statement which accentuates the "free" store of information it offers to the city's population:

> The Los Angeles Public Library provides free and easy access to information, ideas, books and technology that enrich, educate and empower every individual in our city's diverse communities.

The Richard J. Riordan Central Library, built in 1926, is a Los Angeles downtown landmark, with an architectural style described as "Modernist / Beaux Arts." One spectacular attribute is the four-part mural by illustrator Dean Cornwell, depicting the stages of the history of California.

The library prides itself on being a regional history resource, which includes the history and genealogy collection's 50,000 photographs, most taken in Southern California. The Central Library's History Department began collecting photographs before World War II, and had 13,000 images by the late 1950s. When Los Angeles celebrated its 200th anniversary in 1981, Security Pacific National Bank gave its noted collection of 250,000 historical photographs to the city to be archived at the Central Library. Since then, the library has received other major collections and special archives, creating an international resource for photographic images.

LAPL offers many resources in Spanish and English, and its community programs are designed to assist young people and to provide adult literacy services. Twenty literacy centers around the city offer books, videos, audiocassettes, and computer-based tutorials on adult basic education, limited-English proficiency, and test preparation.

The LAPL's 2005–06 circulation from its seventy-one branches was 15.7 million. One of its more notable collections is the Science and Technology Library.

The LAPL suffered major damage in 1986 when an arson fire destroyed some 400,000 volumes. A second fire later that year destroyed the contents of the Music Department Reading Room. Rehabilitation and renovation was completed in 1993, when the library reopened.

National Library of China, Beijing

The National Library of China (NLC), located in Beijing, is the fifth-largest library in the world and the largest in Asia, with more than 23 million volumes. Founded in 1909 as the Capital Library, the library received its legal deposit status in 1916. The holdings do not circulate.

The older buildings of the library—since 1987, the central structures of the National Library of China—house historical and ancient books, documents, and manuscripts. The NLC has inherited the collections of China's imperial libraries, comprised of rare books and manuscripts.

The special collections include ancient titles, genealogical documents, newspapers and periodicals, government documents, local history resources, dissertations, musical documents and resources, and United Nations publications.

Among the most treasured NLC collections are the rare documents and records from past Chinese dynasties. There are 270,000 ancient and rare

Los Angeles Central Library. ▶

Chinese books and historical documents, and more than 1.6 million traditional thread-bound Chinese books. There are more than 16,000 volumes of historical documents and manuscripts from the Mogao Caves in Dunhuang, as well as Buddhist sutras dating to the sixth century. The collections include rare copies of ancient manuscripts and books.

Ancient artifacts—maps, diagrams, and rubbings from ancient inscriptions on metal and stone—include more than 35,000 inscriptions on oracle bones and tortoise shells from the Shang Dynasty (c. sixteenth through eleventh centuries BCE). Books and archives from imperial libraries date to the Southern Song Dynasty (c. 1127).

The library also houses a collection of official publications of the United Nations and foreign governments, and a collection of literature and materials in more than 115 languages.

The National Library of China is augmented by the National Digital Library of China. In 2008, the NLC finalized an agreement with the Library of Congress in the United States to cooperate in developing the World Digital Library. According to the LoC:

> The two libraries agreed to provide content to the World Digital Library and to cooperate in such areas as the development and maintenance of the Chinese-language interface, the convening of international working groups to plan and develop the project, and the formation of an advisory committee of leading scholars and curators to recommend

◀ The National Library of China, Beijing.

important collections about the culture and history of China for inclusion in the World Digital Library.

Shanghai Library, China

The origins of the Shanghai Library hark back to 1847 and the Xu Jiahui Jesuit mission, in a time when this east-coast port city was one of the few cities opened to foreign trade. Shanghai grew to be a major commercial center in the nineteenth century, and is China's largest city. Shanghai's metropolis has a population of 20 million and is a center for science, the arts, and education.

The first library run by the Chinese was founded in 1925 as the Shanghai East Library. In 1950, after decades of foreign invasion and civil war, the library and its supporters launched a major campaign to acquire books, expanding the collection to more than 200,000 volumes in just a year. Shanghai Library was established in 1952, with more than 700,000 volumes. By the 1970s, the library building had exceeded its capacity. In the following decades, work began to build a new home for the Shanghai Library. The first foundation stone was laid in 1993.

With the merging of several other libraries and collections, the Shanghai Library became the second-largest public library in China after the National Library in Beijing. The Shanghai Library is ranked among the world's largest in terms of its collections (including 1.7 million books) and floor space (more than 80,000 square meters). A new library building, opened in 1996, covers almost 8 acres and is a city landmark. At almost 350 feet and 24 stories high, it was the tallest library in the world.

In 1995, Shanghai Library merged with the city's Institute of Scientific and Technological Information, becoming the first Chinese library to combine public library services with such scientific, technical, and industry information-research functions.

German National Library

With locations in Leipzig, Frankfurt am Main, and Berlin, the German National Library (Deutsche Nationalbibliothek) is responsible for collecting, archiving, and comprehensively recording and documenting all German and German-language publications and translations of German works since 1913. This includes the writings of German-speaking emigrants published abroad between 1933 and 1945, termed the Nazi era.

The national library collections total 24.1 million of such items, termed *Germanica*. This library has been a legal deposit institution since 1935. It was established in 1912, with the music archive (printed and recorded) founded in Berlin in 1970. Although these items do not circulate, the national library's visitation in 2007 was more than 880,000.

Plans for a national library were incubated as early as 1848, before there even was a German state. Books were collected and stored in the German National Museum at Nuremberg. In 1912, the Association of German Booksellers joined with the Kingdom of Saxony to found a national library in Leipzig. Decades of war prevented full development, and Germany was divided into east and west (Leipzig in East Germany) after World War II. In 1946, American authorities occupying part of West Germany agreed to a proposal to create an archive reference library at Frankfurt.

With two established national libraries—Leipzig in Communist East Germany and Frankfurt in West Germany—considerable cataloging work was done, but most of it was identical. Upon reunification in 1990, the two libraries merged. The German Music Archive in Berlin had been established in 1970 by West Germany to collect all music published in Germany. The archive, a department of the national library, will occupy new quarters in Leipzig.

The main building in Leipzig was built between 1914 and 1916, with a facade 160 meters long, and decorated with the busts of Johann Wolfgang von Goethe and Johannes Gutenberg, among other famous Germans. Leipzig has 14.3 million items, Frankfurt 8.3 million, and Berlin 1.5. million

Library of the Russian Academy of Sciences

The Library of the Russian Academy of Sciences (RAS), in the city of St. Petersburg, has one of the world's largest research libraries, with a central collection of 20.5 million items. The state-owned RAS is comprised of scientific organizations (institutions), scientific support, and social organizations, with five hundred "full" members and an equal number of "corresponding" members—those who are not fully accredited.

The library was founded by Czar Peter I in 1714 and later incorporated with the RAS, which is headquartered in Moscow. The library is open to employees of the institutions of the Russian Academy of Sciences, and to scholars "with higher education." There is a central collection as well as the collections of specialized academic institutions elsewhere in Russia. The library's mission is described in part as follows:

> [The] [p]rincipal aim of the Russian Academy of Sciences consists in organization and performance of fundamental researches for the purpose of obtaining further knowledge of the natural, social and human development principles that promote technological, economic, social and cultural development in Russia.

Since 1747, all academic institutions in the country have been obliged to provide a copy of all published documents, and since 1783 all publishers have been under the same requirement. After the Russian Revolution and civil war of the early twentieth century, many confiscated items were integrated into the RAS library collections.

During World War II and the horrific Nazi siege and bombardment of the city—then named Leningrad—the collections remained in the city instead of being evacuated, and the library remained open. In 1986, however, a great disaster struck when a catastrophic fire destroyed a large portion of the central collection and subordinate libraries, which at that time numbered 17.3 million items.

Despite the loss, the RAS collection was subsequently built up to become one of the largest in the world by the twenty-first century.

London Library

The world's largest independent lending library refers to itself as a "rare literary refuge in the heart of the capital." This is not a free library, although membership is open to all who pay an annual subscription fee. There are

▲ Library of the Russian Academy of Sciences, St. Petersburg.

more than 8,000 members, including 250 corporate members. The library is self-supporting, with an annual fee of more than 600 dollars in 2009.

Located in the City of Westminster, London, the London Library has a collection of 1 million books, most in open stacks and available for lending. Founded in 1841 by prominent Britons who were generally dissatisfied with the British Library's policies, the library has stood at the northwest corner of St. James Square since 1845. Thomas Carlyle, George Eliot, and Charles Dickens were founding members, and other famous literary figures such as presidents and vice presidents, T. S. Eliot, William Makepeace Thackeray, Rudyard Kipling, Lord Alfred Tennyson, and Rebecca West have joined with many lords and ladies in assuming leading administrative roles.

The library's collections stress literature, history, fine and applied art, philosophy, architecture, religion, topography, and travel. The Library's special collections include hunting and field sports, the Montefiore Collection of material of Jewish interest, and a collection related to the Rubaiyat of Omar Khayyam. Found in the open stacks are "old children's stories, cookery, imaginary history, and foreign impressions of England." And within the "Science and Miscellaneous" collections are sections on subjects such as dancing, dreams, and dueling.

Approximately 8,000 new titles are acquired annually, and the library subscribes to 850 periodicals. Except for losses to war damage in the 1940s, the library has retained almost all the books it has acquired since its establishment. Books are not routinely discarded, as the London Library affirms:

> It is a central tenet of the Library that, as books are never entirely superseded, and therefore never redundant, the collections should not be weeded of material merely because it is old, idiosyncratic or unfashionable: except in the case of exact duplication, almost nothing has ever been discarded from the Library's shelves.

Even rare old books are available for borrowing, with 97 percent of the collection available for loan. That policy, along with an efficient online catalog, combines the London Library's nineteenth-century ambience with a twenty-first century outlook: "With books dating from the 16th century to the latest publications in print and electronic form, the Library has sought to be contemporary in every age."

National Library of Australia

The National Library of Australia, located in the capital city of Canberra, was created by government legislation in 1960 and grew out of the Commonwealth Parliamentary Library, established in 1901. Prior to that, the Parliamentary Library had been functioning as a national library almost since its inception.

The library has more than 5 million items (not counting the manuscript collection), including 2.7 million books (many in microfilm), rare book materials, and formidable Asian and Pacific collections—with the largest Asian-language compilations in the Southern hemisphere. Asian language and research resources, which encompass half a million volumes, augment the Australiana collections.

The national library states one important aspect of its mission thusly:

> We are responsible under the terms of the National Library Act for maintaining and developing a national collection of library material, including a comprehensive collection of library material relating to Australia and the Australian people.

The manuscript collection, with 26 million items, includes documents that have research or exhibition importance. Examples are the *Endeavour* journal of explorer Captain Cook and the notebook kept by Captain William Bligh, who was set adrift on the Pacific after the mutiny on the famed ship, the *Bounty*. Other important collections relate to New Zealand, Papua New Guinea, and the Pacific Ocean.

The archives cover a range of national nongovernmental organizations' documents. Examples are the records of the Federal Secretariat of the Australian Labor Party, the Returned Services League, the Australian Council of Churches, and the Australian Institute of International Affairs. The library

▲ National Library of Australia, Canberra.

also maintains archives of individuals or families who have achieved a degree of national standing and influence. The oral history program collects and preserves recorded interviews and various forms of oral history.

To supplement manuscript holdings, the Oral History Collection was initiated in the late 1950s, recording interviews with eminent Australians. The library has also acquired folklore field tapes, following Australia's twentieth-century folk-culture revival. A substantial number of interviews in the field of social history have been added, contributing to some 58,000 oral history and folk recordings.

The library's Australiana collections are the nation's most important resource of materials recording Australia's cultural heritage. Materials include maps, music, items from the performing arts, and more than 175,000 journal titles. These journals are magazines, newsletters, annual reports, and newspapers produced by all facets of Australian society: academic, ethnic and multicultural, aboriginal, business, society, schools, government departments, and professional associations.

The library also maintains the National Reserve Braille Collection.

National Diet Library of Japan

The national library of Japan is the National Diet Library (NDL), established in 1948 in order to assist members of the Diet (Parliament) in research regarding governmental matters. The library has two facilities: one in Tokyo, Japan's capital, and the other in Kyoto, former imperial capital. There are also twenty-seven branch libraries. Tokyo is the seat of the Japanese government and home of the imperial family, and is the world's most populous metropolitan area, with a population of 35 million.

The NDL has the same traditional function as the Library of Congress in the United States: to serve the governing establishment, to serve as the legal deposit library, and to support research. Its collections acquire works produced inside Japan and works about Japan that were produced in other lands. These include books, journals, newspapers, electronic materials, manuscripts, official publications, Asian materials, doctoral dissertations, maps, and music scores.

The collections also include Japanese statutes and parliamentary documents, publications on Japan, reference materials, materials on science and technology, publications of international organizations and foreign governments, children's literature and related materials, and Asian materials. The library is one of almost 90,000 Japanese libraries, including 40,000 school libraries.

The NDL developed from three separate libraries: the library of the House of Peers, the library of the House of Representatives—both of which were established at the creation of the Imperial Diet in 1890—and the Imperial Library, established in 1872. In general, the NDL has the strongest research collection in the country, followed by university, special, and large public libraries.

After accepting defeat in World War II, Japan was occupied by American forces, which attempted to redirect the formerly totalitarian nation toward democracy. A number of postwar leaders cooperated in this effort, and the NDL was considered a catalyst for change—an educational force for a "peaceful revolution."

Among its 34.5 million items, the NDL houses the former Imperial Library's collection of Japanese-language materials from the Edo Period (1603–1867) and earlier. Included are some 6,000 documents relating to the

▲ National Diet Library of Japan, Tokyo.

Tokugawa Shogunate of the Edo. Library users must be eighteen or older to access the NDL's holdings.

Jewish National and University Library, Israel

The Jewish National and University Library (JNUL) assumes three major roles: It is the National Library of the State of Israel; the Central Library of the Hebrew University in Jerusalem; and also a repository of Jewish heritage from around the world. The JNUL describes this latter role as the "Library of the Jewish People," most of whom live outside the state of Israel.

As the National Library of the State of Israel—with 5 million books and several thousand manuscripts, archives, maps, and musical recordings—the JNUL collects all material published in the country. It also strives to acquire all publications in the world that relate to Israel. In the words of JNUL, in addition to books, the library collects Israeli publications on all subjects, with no distinction as to format, language, age level, literary value, orientation and the like. This includes thousands of periodicals of all type and origin, such as national and local (including kibbutzim) newspapers, government bulletins, organs of trade unions and professional associations, financial reports of corporations, newsletters of youth movements and schools, scholarly and recreational journals, synagogue leaflets, market surveys and television program guides.

As a library of Jewish culture, the JNUL collects "all aspects of Jewish life and cultural expression: history, biography, language, education, religion, folklore, philosophy, *belles lettres*, art, [and] recreation. . . ." The collections of Hebraica and Judaica are the largest in the world.

Founded in 1892 as the first public library in Palestine to serve the Jewish people, the institution was also conceived as an international center for the preservation of books on Jewish culture. It assumed the additional functions of a general university library in 1925.

In 1960, the collection was moved to new quarters as the JNUL, on the Givat Ram campus of the Hebrew University. Over the years, various departmental libraries have been established, including a law library. Among the collections are the personal papers of theoretical physicist Albert Einstein (1879–1955), an "Online Treasury of Talmudic Manuscripts," and 9,000 Hebrew manuscripts.

In 2007, the JNUL was officially recognized as the National Library of Israel, jointly owned by the government and the university in concert with other organizations.

National Library of Brazil

The Biblioteca Nacional (Portuguese) has been the depository of Brazil's bibliographic and documentary heritage since the library's founding in 1810. Located in Rio de Janeiro, it is one of the largest libraries in the Americas, with collections numbering more than 9 million items.

The library's collections originated with books brought to Brazil in the early nineteenth century by Portuguese noble families looking for refuge

during the wars with Napoleonic France. The Portuguese royal family moved to Rio de Janiero, establishing the Royal Library in 1810 with more than 60,000 titles. With the return of the royal family to Portugal, a treaty was signed to leave the collection in Brazil.

In the twentieth century, the National Library of Brazil organized the first library science courses in Latin America. Its staff has taken the lead in modernization of libraries and library services, including the development of online databases. One of the important collections is the archive of 12,000 ten-inch records (78 rpm), which contain part of Brazil's dynamic musical heritage. There is also a "Brazilian Network of Virtual Memory," which includes texts and images on various themes from the history and culture of Brazil. There is also the Virtual Library of Cartography, a collection of rare books and manuscripts, eighteenth-century Brazilian naturalist collections and specimens, and fifteenth-century incunabula.

Jagiellonian University Library, Poland

The Jagiellonian Library (UJ), the library of Jagiellonian University in Cracow, has almost 5.5 million volumes and is one of Poland largest libraries. Popu-

National Library of Brazil, Rio de Janeiro. ▶

larly known as Jagiellonka, it serves as a public library, university library, and as a section of the Polish national library system. Its origins coincide with the university's founding as Cracow Academy in 1364. The university is Central Europe's second oldest.

In the eighteenth century, various small department libraries were centralized into one collection. In World War II, the library staff cooperated with secret underground universities, even though the university had been shut down by the German occupation.

In Polish, Biblioteka Jagiellońska, the UJ has a large collection of medieval manuscripts, including *De Revolutionibus Orbium Coelestium*, the work on astronomy by Polish astronomer Nicolaus Copernicus (1473–1543). There is also a large collection of underground literature from the period of Communist rule in Poland (1945–89). The library collects and preserves all published Polish materials as well as Polonica (items published abroad about Poland or by Poles).

There are more than 1.5 million monographs; half a million volumes of periodicals; more than 100,000 early printed books; almost 3,600 incunabula; 24,000 manuscripts; 13,000 maps; 35,000 music scores; and 77,000 microforms.

An average of 600,000 readers use the library annually. The UJ also has legal deposit status.

National Library of Iran

Iran's national library is situated in Tehran, the capital city, with several branches located throughout the metropolitan area. The National Library of Iran dates its origins to 1852, when the Dar ul-Funun School—the country's first European-style high school—was established in Tehran. A dozen years later, a small library was established for the school. This tiny library would

◀ A page from a work by Copernicus, at Poland's Biblioteka Jagiellońska, in Cracow.

form the nucleus of the Iranian National Library, which was officially inaugurated seventy-three years later in 1941. At that time, the national library was considered a symbol of the advent of modernity in Iran.

Late in the nineteenth century, the Sciences Society was founded in Tehran to promote the establishment of modern schools in the country. In 1898, the Society opened the National Sciences Library at its headquarters, next to Dar ul-Funun School. The term "National" meant the library was a nonprofit institution independent of the government. The Sciences Library can be considered the first public library of Iran, but was not the first national library. It was later merged with the Dar ul-Funun School library, and together, they became known as the Library of Sciences.

Throughout the twentieth century, the school and library served international conferences of scholars, whose individual efforts and donations of books built up the collection and reputation of the library. In the 1930s, it had 5,000 books and an average of 31 daily visitors.

Plans began in earnest to establish a truly national library, and the shah contributed more than 13,000 duplicate titles from the royal library. Thousands of books and manuscripts from private and corporate collections—including Russian and German books—were donated so that when newly built quarters were opened in 1937 and the National Library inaugurated the collection, it totaled more than 30,000 items.

The library grew, but for years it functioned more like a public library than a national library that was charged with cooperating with other libraries and collecting and organizing Iranian works (and works about Iran). The library also cooperated closely with government censors, so legal deposit titles were subject to official scrutiny. One step in directing the operations of the NLI as a true national library was the establishment of library science programs at the University of Tehran.

▼ National Library of Iran, Teheran.

In the 1970s, collaboration with the International Federation of Library Associations and Institutions (IFLA) led to a conference of sixty librarians and architects from around the world to help plan for future development. There followed years of growth, temporary housing of collections, and the Iranian Revolution of the late 1970s, before modern, state-of-the-art facilities were built in the first decade of the twenty-first century.

The library became "The Documents and National Library of the Islamic Republic of Iran," with collections of rare books and manuscripts. The library's mission includes acquiring all works written in Farsi, as well as all works on Iranian and Islamic studies.

National Library of Pakistan

Inaugurated in 1993, the National Library of Pakistan is in the capital, Islamabad. The library is not only the country's leading resource for information—ancient and new—but its staff also works to coordinate library functions and services throughout Pakistan.

The collection includes 130,000 volumes and 1,000 magazines and newspapers. Archived information is maintained on microfiche and microfilms. The holdings include more than 40,000 published items deposited under Pakistan's copyright laws.

A major portion of National Library of Pakistan's main collection is made up of publications about Pakistan, its culture and people, as well as books authored by Pakistanis living abroad. A significant part of the collection consists of manuscripts and rare books. Special collections include manuscripts in Persian relating to the history of Kashmir, and an archive of scholarly dissertations on Pakistan which have been written in American universities.

One of the most important departments is the Model Children's Library (MCL), with more than 9,000 books in English and Urdu, including titles in Braille and in audiocassette format. The library also subscribes to children's periodicals published in Pakistan. The MCL helps children develop learning skills through reading, and teaches the effective use of books and libraries.

Further, the MCL mission includes providing materials to supplement and enrich the schools, with the aim of helping children to develop "intellectual, artistic or practical pursuits" beyond the curriculum. The MCL holds storytelling hours and also sponsors debates and discussions on the necessity of books being available for children.

The library has space for a million volumes, and its reading facilities accommodate 500 patrons. With an auditorium and programming for seminars, workshops, and conferences—including for training and education of librarians and the encouragement of new technologies—the national library serves as a dynamic cultural and educational center for the city of Islamabad.

Bibliotheca Alexandrina, Egypt

The new "Library of Alexandria" (BA) in Egypt opened in 2002, erected as a tribute to the ancient Alexandria Library that faded away in the first centuries of the Common Era. A landmark building standing in the city's historic eastern harbor, the BA is also a keystone in the restoration of the city, an effort led by preservationists and the Egyptian government to revive a former greatness.

New hotels, art museums, and restaurants have been built as part of Alexandria's resurgence, which includes expanding airports and restoring the eastern harbor. In the works are a promenade and an underwater archaeology museum. Much of the ancient city's ruins are under the sea, including the third-century BCE Pharos lighthouse that symbolized the city as much as it did the world's greatest library. The lighthouse is expected to be replicated in one of the new hotels, and the spirit of the ancient library is being imbued into the new by the growing collections, which include many foreign contributions.

In the old days, it was prosperous Alexandria that sent copies of its books throughout the known world.

Although the city declined with the expulsion of many foreign-born residents during the Suez War in 1956 (Egypt versus the United Kingdom, France, and Israel) its former vibrancy is returning. Native Egyptians have always flocked to the twenty-five miles of Mediterranean beaches nearby, and now scholars make their way to Alexandria to use the modern library, originally constructed at a cost of $220 million.

The library has shelf space for 8 million books—although it opened with only 500,000—and a huge main reading room occupying space on eleven levels under a glass-paneled roof that tilts toward the sea. There is also a conference center, libraries for children and for the blind, four art galleries, a planetarium, and a museum of antiquities. A massive wall of Egyptian (Aswan) granite is inscribed with characters from all the world's written languages.

The library states its mission:

> To be a center of excellence in the production and dissemination of knowledge and to be a place of dialogue, learning and understanding between cultures and peoples.

BA Objectives: The unique role of the Library of Alexandria, as that of a great Egyptian Library with international dimensions, will focus on four main aspects that seek to recapture the spirit of the original ancient Library of Alexandria. It aspires to be: the world's window on Egypt; Egypt's window on the world; a leading institution of the digital age; and a center for learning, tolerance, dialogue and understanding.

The administration asserts that the new Library of Alexandria "is dedicated to [recapturing] the spirit of openness and scholarship of the original Biblio-theca Alexandrina." The BA houses several international institutions, including the Arab Regional Office of the Academy of Science for the Developing World, the International Federation for Library Associations

◀ Bibliotheca Alexandrina, Alexandria, Egypt.

(IFLA) Regional Office, and the Secretariat of the Arab National Commissions of UNESCO.

While donations have included documents from Spain concerning the Moors, and French archives regarding construction of the Suez Canal, the Alexandrina Library is ultramodern, serving as the location of the Internet Archive's external backup. Daily tours are offered in Egyptian, English, Arabic, French, Italian, and Spanish. There is a daily admission fee and a separate fee for visiting the galleries.

National Library of India

Situated in the city of Kolkata, the National Library of India is the country's largest library, and the library of public record. Before India's independence from Great Britain in 1947, the library building—the Belvedere Estate—was the official residence of the lieutenant governor of Bengal. Kolkata, formerly Calcutta to Westerners, is capital of the Indian state of West Bengal.

The library's collection numbers more than 2.2 million books. Operating under the national government's Department of Culture, the library is designated to collect, disseminate, and preserve all printed material produced in India, and all foreign works published about the country—where "every work written about India . . . can be seen and read."

With origins in the privately run Calcutta Public Library, founded in 1836, the national library is built upon the institution that resulted from the 1903 merging of the public library with the Imperial Library (an amalgamation of several government libraries). This merged institution, known as the Imperial Library, contained both Indian and foreign (mostly British) titles, and was open to the public. The name was changed to the National Library in 1953, several years after independence.

The library collects books and periodicals in virtually all the Indian languages, with Hindi, Kashmiri, Punjabi, Sindhi, Telugu, and Urdu divisions maintaining their own stacks. Special collections in at least fifteen languages include books in Assamese, Bengali, Gujarati, Kashmiri, and Tamil, with many rare works. The Hindi department has 80,000 books, some from the nineteenth century, and the first book ever printed in that language. The collection includes more than 86,000 maps and 3,200 manuscripts.

▲ National Library of India, Kolkata.

Herzog August Bibliothek, Germany

One of the world's finest libraries, the Herzog August Bibliothek (HBA) in Wolfenbüttel, Germany—also known as Bibliotheca Augusta—is internationally important for its collections from the Middle Ages and early modern Europe.

Of the library's approximately 1 million books, 350,000 were printed between the fifteenth and eighteenth centuries; 3,500 are incunabula; 75,000 are printed works from the sixteenth century; 150,000 are printed works from the seventeenth century; and 120,000 are from the eighteenth century.

Founded in 1572 by Julius, Duke of Brunswick-Lüneburg (1528–86), the ducal library passed down through the generations. The library is named for Duke Augustus (1579–1666), who built up the collection that was mainly kept at Wolfenbüttel. Although armies passed back and forth over the centuries, the collection was protected. So highly regarded was it that generals placed the library under their special protection. The library is one of the oldest in the world to not have suffered loss to its collection.

Its administrators included two especially prominent figures of the seventeenth and eighteenth centuries: Gottfried Wilhelm Leibniz (1646–1716) and Gotthold Ephraim Lessing (1729–81). It is a famed research library where hundreds of international scholars collaborate with the library staff of various research projects. The library's research programs are described as exploring the "history of international relations, or the history of culture, ideas and politics . . . social history, the history of religion, business, science and law, constitutional history, the history of society, [and] women and gender from the Middle Ages to Early Modern Times."

▲ Herzog August Bibliothek, Wolfenbüttel, Germany.

Bibliotheca Philosophica Hermetica, Amsterdam

A private, independent library in Amsterdam, the Netherlands, the Bibliotheca Philosophica Hermetica (BPH) "brings together manuscripts and printed works in the field of the Hermetic tradition, more specifically the 'Christian-Hermetic' tradition."

The library was founded in the 1950s by art and rare-book collector, Joost R. Ritman (b. 1941), whose lifelong book collection became the heart of the BPH holdings. The term *Hermetica*, according to the library,

is used to cover a heterogeneous body of works attributed to the legendary philosopher Hermes Trismegistus, which are mostly philosophical, theosophical, astrological, magical or alchemical in nature. The treatises we now call the *Corpus Hermeticum*, which is today perhaps the best-known Hermetic work, were compiled mainly in the 2nd–3rd centuries CE and have been preserved in Greek codices (although Coptic fragments have also been recovered in Nag Hammadi in 1945).

The emblem of the Bibliotheca Philosophica Hermetica in Amsterdam. ▶

The BPH collection includes some 20,000 volumes: approximately 600 manuscripts (some 70 from before 1550); 5,000 books printed before 1800 (some 300 of which are incunabula); and 15,000 books (primary and secondary sources) printed after 1800. The library seeks the oldest examples of works which fall within its sphere of interest, described as follows:

> The term "Christian-Hermetic" serves as a reminder that the Hermetic works were commented on and/or absorbed in the Christian context, initially in the works of the Church Fathers, notably Augustine and Lactantius. After a long spell of neglect, the Hermetic treatises now known as the *Corpus Hermeticum* were re-discovered in the Renaissance when philosophers like Marsilio Ficino and Giovanni Pico della Mirandola sought to harmonise (Neo)platonism, Pythagoreanism, and other philosophies regarded as part of a *prisca theologia*, with the prevailing Christian heritage.

The BPH collection includes works of Western esotericism, non-Western philosophy and religion, Gnosticism, Kabala, and Sufism, as well as many engravings and artworks—some as old as the sixteenth century, depicting theologians, philosophers, scholars, and various aspects of books and manuscripts.

The library is at Bloemstraat 13-19, Amsterdam, and is open to the public. The library does not lend its holdings, but they are available to researchers on request for use in the reading rooms. The BPH also has a searchable online catalog.

Abbey Library of St. Gall, Switzerland

The Abbey Library of St. Gall in the city of St. Gallen, Switzerland, was established by Saint Othmar, the founder of the Abbey of St. Gall in 719—one of the chief Benedictine monasteries in Europe. Since Othmar's time, letters and the study of sciences have flourished at the Abbey despite its being raided and pillaged over the years, with many books lost.

In 973, the abbey was destroyed by fire—except for the library, which remained undamaged. The oldest library in Switzerland, it is one of the most important monastic libraries in the world. The library's eighteenth-century baroque-style hall is one of the most beautiful non-sacred rooms in Switzerland, and one of the world's most perfect library halls. The library has been described as having the world's richest medieval collection.

The library holds 2,100 manuscripts from the eighth through the fifteenth centuries, more than 1,600 incunabula, and many rare, old printed books. Here, too, is the oldest-known manuscript (thirteenth-century) of the pre-Christian Germanic epic poem, *Nibelungenlied* (*Song of the Nibelungs*). The abbey also possesses the oldest major architectural drawing from the High Middle Ages—the "Plan of St. Gall," from its own design.

In 1983, the library and abbey were named a UNESCO Cultural World Heritage Site: "a perfect example of a great Carolingian monastery." The city itself contains magnificent architecture, including the baroque Cathedral of St. Gallen, which was formerly part of the abbey.

The library offers public exhibitions, concerts, and other events with many visitors, as it states:

> In addition to its role as a modern research library specialising in the medieval period, the Abbey Library is one of Switzerland's leading museums. Each year, some 100,000 visitors come from all over the world to view the exhibitions in the renowned Baroque Library, which is considered by many to be one of the most beautiful library buildings in the world.

▲ Abbey Library of St. Gall, St. Gallen, Switzerland.

There are almost 160,000 volumes, most available for public use—although those printed before 1900 must be kept in the reading room. A virtual library provides access to manuscripts, with a growing number preserved in digital format.

Kederminster Library, England

The Kederminster Library, in the county of Berkshire, is preserved as it was—a rare example of an early seventeenth-century English parish library. Founded at St. Mary's Church, Langley Marish, by Sir John Kederminster in 1613, the library even has its original cupboards from 1620.

The library was presented by Sir John for the education of St. Mary's rector. The library's 1638 catalog lists more than three hundred theological works, and many of the original collection still survive. Kederminster's two most precious titles are on permanent loan to the British Library: one is the eleventh-century illuminated manuscript, *Kederminster Gospels*, and the other is the 1630 "booke of Medicine" manuscript, *Pharmacopolium*.

The library is governed by a charitable trust and open from June to September, or by appointment.

Huntington Library, United States

The Huntington Library, Art Collections, and Botanical Gardens compose a private, nonprofit institution for education and research in San Marino, California. "The Huntington" was established in 1919 by Henry E. Huntington (1850–1927), whose financial empire included railroad companies, utilities, and real estate.

In addition to the library, there is an art collection "strong in English portraits" and eighteenth-century French furniture, and also the renowned botanical gardens.

The Huntington Library contains some 6.5 million manuscripts and more than a million rare books, with the greatest concentration in the English Renaissance era, (about 1500 to 1641). On permanent exhibit are a Gutenberg Bible, printed on vellum, and Chaucer's Ellesmere manuscript of *Canterbury Tales*. The Huntington owns the first two quartos of *Hamlet*, the manuscript of Benjamin Franklin's autobiography, and authors' drafts of Henry David Thoreau's *Walden* and John James Audubon's *Birds of America*. One of the most important collections is composed of several thousand historical documents about Abraham Lincoln.

The Huntington Library's rare books, manuscripts, prints, photographs, maps, and other materials in the fields of British and American history and literature are among the most studied in the United States, with 1,700

▼ Huntington Library, San Marino, California.

scholars visiting annually. Use is extremely restricted, however, because of the delicate and rare nature of the materials. Readers generally require at least candidacy for a doctoral degree. The library often places items from its book and manuscript collections on view for the general public.

The library describes Huntington as "a man of vision":

> During his lifetime, he amassed the core of one of the finest research libraries in the world, established a splendid art collection, and created an array of botanical gardens with plants from a geographic range spanning the globe. These three distinct facets of The Huntington are linked by a devotion to research, education, and beauty.

Folger Shakespeare Library, United States

The Folger Shakespeare Library, on Capitol Hill in Washington, D.C., is an independent research library with the world's largest collection of materials on English playwright William Shakespeare (c. 1564–1616). The library, founded in 1932, has seventy-nine copies of the 1623 Shakespeare *First Folio*—the collection of thirty-six plays titled *Mr. William Shakespeares Comedies, Histories, & Tragedies*. The Folger houses major collections of other rare Renaissance books, manuscripts, and works of art, serving researchers, visitors, teachers, students, and families.

Established by former Standard Oil of New York president (and collector of Shakespeareana) Henry C. Folger (1857–1930), the library possesses more than 256,000 books, 60,000 manuscripts, a quarter of a million playbills, 200 oil paintings, and 50,000 drawings, watercolors, prints, and photographs. The Folger also has musical instruments, costumes, and films. Its two main collections are materials related to the era (in the West) from 1450 to the mid-1700s, and materials related to both Shakespeare and theater to the present age.

The library was a gift to the American people from Folger and his wife, Emily Jordan Folger. It is administered under the auspices of Amherst College, Amherst, Massachusetts, Henry Folger's alma mater. A renowned Shakespeare research center and a resource for scholarship in the early modern

▲ Folger Shakespeare Library, Washington, D.C.

age in the West, its conservation lab is a leader in the preservation of rare materials. Public arts and cultural events include theater, concerts, readings, family activities, exhibitions, and extensive educational programs (including seminars, symposia, and conferences) are offered for students and teachers.

The Folger publishes exhibition catalogs, illustrated editions of Shakespeare's plays, and the journal, *Shakespeare Quarterly*.

American Antiquarian Society, United States

The American Antiquarian Society (AAS) is both a learned society and national research library of the history and culture of pre-twentieth-century United States. Antiquarian Hall, its main building, is located in Worcester, Massachusetts, and is a National Historic Landmark.

Established in 1812 by an act of the Commonwealth of Massachusetts, the society's mission is to collect, preserve, and make available for study the printed records of the United States, including those from the first European settlement through the year 1876.

The AAS offers programs for professional scholars, students, educators, artists, writers, and genealogists, as well as for the general public. Digital collections include "A New Nation Votes: American Election Returns 1788–1824."

The AAS library began with the 8,000 books of founder Isaiah Thomas (1749–1831), Boston-born newspaper publisher, printer, and author. The society's membership has included many distinguished Americans, including a number of presidents. The purpose of the AAS founders, according to the society, was to

> establish an organization to "encourage the collection and preservation of the Antiquities of our country, and of curious and valuable productions in Art and Nature [that] have a tendency to enlarge the sphere of human knowledge." Further, they wished to promote the use of such collections in order to "aid the progress of science, to perpetuate the history of moral and political events, and to improve and interest posterity."

The library collection numbers more than 3 million books, pamphlets, newspapers, periodicals, graphic arts materials, and manuscripts. The AAS holds copies of two-thirds of the books printed before 1820 in the United States. One of the rarest is a copy of the 1640 *Bay Psalm Book*, a book of hymns and the first book printed in British North America (Cambridge, Massachusetts).

Newberry Library, United States

◀ American Antiquarian Society, Worcester, Massachuse

The Newberry Library is a private, noncirculating research library for the humanities and social sciences in Chicago, Illinois. Established in 1887 by a bequest from philanthropist Walter L. Newberry (1804–68), the library is free and open to the public. It is located across from Washington Square Park.

Newberry wished to create a library that would be "the pride and boast of our city." He died at sea in 1868 while en route to Europe. His will provided that, if his two daughters died without issue, half the remaining estate would be used to found a public library in Chicago. Neither married or had children, so the bequest was used to establish the Newberry Library.

The Newberry houses more than 1.5 million books, 5 million manuscript pages, and half a million historic maps. Its major collections include materials from the Renaissance, genealogy, American Indians, early music, cartography, the history of printing, Chicago history, railroad archives, Brazilian history, and manuscripts by Midwestern authors. The Library also offers teacher programs, seminars, programming, and exhibits.

The mission statement reads in part:

> The Newberry acquires and preserves a broad array of special collections research materials relating to the civilizations of Europe and the Americas. [The library fosters] research, teaching, publication, and life-long learning, as well as civic engagement.

▲ The Newberry Library, Chicago.

Among the most valuable works are Thomas Jefferson's copy of the *Feder-alist Papers* and the only copy in existence of the *Popol Vuh* (*Book of the Community*), an eighteenth-century transcription of a book from Guatemala, in the era between the eleventh and thirteenth centuries. Written in Latin and thought to have been copied from an original Mayan codex, the *Popul Vuh* is perhaps the most important extant work of Mesoamerican literature.

Cambridge University Library, England

With 7 million books and more than 1.2 million periodicals, as well as maps, manuscripts, and special collections (including music), Cambridge Univerity Library is the centrally administered library of the University of Cambridge in England. It comprises five separate libraries: the University Library (UL) main building, the Medical Library, the Betty and Gordon Moore Library (Centre for Mathematical Sciences), the Central Science Library (formerly the Scientific Periodicals Library), and the Squire Law Library.

The earliest known references to a library at the university in Cambridge are to be found in the fifteenth-century wills, one of which bequeaths three volumes "to remain forever in the new library at Cambridge for the use of graduates and scholars in residence." In the previous century, library bene-factors donated books along with valuables and monies to the university. Collections of works on canon law and theology were among the first libraries at Cambridge. In the late 1400s there were 330 volumes, mostly of law and religion, very little by classical authors, and no early Christian authors or English chroniclers.

Until the seventeenth century, two rooms were sufficient to house the university library. Many titles were lost during the Reformation era, when theological works in university and ecclesiastical libraries were subject to destruction or removal. New efforts to establish a major library—especially one to challenge the Bodleian at Oxford—resulted in the acquisition of major private collections, some of the purchases financed by acts of Parlia-ment. One private library contained more than 10,000 volumes, another possessed 4,000, and the Royal Library of George I had 30,000 books; all of these were received in 1715. New quarters accommodated the growth, which was matched by the development of the university itself.

The library's status as a legal deposit library brought greater responsibilities to maintain and organize titles sent by English publishers. The library steadily acquired private collections, reorganized its administration along departmental lines, and, by the early twentieth century, was in need of a larger building.

In 1934, the present premises were built, with thanks largely to funding from the Rockefeller Foundation. Several accomplished directors, over the next few years, improved the institution's capacity for the pursuit of scholarship by university students and staff. The library has been extended a number of times to house collections that range from a fifteenth-century Gutenberg Bible to Japanese and Chinese works; ancient Hebrew and Arabic manuscripts; and codices in Arabic, Persian, and Turkish. One of the largest collections is the 60,000 volumes of the library of Lord Acton (1834–1902), professor of modern history at Cambridge from 1885 to 1902.

Cambridge University Library also possesses an archive of the correspondence and books from the working library of English naturalist Charles Darwin (1809–82).

National Library of Medicine, United States

The United States National Library of Medicine (NLM) was established in 1836 as part of the United States Surgeon General's Office, a department of the army. Operated by the federal government's Department of Health, Education, and Welfare, the NLM is the world's largest medical library. The NLM is in Bethesda, Maryland, on the campus of the National Institutes of Health (NIH).

The NIH is responsible for medical and behavioral research "in pursuit of fundamental knowledge about the nature and behavior of living systems and the application of that knowledge."

The National Library of Medicine collects materials and provides information in all areas of biomedicine and health care. The collections, on medicine and related sciences, include more than 7 million books, journals, technical reports, manuscripts, microfilms, photographs, and images. Some items are among the world's oldest and rarest works.

Since 1879, the NLM has published the monthly *Index Medicus*, a guide to articles in nearly 5,000 selected journals. This information is now offered online in the freely accessible search engine, PubMed. More than 15 million MEDLINE journal article references and abstracts go back to the 1960s, and 1.5 million references are from the 1950s.

A division of the NLM provides grants for research in medical information science, as well as for medical institutions to develop computer and communications systems. The NLM also supports research, publications, and exhibitions on the history of medicine and the life sciences.

University of Texas, Austin United States

The University of Texas has twenty-seven libraries whose holdings rank in the national top ten, in terms of volumes, with more than 8.5 million. The main library is especially strong in its Latin American Collection. The library also offers a map collection, with many online.

The research libraries' collections include 320,000 cartographic items, 11.4 million graphic items, 180,000 audio, and 118,000 manuscripts and archives. There are 6.5 million microforms and 40,000 film and video items.

The research libraries concentrate on areas such as architecture and planning, audiovisual, Latin America, chemistry, engineering, fine arts, law, marine science, physics, and geology. The library centers include the Center

for American History and the Harry Ransom Center. The Ransom Center's mission is to further the study of the arts and humanities. The Center was founded in 1957 by university vice president and provost, Harry Huntt Ransom (1908–76), who evoked the French national library when he called for Texas to establish "a center of cultural compass, a research center to be the *Bibliothèque Nationale* of the only state that started out as an independent nation."

The Ransom rare books research collection, built on major donations that started to be received in the late nineteenth century, contains more than a million titles, 36 million leaves of

◀ The landmark Main Building Tower of the University of Texas at Austin.

manuscripts, 5 million photographs, and 100,000 works of art, in addition to major holdings in theater arts and film. The center acquired a Gutenberg Bible copy in 1978 in commemoration of Ransom's service.

In 1971, the first presidential library on a university campus was dedicated at Austin for president Lyndon B. Johnson (1908–73). Constructed on the main campus, the Lyndon Baines Johnson Library and Museum is home to 40 million pages of historical documents, including the papers of President Johnson (a Texan) and his close associates. The library occupies fourteen acres of campus and contains a small-scale replica of the White House Oval Office as it appeared during the Johnson administration of the 1960s.

Harvard University Libraries United States

The Harvard University system includes more than seventy libraries, which serve the university's current faculty, students, staff, and researchers who hold valid Harvard identification for admittance. Some collections are open to the public, but most are reserved for the Harvard community.

Established in 1638, the Harvard system is the oldest in the United States, and its more than 13.1 million books compose the world's largest academic library and the fourth-largest library collection overall. The system is centered in the largest—Widener Library—in Harvard Yard, Cambridge, Massachusetts. Unlike most of the world's largest libraries, the Widener has open stacks, permitting its patrons to browse the collection.

The library and college were founded in colonial Massachusetts at the bequest of English-born clergyman John Harvard, who contributed four hundred books—and his name—to the institution.

More than twenty university libraries are grouped under the Faculty of Arts and Science, including the Biochemical Sciences Tutorial, Biological Laboratories, the Meteorological Observatory, History of Science, Linguistics, Sanskrit, Statistics, and the Peabody Museum Archives. Harvard College libraries include the Cabot Science Library, Fine Arts, Houghton, Loeb Music Library, and the Widener.

The libraries of other Harvard faculties include the Andover-Harvard Theological Library, Baker Library, Countway Library of Medicine, Harvard Law School, Frances Loeb, John F. Kennedy School of Government, and the Schlesinger Library on the History of Women in America.

▲ Widener Library, in Harvard Yard, Cambridge, Massachusetts.

As with all major libraries, the Harvard system is vitally concerned with digitizing its resources and making the results available to users. The Library Digital Initiative (LDI) began in 1998

> to create an infrastructure to support the "collecting" of digital resources at Harvard similar to the infrastructure the libraries have long had for the collecting of research resources in other formats. "Infrastructure" was defined broadly to include not just automated systems, but also staff expertise and service facilities.

The Library Digital Initiative addresses issues arising from the university's decentralized structure and develops "solutions to the technical and organizational challenges of digital collections . . . in a general, sophisticated, and coordinated way." The intent of the Initiative is to simplify the methods of making digital research materials available, and also to ensure that the digital collection is "well organized and accessible as the libraries have always tried to make traditional collections."

Bodleian Library, England

The Bodleian Library, founded in 1602 by bibliophile and retired diplomat Thomas Bodley (1545–1613), is considered "chief" among Oxford University's forty libraries, and is described as holding a "special place" in the university community. Following in the tracks of a defunct fifteenth-century Oxford library, the Bodleian began operations in the same quarters. Those buildings remained intact over the centuries and, for the most part, are still in use.

Bodley's library grew steadily along with the university, enlarged by rich bequests that included major book collections. By the twentieth century, as the library's history narrates it:

▲ The Bodleian Library, Oxford.

> the Bodleian's book collection was growing by more than 30,000 volumes a year, and the number of books had reached the million mark by 1914. To provide extra storage space an underground book store was excavated beneath Radcliffe Square in 1909–12; it was at the time the largest such store in the world, and the first to use modern compact shelving. But with both readers and books inexorably increasing, the pressure on space once more became critical . . .

A new library was built in 1937–40, with book stacks for 5 million volumes and space for library departments and reading rooms. Sixty percent of the book stacks are below ground level. Restoration, renovations, and new construction transformed the facilities and, by 1975, the Bodleian quarters were expanded until they occupied the seventeenth-century structures that had been the "historic core of the University."

The Bodleian, which has legal deposit status, houses 11 million volumes, including those in several off-site storage areas (one a disused salt mine in Cheshire), as well as in nine other libraries at Oxford, among them a Japanese library, law library, the Indian Institute Library, and a science library. The "Bod," as it is known, is the United Kingdom's second-largest library, after the British Library.

The Bodleian's special collections of rare books, manuscripts, archives, maps, and music are undergoing extensive digitization. Every day, hundreds of thousands of scholars download digital resources. As with most Oxford University libraries, the Bodleian is open to the university community, who apply for a reader's card. Others may apply to use the Bodleian "for legitimate purposes of study."

The Vatican Library, Rome

The Vatican Library is the library of the Holy See—the jurisdictional territory of the Bishop of Rome, also known as the Pope, head of the Roman Catholic Church. The Holy See is located in Vatican City, within the city of Rome.

Among the oldest libraries in the world, with some volumes surviving from the earliest days of the Church, the Vatican Library contains one of the greatest collections of historical texts. Until the mid-fifteenth century, Church events and schisms alternately built and scattered the papal collections. The library holdings were moved to the Vatican in 1448, and the Bibliotheca Apostolica Vaticana collection grew in accordance with the wishes of individual popes.

Pope Sixtus IV (1471–84), a bibliophile, formally established the library in 1475, with approximately 3,500 items—then one of the world's largest collections. It was Sixtus IV who first housed the library in the Vatican palace. Pope Sixtus V (1521–90) commissioned the construction of a new library, still in use in the twenty-first century. Acquisitions through purchase and donations built up the collections, especially donations from Catholic military leaders who captured books from Protestant enemies in the Thirty Years' War of the early sixteenth century.

◀ The Vatican library's Sistine Hall.

As centuries passed, successive popes took increased interest in the library, which grew steadily, and the addition of antiquarian non-book treasures—coins, medals, early Christian artifacts (including ivories, enamels, bronzes, glassware, and earthenware) and works of art—led to the establishment of museum collections. The library suffered considerable loss of its museum holdings during the occupation of Rome by French forces between 1798 and 1809.

The Vatican Library grew to have 1.1 million printed books, including some 8,500 incunabula. There are also 75,000 codices. The Vatican Secret Archives, with another 150,000 items, is available to research. There are more than 300,000 coins and medals, and more than 70,000 prints and engravings.

In 2002, the new Periodicals Reading Room, where material is available on open shelves, was opened to the public. In July 2007, the library was closed for refurbishment that was expected to require three years to complete.

The Clark Library, United States

Established in 1962, the library of the Sterling and Francine Clark Art Institute in Williamstown, Massachusetts, is one of the major art reference and research libraries in the United States.

The Clark is a renowned art museum and a center for research and higher education, "dedicated to advancing and extending the public understanding of art," according to its literature. The Clark, which opened in 1955 in rural western Massachusetts, features a collection of more than thirty Pierre-Auguste Renoirs, along with works by Frans Hals, Francisco Goya, Edgar Degas, and Winslow Homer.

Focusing on post–medieval European and American art, the Clark's library collection is outstanding in the Italian and Northern Renaissance, Baroque, and French nineteenth-century

Sterling and Francine Clark Art Institute, Williamstown, Massachusetts. ▶

fields—reflecting the interests of the Clark's founders, Sterling (1877–1956) and Francine Clark (1876–1960), husband and wife and lifelong art collectors. The Clark's library is well balanced in other areas: a recent grant has helped to expand collections of works on contemporary Asian, African, and Latin American art.

The library's resources include approximately 230,000 books, bound periodicals, and auction sales catalogs, with current journal subscriptions numbering around 650. Founded on the libraries of the Duveen Brothers (New York), international art dealers, and of the late Dutch art historian, W. R. Juynboll, the Clark's library holds important collections of books on the decorative arts and on early-twentieth-century art (with particular strengths in Dada, Surrealism, and Conceptual Art).

Sterling Clark's personal library—part of the collection—is notable for its illustrated titles, fine bindings, and rare editions. In addition, the Clark's library holdings include a collection of twentieth-century artists' books.

Arranged in open stacks—unlike most research libraries whose stacks are closed—the library is noncirculating outside the premises, but study areas are available throughout. The library is free and open to the public on weekdays.

Smithsonian Institution Libraries, United States

The Smithsonian Institution Libraries (SIL) is a system of twenty libraries serving the various Smithsonian Institute museums and research centers. Most of the libraries are in Washington, D.C.—as are the museums and research centers—while others are in New York City, Maryland, and Panama. The SIL's main offices are in the National Museum of Natural History in Washington, D.C.

The SIL collections have especially strong holdings in most of the Institution's disciplines: natural history, history of science and technology, anthropology, philately and postal history, African and Asian art, American art and portraiture, aviation, space exploration, botany and horticulture, decorative arts and design, tropical biology, museology (management and organization of museums and museum collections), and Native American and African American history and culture. The holdings include 1.5 million volumes, with 40,000 rare books.

▲ The Smithsonian Institution's headquarters is in "The Castle" on the National Mall, Washington, D.C. The Smithsonian's library system comprises twenty libraries in various research centers and museums.

The SIL system offers a wide array of digital resources. The catalog is part of the Smithsonian Institution Research Information System (SIRIS), of which 1.89 million records of text, images, video, and sound files from across the Smithsonian Institution can be searched. The Digital Library includes publications, collections, online exhibits, webcasts, finding aids, digital versions of print editions, and bibliographies, as well as other resources.

According to SIL:

> Smithsonian Libraries, though a plural noun, is consistently followed by a singular verb because it is considered a system of libraries, with individual locations operating under the aegis of a central administration and adhering to a common mission.

A major aspect of SIL's stated long-range plan is to bring the Smithsonian's many programs and holdings to a wider audience, especially through online technology. The Biodiversity Heritage Library, a "major digital initiative," is a consortium of the world's leading natural history libraries. The Biodiversity Heritage Online Portal links to their resources, which include more than 10,000 titles, 29,000 volumes, and almost 12 million pages:

> The group is developing a strategy and operational plan to digitize the published literature of biodiversity held in their respective collections. This literature will be available through a global "biodiversity commons."

Among the libraries is the National Museum of American History Library in Washington, D.C. The NMAH Branch Library houses more than 120,000 books. At the broadest level, the NMAH Branch Library collections are concerned with the history of science and technology and its impact on Americans.

The Smithsonian American Art Museum / National Portrait Gallery Library in Washington, D.C., has a collection of 180,000 books, exhibition catalogs, *catalogues raisonnés* (scholarly compilations of an artist's body of work), serials, and dissertations. The collection is concentrated on American art, history, and biography, with supportive materials on European art.

The Dibner Library of the History of Science and Technology, founded in 1976, contains 35,000 books and 2,000 manuscripts. The Dibner is housed in the National Museum of American History. Another institution is the Cullman Library of Natural History, which has some 10,000 volumes from before 1840 in the fields of anthropology and natural sciences.

In New York, the Cooper-Hewitt, National Design Museum Library (The Doris and Henry Dreyfuss Study Center) contains 60,000 volumes which document and support the museum's collection of 250,000 objects in decorative arts—including textiles, wall coverings, metalwork, furniture, ceramics, glass, jewelry, prints, and drawings.

ACKNOWLEDGMENTS

SOURCES

The author wishes to thank those who contributed to this book, to acknowledge their part in what is right and to take responsibility for the rest.

Thanks to all the libraries and librarians who offered images for, and insights into, the many libraries mentioned in these pages. And to those who saw the importance of this story from the beginning: book editors Donna Sanzone and Lisa Hacken, who made it possible for us to develop this volume and lay its foundations; to Lisa DiMona of Lark Productions, who represented our work to Skyhorse Publishing, and to those at Skyhorse who took on this project: Tony Lyons, William Wolfsthal, and our hardworking, able editor, Julie Matysik.

For the inner strength of the work, thanks go to Aaron Murray of Lily Book Productions for his picture research and editing and to Donald Davis for keeping us straight with the facts and spirit of the book. And thanks to Nicholas Basbanes for his supportive foreword.

Those who contributed in other important ways include Jeremy A. Murray, Marianne Boersma, Michael Calvello, Elaine and Chris Supkis, and George Engel. And thanks to Irene and Chris Monson, whose encouragement has been invaluable.

These individuals all share with the author certain characteristics—they love books and value libraries. And now we also share this history of the library.

—SM
Berlin, New York

The following abbreviations are used:
Library of Congress, Prints and Photographs Collection—LC
Wikimedia Commons—Wiki

Frontispiece: ii Wiki.

Chapter 1: The Ancient Libraries
2 Wiki; **5** *Asshur and the Land of Nimrod*, by Hormuzd Rassam; **6** John Said/iStockphoto.com; **8** Wiki; **10** Wiki, http://commons.wikimedia.org/wiki/File:Egypte_louvre_144_hieroglyphes.jpg; **11** Wiki; **12** private collection; **13** private collection; **16** Clipart.com; **18** Library of Congress, African and Middle Eastern Division, Hebraic Section; **20** Wiki; **21** private collection.

Chapter 2: European Libraries of the Middle Ages
22 Wiki; **25** Wiki; **26** Wiki; **29** Wiki; **30** *Book of Days*; **32** Wiki; **33** LC; **34** Wiki; **35** Wiki, http://en.wikipedia.org/wiki/File:Abbey_of_Kells.jpg; **36** Wiki, http://en.wikipedia.org/wiki/File:Walraversijde25.jpg; **37** Wiki; **40** LC.

Chapter 3: Asia and Islam
42 Wiki; **44** Wiki; **45** Wiki; **46** Library of Congress, Asian Division, Korean Section; **48** Wiki, http://commons.wikimedia.org/wiki/File:Korea-Haeinsa-Tripitaka_Koreana-03.jpg; **50** Wiki; **51** Wiki; **52** Wiki; **53** Wiki; **54** Wiki/Wolfgang Lettko; **54** Wiki; **56** Wiki.

Chapter 4: Europe's High Middle Ages
58 Wiki; **60** Wiki; **62** Wiki; **63** Wiki; **64** private collection; **66** Wiki; **68** Wiki, http://commons.wikimedia.org/wiki/File:Aristoteles_Logica_1570_Biblioteca_Huelva.jpg; **69** private collection; **69** Wiki; **71** LC; **72** private collection; **73** Wiki, http://en.wikipedia.org/wiki/File:Metal_movable_type.jpg; **74** LC; **75** Wiki.

Chapter 5: Renaissance to Reformation
76 Wiki, http://commons.wikimedia.org/wiki/File:Biblioteca_Duomo_Siena-2_Apr_2008.jpg; **78** private collection; **79** Wiki, http://en.wikipedia.org/wiki/File:IMG_0797_-_Perugia_-_San_Bernardino_-_Agostino_di_Duccio_-1457-61-_-_Falò_delle_vanità_-_Foto_G._Dall%27O2.jpg; **80** private collection; **81** private collection; **82** Wiki; **83** Wiki; **85**

Wiki, http://commons.wikimedia.org/wiki/File:Escorial_-_Biblioteca.jpg; **86-87** Wiki, http://en.wikipedia.org/wiki/File:El_escorial_eingangsseite.jpg; **88** Wiki; **89** Wiki, http://en.wikipedia.org/wiki/File:Wien_Prunksaal_Oesterreichische_Nationalbibliothek.jpg; **91** Wiki, http://en.wikipedia.org/wiki/File:EinFesteBurg.jpg; **92-93** Wiki, http://en.wikipedia.org/wiki/File:Fountains_Abbey_view_crop1_2005-08-27.jpg.

Chapter 6: People of the Book
96 Wiki; **98** Wiki; **99** Wiki, http://en.wikipedia.org/wiki/File:Djingareiber_cour.jpg; **102** Wiki; **103** Wiki; **104** Wiki; **105** Wiki; **106** Wiki, http://en.wikipedia.org/wiki/File:Amritsar-golden-temple-00.JPG; **108** Wiki; **110** Wiki; **111** Wiki; **112** Wiki; **112** Wiki.

Chapter 7: War and a Golden Age
114 private collection; **116** *The Book-Hunter in London*, by William Roberts; **117** Wiki; **118** private collection; **120** Wiki; **121** Wiki; **123** Wiki; **124** Wiki; **125** Wiki; **126** Clipart.com; **129** private collection; **132** Clipart.com; **133** Wiki.

Chapter 8: The Library in Colonial North America
134 LC; **136** LC; **137** The Architect of the Capitol; **138** Wiki; **139** Wiki; **140** LC; **144** LC; **145** private collection; **146** LC; **147** LC; **149** LC; **150** LC; **151** LC.

Chapter 9: The Library in the Young United States
152 LC; **154**LC; **154** LC; **156** LC; **157** LC; **158** LC; **159** LC; **160** LC; **162** LC; **165** private collection; **165** private collection; **169** LC; **170** private collection; **171** Wiki.

Chapter 10: The Library Movement
172 LC; **174** LC; **175** LC; **176** LC; **178** private collection; **181** private collection; **181** LC; **182** LC; **184** LC; **185** LC; **186** Wiki, http://en.wikipedia.org/wiki/File:Teddington_Carnegie_Library.jpg; **188** LC; **191** LC.

Chapter 11: Organizing Knowledge
192 LC; **194** *The Book-Hunter in London*, by William Roberts; **197** LC; **199** LC; **200** LC; **201** LC; **201** LC; **202** private collection; **203** private collection; **204** Wiki; **206** LC; **208** LC; **208** LC; **211** Wiki, http://en.wikipedia.org/wiki/File:Mandalay_kuthodaw.jpg; **212** LC; **213** LC.

Chapter 12: Libraries, Librarians, and Media Centers
214 LC; **216** LC; **217** Wiki/Charlie Fong; **220** Wiki/Erica Kowal, http://commons.wikimedia.org/wiki/File:InstitutIslamiqueDakar2.jpg; **222** LC; **223** Wiki, http://en.wikipedia.org/wiki/File:Evstafiev-bosnia-cello.jpg; **224** LC; **225** Wiki, http://en.wikipedia.org/wiki/File:Biblioburro.jpg; **226** wiki, http://en.wikipedia.org/wiki/File:20041216getty06pano.jpg; **228** LC; **231** LC; **232** "Inquiring Minds" by Kirsten Baker, Liverpool (N.Y.) Public Library (grand prize winner in the American Library Association's Beyond Words Photo Contest).

Libraries of the World
236 Wiki, http://en.wikipedia.org/wiki/File:Bibliotèque_nationale_de_France,_site_Richelieu_(salle_ovale).JPG; **238-239** Wiki, http://commons.wikimedia.org/wiki/File:British_Museum_Reading_Room_Panorama_Feb_2006_edit1.jpg; **241** Wiki, http://commons.wikimedia.org/wiki/File:Wien_Nationalbibliothek5.jpg; **244** LC; **245** Wiki, http://en.wikipedia.org/wiki/File:Library_and_Archives_Canada.JPG; **247** Wiki; **248** Wiki, http://commons.wikimedia.org/wiki/File:Grande_bibliotheque_du_Quebec-mail_hall.jpg; **250** Wiki, http://en.wikipedia.org/wiki/File:Albertine_Bxl.JPG; **251** Wiki; **252**Wiki, http://commons.wikimedia.org/wiki/File:HK_Hong-KongCentralLibrary.JPG; **254** Wiki, http://commons.wikimedia.org/wiki/File:BNCF.JPG; **256** courtesy of the New York Public Library (photo by Don Pollard); **258** Wiki, http://en.wikipedia.org/wiki/File:Brooklyn_Public_Library_by_DS.JPG; Wiki/Douglas Kaye; **259** Wiki, http://en.wikipedia.org/wiki/File:Bates_Hall_Boston.jpg; **261** Wiki; **265** Wiki, http://en.wikipedia.org/wiki/File:Interior_of_LA_Central_Library.jpg; **266** Wiki, http://en.wikipedia.org/wiki/File:National_Library_Beijing_China.jpg; **270** Wiki; **273** http://en.wikipedia.org/wiki/File:NLA_Canberra-01JAC.JPG; **275** Wiki, http://en.wikipedia.org/wiki/File:National_Diet_Library_Japan.jpg; **277** Wiki, http://commons.wikimedia.org/wiki/File:Bibliotecanacional2.jpg; **277** Wiki, http://en.wikipedia.org/wiki/File:Ardon_Windows_JNUL.jpg; **278** Wiki; **279** Wiki/Hessam Armandehi, http://en.wikipedia.org/wiki/File:National-Library.

jpg; **282** Wiki, http://commons.wikimedia.org/wiki/File:GD-EG-BibAlex-Ext_depuis_parvis.jpg; **284** Wiki, http://en.wikipedia.org/wiki/File:India_Education.jpg; **285** Wiki, http://commons.wikimedia.org/wiki/File:Wolfenbuettel_Herzog-August-Bibliothek_Innen1_(2006).jpg; **285** courtesy of the Bibliotheca Philosophica Hermetica, Amsterdam; **287** Wiki, http://en.wikipedia.org/wiki/File:BibliothekSG.jpg; **288-289** Wiki, http://en.wikipedia.org/wiki/File:Huntington_art_gallery_at_huntington_library_california.jpg; **291** LC; **292** wiki, http://en.wikipedia.org/wiki/File:American_Antiquarian_Library1.jpg; **293** Wiki, http://en.wikipedia.org/wiki/File:20070329_Newberry_Library2.JPG; **296** Wiki, http://en.wikipedia.org/wiki/File:UT_Tower_lit_white_with_orange_top.jpg; **298** Wiki, http://commons.wikimedia.org/wiki/File:Harvard_University_Widener_Library.jpg; **299** Wiki, http://en.wikipedia.org/wiki/File:Bodleian_Library.jpg; **300** Wiki, http://commons.wikimedia.org/wiki/File:Sistinehall.jpg; **301** courtesy of the Sterling and Francine Clark Art Institute; **303** Wiki.

Cover Credits:
Front cover: Wiki / David Iliff, http://commons.wikimedia.org/wiki/File:NYC_Public_Library_Research_Room_Jan_2006.jpg

Back cover: Wiki.

FOR FURTHER READING

Basbanes, Nicholas A. *A Gentle Madness: Bibliophiles, Bibliomanes, and the Eternal Passion for Books*. New York: Owl Books, 1999Battles, Matthew. *Library: An Unquiet History*. New York and London: W.W. Norton, 2003.

Birrell, Augustine. *In the Name of the Bodleian, and Other Essays*. London: Elliot Stock, 1905

Casson, Lionel. *Libraries in the Ancient World*. New Haven: Yale University Press, 2002

Davies, D. W. *Public Libraries as Culture and Social Centers: The Origin of the Concept*. Metuchen, N.J.: Scarecrow Press, 1974.

Dixon, Paul. *The Library in America: A Celebration in Words and Pictures*. New York and Oxford: Facts on File, 1986.

Griliches, Diane Asséo. *Library: The Drama Within*. Albuquerque: The University of New Mexico Press, 1996.

Hewins, Caroline M. *A Mid-Century Child and her Books*. New York: MacMillan, 1926.

Hobson, Anthony. *Great Libraries*. New York: G.P. Putnam's Sons 1970.

de Laubier, Guillaume, Jacques Bosser, and James H. Billington. *The Most Beautiful Libraries in the World*. New York: Harry N. Abrams, 2003

Laugher, Charles T. *Thomas Bray's Grand Design: Libraries of the Church of England in America*. Chicago: American Library Association, 1973.

Lerner, Fred. *The Story of Libraries from the Invention of Writing to the Computer Age*. New York: The Continuum International Publishing Group, 1998.

Levinson, David and Karen Christensen, Eds. *Heart of the Community: Libraries We Love*. Great Barrington, Massachusetts: Berkshire Publishing Group, 2006.

Olmert, Michael. *Smithsonian Book of Books*. Washington, D.C.: Smithsonian Books, 1992.

Rassam, Hormuzd, *Asshur and the Land of Nimrod*. New York: Eaton and Mains, 1897.

Schuchat, T. *The Library Book*. Seattle: Madrona Publishers, 1985.

Shera, Jesse H. *Foundations of the Public Library: The origins of the public library movement in New England, 1629-1855*. Chicago: University of Chicago Press, 1952.

Staikos, Konstantinos S., *The Great Libraries: From Antiquity to the Renaissance*. New Castle, Delaware, and London: Oak Knoll Press and the British Library, 2000.

Tolzmann, Don Heinrich, Alfred Hessel, and Reuben Peiss. *The Memory of Mankind*. New Castle, Delaware: Oak Knoll Press, 2001.

Wiegand, Wayne A. and Donald G. Davis, Jr., Eds. *Encyclopedia of Library History*. New York and London: Garland Publishing, Inc., 1994.

Wright, Thomas G. *Literary Culture in Early New England, 1620-1730*. New Haven: Yale University Press. 1920

Papers, Excerpts, and Articles

Augenbraum, Harold. "New York's Oldest Public Libraries." *RBM: A Journal of Rare Books, Manuscripts, and Cultural Heritage*. www.lita.org/ala/mgrps/divs/acrl/publications/rbm/backissuesvol1no/augenbraum.PDF

Bolton, S. K. "Andrew Carnegie and His Libraries," from *Famous Givers and Their Gifts*, edited by S. K. Bolton. New York: Crowell, 1896.

Cort, John E. "Jain Knowledge Warehouse: Traditional Libraries in India." *Journal of the American Oriental Society*, Vol. 115, No. 1 (Jan.-Mar., 1995) pp. 77-87.

Davis, Donald G., Jr., and Mohamed Taher. "Library History in India: Historiographical Assessment and Current Trends." *World Libraries*, Vol. 3, No. 2 (Spring 1993). www.worlib.org/vol03no2/davis_v03n2.shtml

Editors. "Richard de Bury." *Catholic Encyclopedia* www.newadvent.org/cathen/13042b.htm

Galbi, Douglas A. "Book Circulation Per U.S. Public Library User Since 1856." Federal Communications Commission, July 2007. www.galbithink.org/libraries/circulation.htm

Gallop, Annabel. "Is there a Penang Style of Malay Manuscript Illumination?" The British Library, Malay Concordance Project, 1999 http://mcp.anu.edu.au/papers/GallopPenangStyle.html

Hannam, James. "The Foundation and Loss of the Royal and Serapeum Libraries of Alexandria." Bede's Library, 2003. www.bede.org.uk/Library2.htm

"History of the Public Circulating Library" http://rchin.wordpress.com/modernmedia/history-of-public-libraries

Holifield, E. Brooks. "The Renaissance of Sacramental Piety in Colonial New England." *The William and Mary Quarterly*, 3rd Ser., Vol. 29, No. 1. (Jan., 1972), pp. 33-48.

Kanczak, Agnieska, and Karina Stoltysik. "Is there a Place for the Librarian in the Library of the 21st Century?" *World Libraries*, Vol. 16, 1 and 2 (Spring and Fall 2006). www.worlib.org/vol16no1-2/kanczak_v16n1-2.shtml

Koehler, Wallace, "Public Libraries as Institutional Repositories and Stewards in an Historical and Ethical Context." IFLA Seoul, Korea, World Library and Information Conference, 2006.

"Library Lore: Mr. Spofford's Encyclopedic and Indispensable Book—Charming Features of It." *New York Times*, August 25, 1900.

Matthiae, Paolo. "Ebla in the Late Early Syrian Period: The Royal Palace and the State Archives." *The Biblical Archaeologist*, Vol. 39, No. 3. (Sep., 1976), pp. 94-113.

Neves, Carol M.P., et al. "Key Trends Affecting Libraries." Office of Policy and Analysis, Smithsonian Institution, Washington, D.C., July 2004. www.si.edu/opanda/Reports/Reports/SIL.keytrends.pdf

Riedlemayer, Andras J. "Crimes of War, Crimes of Peace: destruction of libraries during and after the Balkan wars of the 1990s." *Library Trends* (June 2007). http://goliath.ecnext.com/coms2/summary_0199-7196052_ITM

Smart, George K. "Private Libraries in Colonial Virginia." *American Literature*, Vol. 10, No. 1. (Mar., 1938), pp. 25-52.

Online Resources

American Colonist's Library, The: A Treasury of Primary Documents. www.freerepublic.com/focus/f-news/1294965/posts

American Library Association, The. www.ala.org

The Cambridge History of English and American Literature: An Encyclopedia in Eighteen Volumes. New York: Putnam, 1907-21. www.bartleby.com/cambridge

Centre for the History of the Book. The University of Edinburgh. www.hss.ed.ac.uk/chb

Editors, et al. "Library (institution)." Microsoft Encarta Online Encyclopedia 2008. http://encarta.msn.com/text_761564555__1/Library_(institution).html

European Library, The. A portal to Europe's libraries. http://search.theeuropeanlibrary.org/portal/en/index.html

International Federation of Library Associations and Institutions (IFLA). www.ifla.org

Libraries: Wikipedia. http://en.wikipedia.org/wiki/Category:Libraries

Libraries and the Cultural Record. Journal published by the University of Texas at Austin. http://sentra.ischool.utexas.edu/~lcr/index.php

Library History Buff, The. Website of Larry T. Nix, aficionado of library history, libraria, and especially "postal librariana." www.libraryhistorybuff.com

Library of Congress Center for the Book. www.loc.gov/loc/cfbook

"A Library Primer," by John Cotton Dana. www.gutenberg.org/etext/15327

Library: Wikipedia. http://en.wikipedia.org/wiki/Library

Lib-web-cats: A directory of libraries throughout the world. www.librarytechnology.org/libwebcats

UNESCO Libraries Portal. www.unesco-ci.org/cgi-bin/portals/libraries/page.cgi?d=1

University of Texas at Austin/The University of Texas Libraries. "Statistical Overview of the Library Collections." American university library statistics. www.lib.utexas.edu/admin/cird/statisticaloverview2005.html

World Libraries, an international online journal focusing on libraries and socio-economic development. www.worlib.org

INDEX